The Building and Breaking of Peace

The Building and Breaking of Peace

Corporate Activities in Civil War Prevention and Resolution

MOLLY M. MELIN

(Loyola University Chicago)

OXFORD

UNIVERSITY PRESS

OXFORD
UNIVERSITY PRESS

Oxford University Press is a department of the University of Oxford. It furthers
the University's objective of excellence in research, scholarship, and education
by publishing worldwide. Oxford is a registered trade mark of Oxford University
Press in the UK and certain other countries.

Published in the United States of America by Oxford University Press
198 Madison Avenue, New York, NY 10016, United States of America.

CIP data is on file at the Library of Congress
ISBN 978-0-19-757936-7

DOI: 10.1093/oso/9780197579367.001.0001

1 3 5 7 9 8 6 4 2

Printed by Integrated Books International, United States of America

To Philippe, my partner in crime,
and Charlie and Maizy, our willing accomplices

Contents

Acknowledgments

Many midcareer academics face a crossroads: dig deeper into their current research topics or move to a new area of curiosity, building a research agenda from the ground. Certainly, some scholars are not like this—they can dip their toes in the ponds of an impressive variety of topics. I never worked this way though, I needed to really dive deep to feel comfortable conducting research on a subject. So, after tenure, I faced the choice of expanding my research on traditional conflict management mechanisms or moving to something new. In a way, this book merges these options: examining actors and activities that are not discussed in the mainstream conflict management scholarship and diving into the work that does discuss them.

Tackling a new topic can be daunting and, especially when there is little work in your discipline on it, terrifying. There were many days that I feared nothing would come of the work I was doing, the data collection, the interviews. Throughout my career, however, I have been blessed to have people in both my personal and professional life who believed the work I was doing was important. Scott Gartner has always encouraged me to take the path less traveled. My department at Loyola has been incredibly supportive. Alex Grigorescu read early drafts and, more importantly, walked me through the complexities of the book publishing process. David Doherty and Eric Hansen helped with my methodology questions. Olga Avdeyeva talked me through case selection. Peter Schraeder and Tofigh Maboudi helped me arrange interviews in Tunisia and read the case study. The College of Arts and Sciences assisted with startup funds.

Because the business and peace literature has a strong footing in business ethics, my study began there. Kathleen Getz, former Dean of Loyola's business school, and Tim Fort, one of the foremost scholars in this field, were incredibly kind and generous with their time and knowledge as I began. I am also grateful for formative conversations with Jennifer Oetzel, John Katsos, and Jason Miklian. These scholars helped encourage and inform the departure point for this project.

None of this work would have been possible without the generous funding and workshops hosted by the Folke Bernadotte Academy. Their support enabled me to collect the data, conduct field interviews, and get productive feedback from both scholars and practitioners. I am indebted to the members of their working groups, who are always open to new ideas and constructively pushed this project forward.

I am lucky to have a community of supportive scholars in and around Chicago. Paul Poast arranged for me to have office space and an engaged audience at the University of Chicago. I also am grateful for the visiting scholar position through Northwestern's Latin American and Caribbean Studies Program and Jorge Coronado's kindness during my time there.

Research assistance was a major part of this data collection effort, and I am grateful to Paul Olander, Caglayan Basar, Sabrina Minhas, Lindsay Dun, Dylan Reel, Rami Khadra, Muhammud Asil, and Benjamin Collings for their careful work.

Finally, these ideas would have died in my head but for my home team. I am incredibly blessed with an adventurous crew, who happily gallivant the world with me. Thank you, Team Melin: Philippe, Charlie, and Maizy, for putting up with me. Philippe has always encouraged me to think outside academic silos, in both his words and his actions. Charlie and Maizy were so excited that I was writing a book that I had to write the book. I hope that this research will help to build a better world for them and their peers.

1

Introduction

The Puzzle of Corporations, Conflict Prevention, and Conflict Resolution

In 2006, the United Nations established the Mediation Support Unit, a department exclusively focused on mediation services, and UN Peacemaker, a support network for peacemaking professionals. The United Nations, along with multiple regional organizations, is also simultaneously engaged in numerous peacekeeping missions around the globe. An astounding number of nongovernmental organizations (NGOs) are working in peace advocacy, such as Search for Common Ground, Interpeace, and Alliance for Peacebuilding. Norway and Sweden have built a niche around facilitating and mediating challenging conflicts and, with a long tradition of employing alternative conflict resolution mechanisms, have made this a cornerstone to their foreign policies (Lieberfeld 1995; Sperr 2013). Academic research offers substantial evidence that these efforts are not for nothing: they help protect civilians (Hultman, Kathman, and Shannon 2013), reduce casualties (Beardsley, Cunningham, and White 2018), increase the likelihood of a peace agreement (DeRouen and Sobek 2004; Gartner 2011), and prolong agreements (Mattes and Savun 2009; Fortna 2004).

And yet, peace remains elusive.

In 2018, the Uppsala Conflict Data Project recorded over 77,000 deaths and a new peak in the number of active conflicts (Pettersson, Hogbladh, and Oberg 2019b). This is not to suggest that 2018 was a particularly violent year, but offers evidence that conflicts are not successfully being prevented. The trends present in Figure 1.1 echo this story: violence between governments and rebel groups, as well as that between nonstate actors, continues to plague peacebuilders.

If we want to further reduce violence and conflict, we need to look beyond the actors that peace science scholars traditionally discuss: states, intergovernmental organizations (IGOs), and NGOs. This book argues that bringing corporations into the discussion of peace and conflict can contribute to

The Building and Breaking of Peace. Molly M. Melin, Oxford University Press. © Oxford University Press 2021.
DOI: 10.1093/oso/9780197579367.003.0001

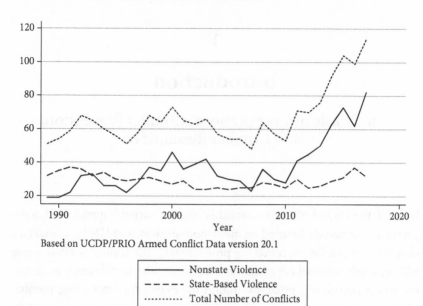

Based on UCDP/PRIO Armed Conflict Data version 20.1

——————— Nonstate Violence
– – – – – State-Based Violence
··········· Total Number of Conflicts

Figure 1.1 The Number of Ongoing Violent Conflicts Globally

resolving the challenge of violence. Business and politics are linked to the extent that one cannot be extracted from the other. Since the colonial days of the British East India Company and Cecil Rhodes, large companies have engaged in political activities. This linkage between the business community and politics has only grown with globalization. Alongside the increasing roles of the private sector in global politics come increasing challenges and opportunities. One of those includes conducting business in volatile locations.

There is evidence suggesting corporations are increasingly recognizing the challenges posed by operating in conflict-prone environments and are acting to prevent the outbreak of violence. While corporations did little to actively engage issues of human rights, environmental pollution, or corruption twenty years ago, *Forbes* now reports that integrating environmental, social, and governance factors "has become part of normal business practice" (Kell 2018). Capitalism, they report, can now sit side by side as a partner with the peace movement. The *Harvard Business Review* even suggests that efforts to revitalize the Palestinian economy through increased access to education, fair wages, and infrastructure, all common parts of corporate social responsibility (CSR) programs, could end the long-lasting conflict with Israel (Alamaro 2002).

The international community, overburdened with tackling a multitude of global challenges, is both encouraging and promoting such corporate engagement. For example, in 2013, the UN Global Compact launched Business for Peace as a leadership platform to assist companies in implementing responsible business practices that contribute to peace in conflict-affected and high-risk areas. Advice and practical guides for companies operating in such environments, such as the UN Global Compact, the Organization for Economic Cooperation and Development's (OECD) Guidelines for Multinational Enterprises, and International Alert's country-specific recommendations as well as stakeholder- and industry-led initiatives, are proliferating. As the head of Blackrock, the world's largest investment firm, recently wrote in a letter to CEOs, "the world needs your leadership" (Fink 2019).

Academics across disciplines are beginning to emphasize the role of businesses in violence reduction, leading to a new research agenda on business and peacebuilding (Miklian and Schouten 2019; Miklian, Alluri, and Katsos 2019). There is a growing collection of work on business contributions to building more peaceful communities (Deitelhoff and Wolf 2010; Fort 2007; Bond 2018; Miklian, Alluri, and Katsos 2019; Nelson 2000; Wenger and Möckli 2003; Ford 2015; Forrer and Seyle 2016). This research offers evidence from surveys (Oetzel and Getz 2012) and single case studies (Austin and Wennmann 2017; Rettberg 2009; Hanieh 2015; Tevault 2013; Miklian and Schouten 2019). The findings offer many "frameworks for action" (Banfield, Gündüz, and Killick 2006; Ganson 2011; Haufler 2001a; Wenger and Möckli 2003), but lack broad evidence of the positive and negative implications of corporate engagement. We lack cross-national, large N evidence of corporate engagement and its outcomes.

While practitioners have embraced the concept of corporations working for peace, and the business and peace literature discusses the work these actors can do to reduce tensions in conflict zones (Getz and Oetzel 2009; Oetzel, Getz and Ladek 2007), the role of these actors is notably absent in studies of violent conflict. Thus, we have an incomplete picture of the prevention and causes of violence. Private firms also have a role in preventing the outbreak of violence since they shape individuals' opportunities and incentives. This book endeavors to bring the increasingly powerful corporate world into conversations on the causes of conflict, conflict prevention, conflict duration, and conflict management.

Driving Questions of Peace, Violence, and Conflict Resolution

Civil wars occur because individual citizens choose to join a rebel group over peaceful political processes. Increasing quality of life and access to political participation provide opportunity costs that make violence a less attractive alternative (Walter 2004). Governments can and must create policies and institutions that provide opportunity and create growth (such as guaranteeing property rights, see North 1990; Acemoglu and Robinson 2013), as such strong and inclusive institutions incentivize peaceful means of resolving conflict. When the government is unable or unwilling to properly incentivize peace, violent conflict is more likely to erupt.

In whose interest is it to prevent and resolve violent conflict? Research on conflict processes suggests multiple actors can serve the role of peacemaker. While peace is in the interests of the disputants themselves, as war is costly, wars still occur due to private information, issue indivisibility, and commitment problems (Fearon 1995). There are also actors outside the conflict that have an interest in maintaining peace and stability. For example, states with strong trade and alliance ties with one of the disputants are likely to act quickly to help resolve conflict and avoid the negative broader implications conflict can have (Melin 2011). State actors often face tight constraints on financial policy (Zielinski 2016), however, and must be strategic about where they become involved. Organizations with relevant missions also play a key role in active peacebuilding (Beardsley and Lo 2013; Gartner 2011) but also face budgetary and organizational constraints (Gaibulloev et al. 2015). Thus, each of these actors face limitations on their ability to prevent and resolve conflict.

This leaves the question of how the private sector, such as small businesses and large corporations, plays into conflict dynamics. Private firms are invested organizations that can stand to lose financially from instability. Conflict often damages the infrastructure necessary to get products to market, and rebel groups often target companies seen as close to the government (such as Colombia's oil lines, which the National Liberation Army [ELN] has regularly attacked, and many businesses in Northern Ireland, which the Irish Republican Army [IRA] viewed as symbols of British power). Indeed, the business model of risk management firms is based on predicting and preparing corporations for possible violence (Aon 2015; Haufler 1997). Firms also have an ethical obligation to operate in ways that promote peace in their areas of operation (Fort 2015), often doing so in response to pressure from local and international stakeholders (Oetzel and Getz 2012). In addition, a firm's peacebuilding efforts, community engagement, and ethical behavior have an indirect effect that generates increased profit margins. Consultants are increasingly providing business leaders with evidence that diligent business practices enhance a company's financial performance (Bonini, Koller, and Mirvis 2009; Clark, Feiner, and Viehs 2015).

Despite these motives for private firms to help prevent and resolve violence, they are often distrusted and viewed as negatively impacting volatile environments (Dedeke 2019; Walker 2013; Yoon, Gürhan-Canli, and Schwarz 2006). There are cases of firms instigating and escalating violence as well as cases where firms have benefited from instability and conflict.

That said, recent scholarship suggests there may be shifts in the way firms respond to conflict: actors often viewed as exacerbating tensions due to gaps in accountability (Koenig-Archibugi 2004) are now discussed as engaging in both commerce and peacemaking (Fort 2007, 2015; Bais and Huijser 2005). Given the high costs firms face in the event of political violence, being proactive in facing these threats is imperative. Firms are therefore increasingly thinking about stability where they operate. Examples of this include CSR programs focusing on a wide range of issues (Smith 2015), the establishment of separate foundations with funding from firms (Westhues and Einwiller 2006; Walker 2013), a rise in the requirements of ethics and CSR subjects in management education programs (Wright and Bennett 2011), and the establishment of NGOs and IGOs that work with and consult business operations in adverse conditions (such as the UNs' Business for Peace leadership platform). What effect, if any, do such programs have on the occurrence of violence?

If we are to understand the effects of corporate engagement, we must first understand when they become involved. Which private firms act beyond "business as usual" and proactively build peace? In first examining the corporate motives for peacebuilding, then examining the implications of these activities for preventing violence and conflict resolution, this book builds a more holistic picture of the peace and conflict process. This book therefore examines two main research questions. First, when are we likely to see corporations engaging in communities beyond normal business operations? Second, what are the implications of this engagement for peace and conflict? Creating value, encouraging development, community building, promoting the rule of law, and engaging in unofficial (track two) diplomacy are ways the private sector can help build peaceful societies and reduce conflict (Oetzel et al. 2009). As we do not have a strong understanding of when corporations engage in peacebuilding activities or the effects of such efforts, exploring this topic promises to help us understand why conflict persists despite the proliferation of peacemakers.

The Challenge: Perspectives on Peace and Conflict since World War II

Conflict management, like conflict, spans both history and the globe. It is as old as conflict itself. In 1492, following Columbus' discovery of the West Indies, a delimitation of the Spanish and Portuguese spheres of exploration was desired. European imperial rivalries and colonial pressures made clear that conflict would soon arise over the land claims of Spain and Portugal (Elliott 2006). In May 1493, after vigorous petitioning by both Spain and Portugal, the Vatican acted to set a boundary between their respective spheres of interest (Davies 1996). Pope Alexander VI issued a decree that established an imaginary line running north and south through the mid-Atlantic. Spain would have possession of any unclaimed territories to the west of the line, and Portugal would have possession of any unclaimed territory to the east of the line. The New World was thus neatly bifurcated by the sole authority of a third party (Davies 1996).

There are other examples of third-party actors stepping in to help resolve conflict throughout history. In 1905, Theodore Roosevelt offered to act as an intermediary between the claims of Russia and Japan over interests in northern China and Korea (Roosevelt 1985). Japanese and Russian delegates met with the president on board a US Naval ship in Oyster Bay and later in Portsmouth, New Hampshire. For his mediation efforts, President Roosevelt became the first American to receive the Nobel Peace Prize. Roosevelt later arbitrated a dispute between France and Germany over the division of Morocco. These actions possibly helped to postpone a world war.

These examples suggest third parties can take various actions toward helping to resolve a conflict. In effect, such actors are building peace through conflict management. A conflict manager is an outside actor that chooses to become involved in a dispute and has a preference for deescalating the dispute that exceeds their preference for one side's victory. Conflict management can include a variety of actors, including nation-states, coalitions of states, regional or international organizations, and individuals (Dixon 1996). It does not exclude third parties that prefer that a certain disputant prevails, but this preference is not as strong as that for conflict resolution (Butterworth 1978). Conflict managers are not required to be neutral or unallied with a disputant; however, the third party does not overtly join the conflict on the side of a disputant.

The challenge in understanding peace and conflict is that there are different perspectives on the actors that influence conflict dynamics. The conflict management perspective tends to focus on states and their representatives, and regional and global organizations. The business and peace perspective tends to focus exclusively on various sized businesses, with an occasional discussion of partnerships with other actors. The result is an incomplete picture of the widespread engagement in peacemaking, the lost opportunities that lead to violence, and the possibilities for a more peaceful future. In what follows, I outline the findings from the political science and business and peace perspectives, discuss the problems of having two perspectives, and then offer a theory that endeavors to form a picture of peace and violence that incorporates these varied perspectives.

Theory

With the numerous efforts and methodologies used to prevent and resolve violent conflict, why does it persist? Bringing corporations into the discussion of peace and conflict can help us understand the continued challenge of armed conflict. Given arguments that corporations are increasingly acting in ways that help build more peaceful societies, why have we not observed a downturn in violence? Answering these questions requires first examining the conditions that prompt companies to behave in a way that builds peace, then studying how these efforts affect long term prospects for peace.

The Supply of Peacebuilding

Not all businesses are proactive in building more peaceful communities. Given that profit is the very purpose of engaging in economic exchange, why would a corporation engage in efforts to build peace? While there are many examples of private sector contributions to peace, we do not understand under what conditions they occur. This book argues that a firm's operating environment is the source of conditions that can either encourage or discourage their investment in building peace. I offer a thorough exploration of such conditions in chapter 4. Corporate engagement is likely when the operating environment creates the demand for action and allows for its supply. Specifically, there are two main environmental factors that promote firm-led peacebuilding activities:

1. **Government Capacity**—the government must have some ability to enforce the rule of law for companies to be willing to invest in peace. When lawlessness persists, firms are more likely to shutter, flee, or behave unethically. In moderately capable states, corporations can most influence political and social stability by helping to fill "gaps" in governance. This has been the case in Colombia, where topographical challenges minimize the government's provision of goods and services, and companies are contributing to rural development projects.

2. **Political Stability**—when a government adopts policies that are less democratic or violence threatens stability, companies must shift their concerns to survival. Instability and violence interrupt business activities and depress economic growth. Firms invest in peacebuilding during periods of peace, since peace stimulates investment and economic growth. While recent violence may instigate discussions toward policy adjustments, corporations are more likely to invest in building peace in long periods of peace, since this allows for investment and innovation.

In addition, certain companies have a culture that makes them more prone to proactive community engagement. These companies are more likely to work with IGOs and be responsive to challenges facing the communities where they operate. This adds a final, corporate characteristic–based factor that increases the likelihood that we observe active community engagement.

3. **Norm entrepreneurs**—companies that are on the forefront of CSR, joining international dialogue on these topics, are more responsive to the needs of local communities. Firms are primarily concerned with ensuring the future marketability of their products. This is especially the case when a firm has been caught being a "bad" actor, as peacebuilding helps a firm to build "reputation capital" and suffer less

harm to its image from negative publicity than a firm that does not have a good image. The extractive sector has been especially responsive to public pressure, as with the creation of the Kimberly Process for certification of diamonds as conflict-free.

This argument is summarized in Figure 1.2. Variations in corporate conflict prevention result from changing local dynamics and shifts in political capacity, as well as threats to the ability to conduct business. Corporations engage in peacebuilding when their investments are threatened, when there is a gap in the state's capacity to enforce laws, and when there is political instability. The environmental factors effecting firm-led peacebuilding stem from the characteristics and actions of the local government where a company is operating. Below a certain threshold of stability and capacity, corporations are likely to shutter or flee. This disengagement has an even more destabilizing effect on already volatile environments. This helps us understand why violence persists in a world that is working so hard to prevent it.

That norm entrepreneurs are open to new ideas about firm engagement offers hope for this puzzle, however. These firms work with international actors and take part in forums to operate ethically and employ best practices. The international community, such as IGOs, heavily affects the characteristics of the firm and its willingness to engage. The smaller circles represent other firm characteristics that affect a firm's willingness and opportunity to invest in peacebuilding: things like size of profits, number of employees, and sector. This means efforts to more broadly and effectively engage corporations can help prevent violence.

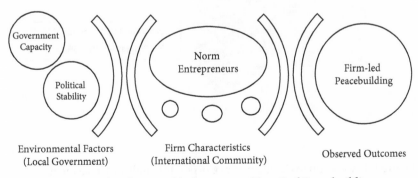

Figure 1.2 External and Internal Influences on Firm-Led Peacebuilding

Recent research on variation in business responses to crises in Africa provides examples of how the dynamics between environmental factors and firm characteristics lead to vast differences in proactive engagement (Handley 2019). In Kenya, businesses were unable to effectively organize to help resolve the political dispute at the heart of election-related violence, and some businesses were complicit in these tensions. Conversely, in South Africa, while many businesses remained complicit, a small group acted in important and concerted ways to resolve the political conflict during the transition from apartheid. In both places, political instability was at the heart of the conflict. What differed for those who acted, however, was the ability of corporate leaders in South Africa to develop political autonomy and link its interests with those of broader society. These norm entrepreneurs incorporated such policies into corporate practices and behaviors. The same was true of Botswana's businesses in actively fighting the AIDs epidemic. The capacity of business to define its interests as linked to the welfare of society as a whole can encourage positive firm contributions even during political instability.

As Figure 1.3 shows, there is significant opportunity to engage more companies in peacebuilding. While the Company of Peace and Conflict (COPC) data show there is variation in engagement mechanisms, the majority of firms have no programs that help build peace in the communities where they operate. By creating an understanding of influences on firm-led peacebuilding, policymakers can work to more encourage widespread

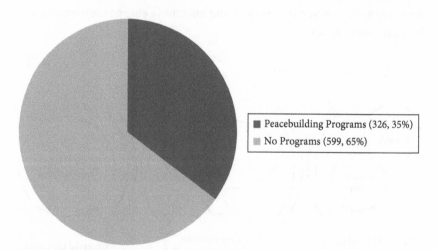

Figure 1.3 Variation in Occurrence of Corporate Conflict Management
Based on the Company of Peace and Conflict data.

corporate engagement. Before doing so, however, it is imperative to consider whether these efforts are in fact having a positive effect.

Peacebuilding and Breaking

When firms are proactively working to build peace in a country, what effect do they have on levels of violence there? Chapter 5 explores the implications of firm engagement in terms of peace and conflict. I argue that companies are uniquely situated in their ability to raise the cost of violence. Given that increased quality of life provides opportunity costs that make violence a less attractive alternative (Walter 2004), companies that invest in their workers and communities can help ensure peaceful conflict resolution is an attractive alternative to violence. Scholars often cite the importance of opportunity costs for potential rebel recruits as a way to understand motives for rebelling (Walter 2004; Collier and Hoeffler 2000), which can be seen as changing the payoffs of war in comparison to peace. How groups perceive such preferences and opportunities can also help us understand when groups choose conflict (Hirshleifer 1995, 2001). States with poor living conditions (Walter 2004) and low average income or high inequality (Collier, Hoeffler, and Söderbom 2004) are at a higher risk of civil war. The incentives to join a rebellion increase when individuals have poor access to alternative employment (Hegre 2004) and when rebellion is economically viable (Collier and Hoeffler 2000).

Each of the correlates offers areas where private sector engagement can raise opportunity costs, thereby altering the payoffs each party expects from conflict and disincentivizing violence. One approach is to reduce the incentives for rebellion, which is the product of the probability of victory and its consequences. For example, initiatives like the Kimberly Process, which limits the access to funding for rebel organizations by shutting diamonds from conflict zones out of the market, can limit rebel funding. Another approach is to raise the costs of rebellion, through loss of income and the costs of coordination. In Colombia, companies like Electrolux, Coltabaco, and Exito[1] are training and hiring ex-combatants, thereby shifting opportunity costs for would-be rebels: individuals who might otherwise take up arms instead have peaceful means for bettering their lives and more to lose with violence. In post-conflict societies, reintegration programs add social ties and educational opportunities that decrease recidivism among ex-combatants

(Kaplan and Nussio 2018). Programs that offer job training, educational opportunities, and employment create incentives for would-be rebels to engage in legal forms of commerce. This book shows that such efforts significantly reduce the likelihood that a country erupts into violence.

Active firm engagement that occurs once violence has begun, however, does not necessarily help end the conflicts. A strong and proactive private sector often plays a role in the peace process, even being a part of the negotiations, as was the case in Colombia and Tunisia. In Tunisia, this engagement was able to prevent violence from erupting, but in Colombia, where civil war had been ongoing for years before corporations became involved, this engagement complicated negotiations. When these companies were not happy with the terms of the agreement, they worked to ensure the public voted against the deal. When companies work for peace after prolonged violence, their efforts do not help build peace when they add an additional veto player to negotiations.

Figure 1.4 depicts these outcomes, which vary in effectiveness according to when they occur. Firm-led peacebuilding effectively preserves peace when it occurs before violence has begun, but it does not help societies that are experiencing violence move to peace.

What does this mean for the puzzle of continued violence? Private corporations offer an answer to why some would-be civil wars are avoided and others continue for years. In periods of instability, active firm engagement can help avoid violence. Countries that do not have the capacity to enforce the rule of law, however, are unlikely to have an environment that encourages corporate engagement. Yet once violence has escalated, companies are not effective peacemakers. This book offers evidence that companies

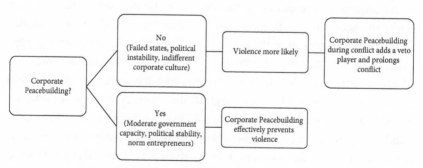

Figure 1.4 Corporate Peacebuilding Outcomes

can effectively prolong peace when they work to invest in peace in their communities prior to conflicts escalating.

Conclusion

The purpose of this book is to highlight the role of corporations in peace and conflict, especially as it relates to research in the fields of political science and international relations on the topic of third-party conflict resolution. This chapter highlights how business and peace scholars approach this topic and how merging the findings from these studies and those within international relations are both warranted and desirable. Moving this research forward requires scholarship that offers a theoretically and methodologically sound examination of the roles that diverse actors play in preventing and resolving violent conflict. More systematic analysis is necessary to understand how corporations can be constructively engaged in volatile conflict environments. Creating an understanding of the roles these actors play and the outcomes of their efforts will enable policymakers to encourage future involvement where opportunities for engagement might otherwise be missed. This book increases our knowledge of the corporate role in promoting peace and generates evidence useful for encouraging positive corporate involvement into the future.

This book offers a first step in producing a systematic analysis of the role of corporations in peace and conflict. The next chapter presents a thorough discussion of existing literature related to this topic. Chapter 3 presents the definitions and the data: sources, coding rules, and trends. Chapter 4 assesses the supply and demand factors that encourage corporate involvement, presenting and testing a theoretic approach based on contextual factors that provide the opportunity for engagement and demand for action from firms. I argue certain corporations are more likely to engage based on their willingness to respond to the need for corporate engagement. Chapter 5 argues that the factors effecting supply and demand have implications for the likelihood of peace and violence. In the next three chapters, I assess these arguments in the context of Colombia, Tunisia, and Northern Ireland. The concluding chapter presents an overview and implications of the findings and offers suggestions for corporate actors that wish to have a stronger effect on the communities in which they operate and the policymakers that wish to engage them.

The path to peace is neither straight nor narrow. Peace does not rest on the shoulders of a single peacemaker, nor does violence. Building and sustaining societies that choose peaceful methods of dispute resolution requires widespread efforts. Private corporations, when properly engaged, can help realize this goal.

2

The State of Our Knowledge

Varied Approaches to Understanding Corporate Engagement

Business and politics are linked to the extent that one cannot be extracted from the other. Since at least the colonial era, large companies have engaged in political activities. With the spread of globalization, the overlap between business and politics has only grown. The private sector's involvement in global politics offers both challenges and opportunities, such as conducting business in pre- and post-conflict environments.

Both corporations and international organizations are increasingly recognizing the challenges operations in conflict-prone environments pose (Kolk and Lenfant 2010). As exit from environments experiencing conflict is not always desirable or feasible, corporations are increasingly being called to proactively engage in collaborative practical action to advance peace. For example, in 2013, the UN Global Compact launched Business for Peace as a leadership platform to assist companies in implementing responsible business practices that contribute to peace in conflict affected and high-risk areas. There is a proliferation of advice and practical guides for companies operating in such environments, such as the UN Global Compact (2008), Organization for Economic Cooperation and Development's (OECD) Guidelines for Multinational Enterprises (2011), and International Alert's multitude of country specific publications as well as stakeholder and industry-led initiatives. These suggest that corporations can and will act if given the expertise (Ganson 2011). Indeed, risk management firms spend significant resources predicting and preparing for possible violence (Haufler 1997). While there are successful cases of corporations preventing conflict (such as Tesco's mechanisms addressing labor grievances in South Africa, see Boudreaux 2008) and solidifying peace (as in the transformation of Rwanda's coffee industry, see Boudreaux 2008), some corporations remain bystanders to atrocities and human rights abuses (as in Talisman Energy's experiences in Sudan, see

The Building and Breaking of Peace. Molly M. Melin, Oxford University Press. © Oxford University Press 2021.
DOI: 10.1093/oso/9780197579367.003.0002

Leary 2007). Fort (2007) shows corporations need not be removed from the peace process, as there is a positive correlation between commerce, peace, and engagement. Capitalism, according to a Forbes report on corporate responsibility, can now sit side by side as a partner with the peace movement (Guthrie 2014).

The Swedish Institute of International Affairs distinguishes among the phases of conflict during which third-party actors may help to promote peace: peacemaking, peacekeeping, and peacebuilding (Andersson et al. 2011). *Peacemaking* involves efforts to separate the warring parties and find ways for them to work out their disagreements, such as the US and EU-led mediation of the peace conference that generated the Dayton Peace Accords. Following such agreements, *peacekeeping* seeks to maintain truces among factions after a peace accord has been adopted. *Peacebuilding* activities are preventative in nature, helping address the various social and economic causes of conflict and creating an atmosphere for peaceful dispute resolution. The focus of this chapter is on peacebuilding: making peace after violent conflict has arisen. While public and private third parties have roles to play in each stage of creating peace, the literature on peacemaking within political science is one of the more robust and developed areas of research. This is also the arena where we are likely to be able to observe both third-party engagement and the greatest costs for inaction. As Fort (2015) highlights, however, we must not think only actors in conflict zones deal with issue of peace, since technologies and practices can spread and can have a broader impact on peacebuilding than we might initially think.

While practitioners have embraced the concept of corporations working for peace and the business literature discusses the work these actors can do to reduce tensions in conflict zones (Getz and Oetzel 2009; Oetzel, Getz, and Ladek 2007), the role of these actors is notably absent in studies of conflict resolution. In this chapter, I offer an overview of the findings on conflict resolution processes by scholars in the field of political science. I then draw from business scholarship and overview research suggesting the positive contributions the private sector can and does make toward peace. I conclude by highlighting the problems of having disjointed approaches and offering a conceptual framework for how these distinct approaches can be combined to generate a more comprehensive understanding of conflict resolution.

The Conflict Management Perspective

Outside actors may play varied roles in a dispute. They may join a conflict as a disputant, may express preferences for seeing a certain side prevail, may act to resolve the conflict, or may play a role that is somewhere in between. For purposes of this book, it is necessary to distinguish between the two primary roles third parties have in ongoing disputes. First, third parties may join a conflict as an additional disputant (Siverson and Starr 1991; Most and Harvey 1980; Heldt and Hammarström 2002; Melin 2005). The expectation of possible third-party assistance can influence decisions to go to war (Blainey 1973; Gartner and Siverson 1996). Even a third party's affinity for one actor over another can influence the outcome of a crisis, regardless of whether actual intervention occurs (Favretto 2005).

The second role outside actors can play, the role of conflict manager, focuses on helping disputants deal with the information asymmetries and credible commitment problems that often lead to conflict (Beardsley 2006b). Conflict management constitutes any course of action taken by a nondisputant aimed at either preventing the further escalation of the conflict or resolving it completely (Dixon 1996; Butterworth 1978). Conflict managers work to reduce, limit, or eliminate the level, scope, and intensity of violence in conflict and build structures that control the need to resort to violence in future conflicts (Deutsch 1973; Maoz 2004). Management activities are varied, spanning from verbal condemnation of a conflict to direct military intervention (Regan 2000). Figure 2.1 shows the usage of nonbinding conflict management mechanisms. Each approach may be suited to different conflicts and each has different consequences that entail different costs and resources and may be effective under different circumstances.

Third-party interventions, especially mediation, have increasingly become a topic of study (see Beardsley et al. 2006; Greig 2005; Regan and Stam 2000; Bercovitch 1997). Unlike sanctions or military intervention, a prerequisite to the occurrence of mediation is the acceptability of mediation to all involved parties. An often-cited definition of mediation highlights this characteristic, describing mediation as "a reactive process of conflict management whereby parties seek the assistance of, or accept an offer of help from, an individual, group, or organization to change their behavior, settle their conflict, or resolve their problem without resorting to physical force or invoking the authority of the law" (Bercovitch and Houston 1996, 11).

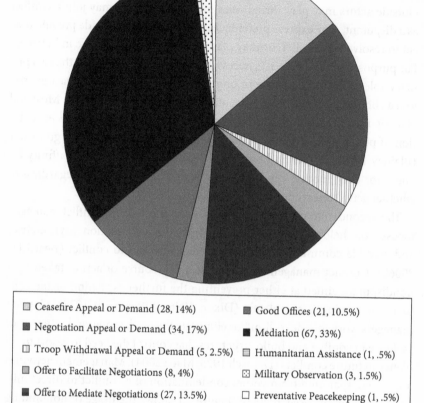

□ Ceasefire Appeal or Demand (28, 14%)   ■ Good Offices (21, 10.5%)

■ Negotiation Appeal or Demand (34, 17%)   ■ Mediation (67, 33%)

▥ Troop Withdrawal Appeal or Demand (5, 2.5%) ▤ Humanitarian Assistance (1, .5%)

□ Offer to Facilitate Negotiations (8, 4%)   ⊡ Military Observation (3, 1.5%)

■ Offer to Mediate Negotiations (27, 13.5%)   □ Preventative Peacekeeping (1, .5%)

▨ Inquiry/Fact Finding (6, 3%)

Figure 2.1 Variation in Nonbinding Conflict Management Mechanisms

Based on the Third Party Intervention (Frazier and Dixon 2006) and International Conflict
Management data (Bercovitch 1999).

The majority of the research on mediation focuses on the determinants
of successful mediation (Mack and Snyder 1957; Bercovitch 1998; Kleiboer
1996; Pruitt 1981; Ott 1972; Regan 2000). Although it remains unclear which
management efforts are the most effective and why, there are various explanatory variables that reappear throughout the literature. These include characteristics of the mediator, characteristics of the conflict, and characteristics
of the disputants. The mediation literature is not the only conflict management literature to focus on the effectiveness of third-party efforts. Similar

debates exist in the economic sanctions literature (Li 1993; Hufbauer and Schott 1983; Martin 1993) and work on military interventions (Regan 1996). It remains unclear which management efforts are the most effective and why, and the different methods of management are rarely considered together (for notable exceptions, see Clayton and Dorussen 2021; Owsiak 2020, 2014; Melin 2011).

Authors also consider the third party's decision to manage a conflict. The majority of the research looks at the determinants of military intervention. Authors cite the presence of a ready military option (Allison 1973), the distance of the state from the intervener (Pearson 1974), strategic interests (Yoon 1997), disputant regime type (Schmidt 2004), major power status (Gent 2003), attacker demands (Werner 2000), and how "solvable" the conflict is (Terris and Maoz 2005). More recently, a similar research agenda is appearing in the mediation literature, examining the mediator's decision to mediate (Beardsley 2006a; Kydd 2006; Savun 2005; Svensson 2006) and the implications of this process for long-term peace (Beardsley 2011).

Conflict resolution scholars, including this author, generally examine four categories of conflict managers (Melin 2013): global intergovernmental organizations (IGOs) like the United Nations, regional IGOs like the Arab League, individuals like former US President Jimmy Carter, and countries like Sweden. The actual practice of managing conflicts operates differently across actor types. Differing motives of states for offering conflict management assistance in comparison to those of the other actors is of particular note. States carefully consider when and where they become involved, and often consider the strategic benefits when deciding whether to take on the role as conflict manager (Melin 2011). Potential gains include establishing a reputation as a peacemaker (as have Norway and Sweden) and advancing the state's ability to influence the dispute's outcome, either by changing an unfavorable situation or maintaining a favorable status quo. States often take on the role of conflict manager as a way to expand their influence, resources, and power.

Many international IGOs, like the United Nations, have encouraging peaceful dispute resolution written into their charters. These IGOs can enable peace processes to overcome the challenges that low-capacity states with high levels of hostility create (Doyle and Sambanis 2000). Indirectly, IGOs encourage multiparty talks between member countries but not direct, bilateral negotiations (Shannon 2009). An organizations' institutional setup and the characteristics of its member states determine in part the impact that an organization has on generating peace (Hansen et al. 2008). And IGOs are known to get particularly hard-to-resolve cases (Bercovitch and Gartner 2006), especially regional organizations (Gartner 2011). However, when we account for the challenges these organizations face, both actors positively contribute to dispute resolution and peacebuilding.

Conflict research does not directly address private firms and their role in this process. Instead, links between the corporate world and peace are addressed at a much broader level, focusing on the relationship between trade and peace rather than businesses. Trade can increase peaceful bilateral relationships through several avenues, including offering nonmilitary ways of communicating resolve (Gartzke et al. 2001) and forcing leaders to choose between economic stability and political goals (Gartzke and Li 2003). Others have highlighted the role of the private sector in conflict prevention as a shift in global governance resulting from the use of natural resource revenues to finance conflict (Haufler 2010a).

Despite the explosion of research on conflict management and resolution, the vast majority of this literature focuses on the roles of state actors and international organizations. And yet many global and transnational firms function as diplomatic actors in ways that are analogous to states (Pigman 2013). There is evidence that corporations can promote fair trade and human rights (Marshall and Macdonald 2013), order (Reno 2004), and public accountability (Koenig-Archibugi 2004). This area has begun to attract the attention of business and peace scholars, as I discuss further in the next section.

The Business and Peace Perspective

Scholars in fields as varied as business, sociology, anthropology, and geography have noted that private firms can contribute to governance and public goods provision, often taking on responsibilities beyond those required by legal and profit-making concerns. Much of this research is based on analysis of cases without scientific selection criteria, especially work seeking to change corporate policy. For example, Nelson (2000) uses various examples of business engagement to develop five principals of corporate engagement in conflict prevention and resolution. She and Jackson (2004) expand on this research to show businesses can offer value and simultaneously profit. Similarly, policy-oriented research shows governments and institutions (Banfield, Haufler, and Lilly 2005b), as well as NGOs (Kolk and Lenfant 2012;

Schepers 2006) and industry-led initiatives (Haufler 2001b) can encourage firms to contribute to peacebuilding. Evidence from multinational mining companies in the Democratic Republic of Congo, South Africa, Europe, and North America suggests contemporary companies are committing to norms of corporate social and security responsibility (Hönke 2013). Research on business-NGO partnerships in the Democratic Republic of Congo reveals corporations can build trust and capacity in addressing governance problems (Kolk and Lenfant 2012). The tourism industry in post-conflict Rwanda suggests businesses contribute to economic growth and physical reconstruction as well as reconciliation and justice (Alluri 2009). Research on Azerbaijan, Bosnia, and Rwanda shows the host governments, international agencies, and international companies coordinated successful post-conflict reconstruction (Davis 2012). These case studies suggest firm-led peacebuilding merits further examination.

The business scholarship on the topic of business and peace generally falls into one of two frameworks "corporate social responsibility" (CSR) or "creating shared values." The CSR framework refers to firms considering issues beyond the narrow economic, technical, and legal requirements. In other words, CSR is considering social obligations beyond the requirements of the law. Social movements of the 1960s and 1970s in civil rights, antiwar, women's rights, and environmentalism created a push to rethink the role of business in society. The CSR scholarship moved the focus from satisfying owners to consideration for the public, communities, and employees. The related scholarship on this topic is too wide-ranging to fully engage here, but has been cataloged (Preston and Post 1981; Preston 1981). This research generated many new approaches, concepts, and ways of conducting business.

This approach to corporate behavior is not without its critics, with Milton Friedman's well-known argument that "the social responsibility of business is to increase its profits" (Friedman 1970). The so-called Friedman doctrine is based in classical economics, which focuses on the free market. Proponents of CSR argue that it is in the long-term self-interests of business, since a better society creates a better environment for business (Davis 1973). Companies can also benefit from having a strong self-image, greater visibility, proactively avoiding new government regulations, improving business sociocultural norms, and increasing stockholder interests.

Despite these arguments, the topics and operations of profits and social issues remain distinct. Often the "socially responsible" part of a business is split from the "profit-making" part of business both in the academy (with different divisions for "social issues in management" and a division for "business policy and strategy"). In the 1970s, scholarship began to examine the relationship between CSR and profitability, although without generating consensus (Ullmann 1985; Starik and Carroll 1990). Researchers faced challenges of measurement, especially given the diversity of CSR definitions. Contemporary corporate leadership seems to be shifting toward a view that CSR does not involve a strict trade-off with corporate economic interests (Dealbook 2020).

The CSR literature shifted conversations from a focus exclusively on shareholders to include stakeholders, those actors affected by corporate activities. The "stakeholder approach" emerged in the mid-1980s, as a way to strategically deal with the myriad of different groups and relationships that resulted from the volatile business environment of this time. Stakeholder theory argues that business can be understood as a system of how we create value for stakeholders. This approach connects business and capitalism with ethics, providing a framework for strategic management that emphasizes investing in relationships with those who have a stake in the firm (Freeman 2010; Freeman and McVea 2001). Such an approach requires managers to consider the values of their corporation, the expectation of stakeholders, and societal issues. Thus, CSR programs are mostly a response to external pressure and largely focus on improving a firm's reputation. Evidence suggests many companies have applied these concepts to their operations and that companies incorporating a strong set of business values are able to maintain stakeholder support (Svendsen 1998; Wheeler and Sillanpää 1997).

Related is the emerging framework of "creating shared value" (CSV), which suggests opportunities for both private firms and the communities where they operate to benefit. This sees a company's competitiveness and a community's health as intertwined. Successful communities provide companies with a demand for their products, public assets, and a supportive environment. At the same time, companies provide citizens with employment and opportunities to create wealth. "Shared value" refers to policies that both enhance a company's competitiveness and the community's economic and social conditions (Porter and Kramer 2019, 2006). And CSV differs from the CSR framework in that CSR programs focus mostly on reputation without having a strong connection to the business, creating challenges for sustaining these programs in the long term. In contrast, CSV is directly linked with a company's profitability and competitiveness, leveraging the company's resources and expertise to create both economic and social value.

A separate, but related, line of research explores the challenges and potential for companies operating in conflict environments as they can build "peace through commerce." Stemming from business ethics scholars, this research seeks to offer ways that firms operating in zones of violent can avoid the negative impact of violent conflict and assist in conflict mitigation (Oetzel et al. 2009). This scholarship suggests that there are opportunities for "business-based peacebuilding," wherein businesses can contribute to peaceful societies by filling some of the needs in conflict-prone states (Sweetman 2009). Much of this work views businesses as a partner, working with NGOs, national governments, and local actors to build peace in fragile states (Kolk and Lenfant 2015; Fort 2009). Efforts can include fostering economic development through positive economic spillover of job creation and local investment (Fort and Schipani 2004; Oetzel, Getz, and Ladek 2007), promoting a sense of community (Fort 2008), adopting international operations standards (Steelman and Rivera 2006; Getz 1990), community building (Spreitzer 2007), track two and corporate diplomacy (Lieberfeld 2002; Iff et al. 2010; Westermann-Behaylo, Rehbein, and Fort 2015), and adopting conflict-sensitive practices and risk assessment (Guáqueta 2013; Ballentine and Haufler 2005; Guáqueta and Orsini 2007). Each of these literatures suggests opportunities for the private sector to effect more than a country's economy.

Firm Peacebuilding Activities

One thing is clear: the roles of private firms are shifting in the highly globalized world economy. Businesses face difficult trade-offs when operating in volatile environments. As a result of these challenges, academics, international organizations and trade groups offer analysis and advice for making ethical choices. Generally speaking, private companies have three mechanisms through which they can contribute to conflict prevention: "through its core business activities, social investment programs, and engagement in policy dialogue and civic institution building," and, in exceptionally high risk environments, "preventative diplomacy, fact-finding, and mediation missions" (Nelson 2000, 45). Engagement often involves NGO groups with expertise in conflict resolution, such as International Alert. These partnerships target corruption, poverty, and social inequality, some of the main causes of conflict (Bennett 2002).

Business scholars, and increasingly political scientists, reveal significant opportunities for private actors to strengthen preventive diplomacy (Eskandarpour and Wennmann 2011; Iff et al. 2010), support emerging economies (Hoskisson et al. 2000), and minimize negative company impacts (Ganson 2011). Companies can promote economic development, the rule of law, and principles of external valuation. They can add to a sense of community and engage in track two diplomacy and conflict sensitive practices (Deitelhoff and Wolf 2010; Oetzel et al. 2009). There is also evidence that businesses can contribute to the mediation process (Iff et al. 2010; Iff and Alluri 2016).

Corporations have a range of available mechanisms for addressing conflict, some of which are aimed at resolving the conflict directly and some of which are aimed at preventing violence through addressing its causes. Conflict resolution tactics may include lobbying or publicly speaking out against violence (Lieberfeld 2002). Companies may in fact reach out to conflicting parties directly to actively mediate, arbitrate, or facilitate negotiations (Ballentine and Nitzschke 2004). For example, the Anglo-American Mining Company is seen as facilitating negotiations between the African National Congress (ANC) and the South African government (Lieberfeld 2002). Conflict prevention tactics may include human resource policies aimed at relieving social tensions, supporting small businesses through microfinance, avoiding business with those who facilitate conflict (Collier 2007), and engaging in philanthropic activities aiding victims of conflict (van Tulder and Kolk 2001). Often, these activities are conducted along with NGO, IGO, or local partners, as these actors can help provide knowledge, skills, and access (Doh and Teegan 2003).

One of the challenges for those looking to understand corporate contributions to peacebuilding is the diversity of the actors that make up the corporate world. These actors vary in terms of their scope of operations, sectors, and their peace-related activities. Some research distinguishes between these actors, suggesting these differences have implications for the nature of corporate engagement. Heterogeneity exists across firms' desire to protect their investment and influence the conflict environment, varying across size, corporate culture, and industry. Large firms are motivated by stakeholders to invest in social programs (Russo and Perrini 2010) and have greater access to financial, human, technological, and organizational resources (Kindleberger 1969). Having access to resources, expertise, and efficacy can even translate into the authority to act, which often derives from the delegation of this authority by powerful states and international organizations (Haufler 2004, 2010b).

One source of heterogeneity is the corporation's local relationships. These relationships can involve strong, long-term commitments to investments, public-private partnerships, or an organizational structure that recognizes local challenges. Conversely, some corporations can thrive from local instability and conflict. King shows "There is a political economy to warfare that produces positive externalities for its perpetrators" (2001, 528). The wartime environment may have spoils that discourage peaceful settlement, as happened in Angola's diamond industry, Cambodia's timber industry, and coca in Colombia. In addition, companies may work outside the law to ensure the security of immobile investments, as with Del Monte, Dole, and Chiquita's financing of right-wing paramilitary groups in Colombia. A significant body of research sees business as part of the problem facing countries embroiled in conflict, particularly in those states with natural resources (Switzer 2002).

Variation in corporate culture has broader implications. These are the key values, beliefs, and norms of the corporation (Reidenbach and Robin 1991). Corporations have personalities that are stable over time and independent of their members (Crèmer 1993). Corporate culture can promote various behaviors at the organizational and individual levels (Deshpande and Farley 1999). For example, a culture explicitly promoting and encouraging ethical decision-making encourages ethical behavior throughout a firm (Chen, Sawyers, and Williams 1997). Corporate cultures can create positive or negative influences depending on their goals, policies, structures, and strategies (Brown 1987).

Finally, there is important variation in the mobility of firms. As civil war damages resources and the economy, mobile firms can shift investments and relocate capital outside the deteriorating economic environment (Collier 1999). Equipment and livestock are relatively easy to move during a conflict, as with Mozambique's 80 percent decline in cattle stock in the 1980s (Brück 1996). A common mechanism of distinguishing among sectors is to differentiate among those corporations that operate in the extractive sector, which consists of any operations removing metals, minerals, and aggregates from the earth. There is a large amount of scholarship on the link between natural resources and civil war (for a review, see Ross 2004).

To overcome the challenges of the corporate heterogeneity, the research on business and peace to this point generally takes one of two

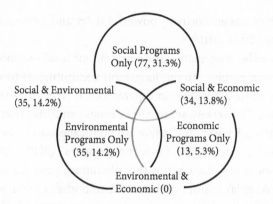

Figure 2.2 Variation in Corporate Conflict Management Mechanisms
Based on the Company of Peace and Conflict data.

approaches: building a theoretical understanding of why and how private firms can contribute to peace (Fort 2007, 2015) or examining individual cases of corporate engagement (Miklian and Schouten 2019). This book fills the empirical gap of descriptive examples using both comparative case studies and the large-N cross-national data. Without such analysis, it is difficult to produce conclusions that can be generalized more broadly to understand how and when firms contribute to peace. Figure 2.2 shows the variation in the methods that firms use to prevent violence, based on the data discussed in the next chapter. While I do not delve into the complexities of variation in corporations, I offer a theoretical and empirical launching pad for future researchers to address such heterogeneity.

Moving Forward with a United Perspective

Reports on the role of private actors in preventative diplomacy suggest that private actors have a comparative advantage in some aspects of building peace (Eskandarpour and Wennmann 2011). Many of the emerging practices in the fields of armed violence reduction, peace mediation, and human rights protection offer significant opportunities for private actors to strengthen preventative diplomacy. Corporations have the capabilities for conflict prevention through stopping predatory behaviors, minimizing negative impacts, creating positive externalities, and being peacemakers and peacebuilders, but these skills must be fostered (Ganson 2011).

Failing to account for the role that corporate actors play in conflict processes is likely to bias research findings about the causes of peace and violence, as their substantial power could significantly affect the levels of peace and violence experienced in a society. Scholarship on different actors and their mechanisms for conflict prevention, management, and resolution study different actors in isolation from one another. To adequately understand the puzzle of continued violence, there is a need for a more holistic approach. The substitutability framework developed by Most and Starr (1984, 1989) offers warnings of the problems associated with failure to integrate actors, their actions, and the associated outcomes. That is, research that does not include all of the factors that may the trigger the events we observe suffers from biases that limit our ability to develop an integrative understanding of phenomena. Various actors have a wide array of available options for approaching any range of policy issues, since any cause may have a number of effects and any effect can stem from several causes (Morgan and Palmer 2000). Different conflicts may lead to similar responses (as in mediation efforts by the United States with Israel and Egypt in the 1970s, by the Vatican in the Falkland conflict between Argentina and the United Kingdom in 1982, and by Congo with Burundi and Rwanda in 1966), and there are multiple ways to respond to similar conflicts (as was the case of the UN observers sent in 1992 to Yugoslavia compared to the later NATO military intervention in Kosovo and postagreement engagement of businesses). The framework of substitutability is applicable to third-party reactions to violence: economic sanctions, diplomatic efforts, grassroots programs, and military operations are substitutable policy instruments, all of which can be triggered in response to conflict.

Not accounting for business-led peace efforts leaves scholars with an incomplete picture of the influences on peace and violence. Research ignoring substitutability in conflict prevention and resolution activities and actors risks producing inaccurate results and unconvincing conclusions. Adequate analysis of the complex decision process involved in choosing a response to conflict requires the inclusion of the various actors and instruments available and is "essential" for the comparison of policies (Palmer and Bhandari 2000, 6). Accounting for substitutability captures some of the complexity of actor choices omitted in much of the existing research and reflects intuition of how policy is made (Morgan and Palmer 2000). Studies of conflict resolution that do not include all possible actors and actions prevent the true accumulation of knowledge:

Focusing on only one [actor] would mean a failure to provide full coverage of the possible outcomes and lead to incomplete results that fail to cumulate (or even make sense when compared). The results would fail to capture the theory or model being tested (as only part was being tested). And [...] focusing on only one possible outcome (the successful outcome that is observed) leads to the logical problems that exclude the study of sufficient relationships. (Starr 2000, 129)

The lack of scholarship merging conflict management research with that on business and peace can account for the weakness of many empirical findings and failure to better understand the puzzle of continued violence (see also Most and Starr 1989).

The problems associated with isolated research programs are endemic in both the conflict management and business and peace literatures. Within conflict management research, studies examine policies of military intervention (see Regan 1996), diplomatic approaches (see Mack and Snyder 1957; Bercovitch 1998; Kleiboer 1996; Pruitt 1981; Ott 1972), and economic sanctions (see Hufbauer and Schott 1983; Li 1993; Weiss 1999) independent of one another. Similarly, much of the scholarship on corporate activities focuses exclusively on the actions of one corporation. Responses to violence, whether by a government representative, a corporate executive, or an international mediator, rarely occur in isolation. Yet academic research treats these varied actors and their actions as completely separate choices, policies, and outcomes. It is unclear how different conflict management activities work together both theoretically and in practice. For example, the United States and European Union used economic sanctions, mediation, and eventually military intervention to help end the bloody conflict that arose during the breakup of Yugoslavia. Mercy Corps worked to build business links across ethnic groups in Kosovo. Citing the bombing of Bosnia-Herzegovina as the reason for the end of the conflict and what seems to be sustained peace ignores the possibility that earlier sanctions, mediation, and NGO grassroots work may have paved the way for a successful NATO bombing campaign. The same is true if we ignore the role that the private sector played. For example, the conflict shrunk Bosnia-Herzegovina's GDP to a third of its prewar levels, obliterated the infrastructure, and restricted the private sector to microbusiness (Banfield, Gündüz, and Killick 2006). Nova Banka is a bank that focused on enabling access to capital for businesses, critical for developing the postwar economy. Organic Medici, a twig broom company that expanded to processing products from Bosnia's hills into tea, herbs, and essential oils, works with farmers and employees from diverse ethnic backgrounds. Many businesses, through investments, hiring practices, and expansion, have taken proactive steps to consolidating peace. Ignoring their role leaves us with an incomplete picture of the process involved in building a lasting peace.

3

Peacebuilding

Definition, Actors, Framework, and Measurement

What does it mean to build peace? How is it done in practice, and who does it? Is it possible to create a broad understanding of this process? This book argues that we can create generalized knowledge about the ways different actors build peace, but to do so requires we move beyond more traditional actors and reconsider how private firms contribute to peace. It also requires precise definitions, logically sound theoretical frameworks, and measures of corporate peacebuilding grounded in the strong scholarship on peace and conflict. I build from existing knowledge on the causes of conflict and its resolution to understand the role of private business, thereby creating an argument and evidence that speak across fields.

I situate firm-led peacebuilding occurrence and outcomes within the rational choice framework of civil war. Violence, rebellion, and war can all be understood as part of a rational decision-making process despite the fact that they are suboptimal. That is, would-be disputants consider the costs, benefits, and likely outcomes of violence before engaging. Peacebuilding efforts can change actor's decision calculus, making violence a less attractive choice. Similarly, private firms weigh the opportunity costs of investing in peacebuilding activities, responding to demand when the conditions enable its supply. Considering these incentives reveals information about when peacebuilding occurs, its effects, and its outcomes.

This chapter begins by defining the term "peacebuilding," an admittedly broad and abstract concept. I then outline the varied actors that have the opportunity to engage in this process with a focus on the role and attributes of private firms. I overview the rational choice framework and apply it to the incentives for private firms to build peace and the outcomes of these efforts. Finally, I describe the data used to test these arguments and show trends in the occurrence of firm-led efforts to build peace.

The Building and Breaking of Peace. Molly M. Melin, Oxford University Press. © Oxford University Press 2021.
DOI: 10.1093/oso/9780197579367.003.0003

Defining Peacebuilding

The concept of peacebuilding was first introduced in the former UN Secretary-General Boutros Boutros-Ghali's 1992 report, "An Agenda for Peace." His definition involved "action to identify and support structures, which will tend to strengthen and solidify peace in order to avoid a relapse into conflict" (Boutros-Ghali 1992, 204). The concept was further developed in the Brahimi Report as "activities undertaken on the far side of conflict to reassemble the foundations of peace and provide the tools for building on those foundations something that is more than the absence of war" (Brahimi 2000, 2). Reports that followed identified five main priority areas for peacebuilding: (1) support to basic security and safety, (2) political processes, (3) provision of basic services, (4) restoration of core government functions, and (5) economic revitalization (United Nations).

Thus, peacebuilding is a broad concept that can include any activity meant to help create a less violent society. Doyle and Sabanis offer a useful description of such actions:

> Peacebuilding is an attempt . . . to address the sources of current hostility and build local capacities for conflict resolution. Stronger state institutions, broader political participation, land reform, a deepening of civil society, and respect for ethnic identities are all seen as ways to improve the prospects for peaceful governance. In plural societies, conflicts are inevitable. The aim of peacebuilding is to foster the social, economic, and political institutions and attitudes that will prevent these conflicts from turning violent. In effect, peacebuilding is the front line of preventive action. (2000, 779)

What peacebuilding looks like in action might range from large-scale government reform (which often includes democratization, see Jarstad and Sisk 2008), to grassroots programs engaging civil society (Lederach 1997).

Scholarship on the topic of peacebuilding explores activities that occur following the aftermath of conflict. While countries that are recovering from conflict certainly face challenges, many of these are not unique to the post-conflict environment. Conflict prevention and preventative diplomacy involve "action to prevent disputes from arising between parties, to prevent existing disputes from escalating into conflicts and to limit the spread of the latter when they occur" (Boutros-Ghali 1992, 204). As with peacebuilding, conflict prevention and preventative diplomacy include actions that address the underlying causes of violent conflict, especially addressing economic and social development. Together, they offer a coherent way to secure peace, as envisioned by the UN Charter. I therefore consider corporate contributions to peace in both the preventative and post-conflict settings.

I link the scholarship on peacebuilding and conflict prevention to the rational choice framework, thereby considering how national contexts affect individual and group decisions. Drawing from the rational choice approach, which I outline further in what follows, I define the peacebuilding-related[1] activities examined in this study as *any activity that raises the opportunity costs of violence, thereby preventing the occurrence or recurrence of war*. More precisely, this includes programs that help increase factors associated with positive peace: a well-functioning government, a sound business environment, low levels of corruption, high levels of human capital, free flow of information, good relations with neighbors, equitable distribution of resources, and the acceptance of the rights of others (Institute for Economics and Peace 2017). Such structures help to create and sustain peaceful societies through making violence a less attractive alternative. When these are absent, violence or fear of violence increases. Firms can work to create more peaceful societies through programs that increase societal safety and security and reduce domestic unrest. Investment in education programs (Thyne 2006) and programs that increase economic opportunities (Collier and Hoeffler 2002a) are two ways by which firms can reduce conflict, since these factors increase the opportunity costs of violence, thereby encouraging political participation and reducing the risk of political violence.

The Builders of Peace

Peacebuilding-related activities can involve a wide variety of actors and actions. Moving a society away from violence usually involves state-building and institutional reform, such as in Afghanistan and Liberia. Such activities occur at the elite level, where formal negotiations occur. In addition, so-called track two diplomacy involves church leaders, intellectuals, and party members. To say that corporate actors can play a role in peace and conflict is not to say that they play the same role that other prominent actors play. It is possible to distinguish the corporate roles on several fronts: (1) the level at which corporate engagement occurs, (2) corporate intentions, (3) the publicity of corporate involvement, and (4) the outcomes resulting from corporate involvement. As these attributes can have implications for when, where, and how corporate engagement occurs, I discuss each of these factors more thoroughly in this section.

Level of Engagement

Conflict prevention and resolution techniques are often discussed in terms of their level of engagement, distinguishing between tracks one (official, high-level political and military leaders focused on ceasefires and treaties), two (unofficial dialogue that engages civil society in building relationships), and three (grassroots levels meetings and events designed to bring together conflicting communities). Involvement of corporate actors occurs at all three levels but often involves tracks two and three diplomacy, working in the community. For example, Richard Holbrooke worked with the International Peace Research Institute in Oslo and helped convene groups of business people from Cyprus, Greece, and Turkey as a way to build trust and improve negotiations. More broadly, the peacebuilding work of the business community in Cyprus has been indirect, aiming to increase interaction between groups and generate economic gains from greater interdependence (Portland Trust 2013). Efforts in Northern Ireland were more formally political, especially through the Confederation of British Industry and other business and trade organizations, quantifying the costs of conflict and lobbying politicians and the public to support peace as a way to generate prosperity. In South Africa, the business community both engaged directly in helping broker peace, facilitating negotiations, and providing administrative support to the talks that led to the first democratic election, and indirectly engaging in community building projects that range from education to criminal justice.

Intentions

Since the purpose of a business is to generate profit, peacebuilding is not necessarily an intended outcome for firms. Corporate engagement in the peace process often involves an intention–consequence gap, wherein peaceful interactions can be a positive externality rather than a direct goal. While businesses may do the right things for the wrong reason, these acts can still benefit the greater good (Williams 2008). While it is preferable that companies are motivated by positive values, it may not be necessary. Indeed, the question of motives has no easy answer.

The business strategy of shared value, wherein companies find business opportunities in social problems, offers evidence that creating both social value and business value are not mutually exclusive. For example, Grupo Exito adjusted its employment policies to hire and retain victims of conflict and former combatants following the peace accord. Supporting the unique needs of these employees through continuing education scholarships, access to credit, and parental leave has increased employee productivity while improving the work environment. Businesses are increasingly seeing the advantages of shared-value approaches and taking intentional steps to address social problems.

Publicity

Corporate engagement varies from being very public to completely behind closed doors. This can create challenges for the scientific study of such activities, which is somewhat dependent on the availability of information to examine. While high profile activities and public corporate policies are easily accessible, unofficial acts are more difficult to examine. Playing an unofficial role in peacebuilding does not necessarily distinguish corporate activities from those of states and diplomats, as their negotiations often occur privately as well. This fact has not prevented a huge amount of research on the topic of state-led mediation efforts, international arbitration and adjudication, and negotiations. While businesses may be more likely to tout their "good" actions as a way to improve their brand image, governments and officials also have an incentive to improve their global reputation. Thus, scholars must make do with the available information about peacebuilding and try to extrapolate knowledge from there.

Outcomes

The outcomes from corporate engagement also tend to differ from those of other actors engaged in the peace and conflict process. While state and international organization-led efforts often produce highly publicized agreements, such as ceasefires and treaties, corporate involvement tends to have more of an incremental, less dramatic effect. Additionally, when businesses are involved in higher profile negotiations, they are more likely to include many diverse actors, which makes attributing outcomes to actors and their actions challenging. To further complicate this process, examining the successful promotion of peace poses its own challenges. Thus, we are once again faced with the suboptimal availability of information, but can still examine shifts in behavior and conflict dynamics.

Theoretical Framework

Which firms act to build peace in their countries, and what are the outcomes of such engagement? Research has shown that private sector activity can play an important role in conflict prevention (Banfield, Haufler, and Lilly 2005a; Ballentine and Haufler 2005). In what follows, I develop a theoretical argument and hypotheses about when corporate actors engage in building peace and the resulting outcomes. I assume corporations are rational actors seeking to maximize the benefits and minimize the costs of any policies they implement or actions they take. Thus, in considering any peacebuilding policy, business leaders will account for the demand for and utility of peacebuilding, as well as the supply or cost of peacebuilding before choosing a policy. Within the conflict literature, expected utility arguments have been used to help explain a wide range of decision processes, such as rebellion and revolution (Weede and Muller 1998), civil wars (Mason and Fett 1996a), international conflict (De Mesquita 1988), third-party mediation (Terris and Maoz 2005), and conflict management (Melin 2011). The rational choice framework also helps us understand private firm actions, such as corporate deterrence (Braithwaite and Makkai 1991), corporate responses to activist campaigns (Baron 2001), and social responsibility policies (Baron 2007).

Investing in Peacebuilding

As profit-maximizing firms, corporations can use engagement as a way to maximize profits and market value while decreasing the costs of doing business. Peacebuilding and profit maximizing are not mutually exclusive processes. In fact, because firms operate in complex social, market, and political environments, they must take into account concerns beyond short-term profit maximization (Wolf, Deitelhoff, and Engert 2007). The concept of complex market rationality requires firms to consider reputational costs and normative expectations in their cost-benefit calculations. At the same time, firms are under pressure to keep their costs low. Peacebuilding involves opportunity costs: investing in a community engagement program means that time, talent, and money cannot be spent on product development, marketing, salaries, or production.

Given these trade-offs, what conditions might encourage firms to invest in peace? What circumstances make engagement an attractive corporate policy? As internal motives for peacebuilding, such as firm industry and size, tend to be slow to change and relatively constant over time, I focus on external causes. External dynamics can create an operating environment that demands active corporate engagement, as when a government is unable to provide the infrastructure that allows corporations to get goods to market in a safe and timely manner. Such conditions define the setting in which the corporation operates: does that environment demand that the company engage stakeholders beyond simple economic transactions?

Environmental conditions create both the demand for and supply of peacebuilding. The demand for corporate peacebuilding is highest when corporations can fill "gaps" in governance left by a weak state. Only some conditions foster the supply side of this calculus, however. Firms are better situated to invest in peacebuilding when conditions foster economic growth, investment, and innovation. Firms are less able to supply peacebuilding in uncertain conditions, making engagement a less attractive policy for a firm to pursue due to untenable opportunity costs. These variations in a corporation's operating environment offer insights into how state characteristics foster or hinder corporate engagement.

Table 3.1 outlines the conditions that create the demand for corporate peacebuilding and foster a firm's ability to supply it. A weak state is one that lacks government effectiveness, the ability to enforce the rule of law, and regulatory quality. Each of these conditions creates a gap in governance, or a demand for corporate peacebuilding. A stable environment is one that has experienced years of peace rather than violence, which allows firms to increase investments and adopt innovative policies that supply peacebuilding. The opportunity costs of peacebuilding will be lowest when conditions foster a firm's ability to supply peacebuilding in response to a present demand for it.

Alternative explanations point to the reputational benefits a company gains from community engagement projects like peacebuilding. Companies

Table 3.1 Causal Paths and Definitions in the Demand for and Supply of Peacebuilding

Increased Demand for Peacebuilding	Increased Supply of Peacebuilding
Operating Under a Weak State	Operating in Stability
Government effectiveness—quality of public services, civil services, policy formulations and implementation, and credibility	Years of Peace—Years without violence leading to at least 25 battle-related deaths Years of violence—Years with violence leading to at least 25 battle-related deaths
Rule of law—quality of contract enforcement, police, and the courts	
Regulatory quality—developing and implementing sound policies and regulations promoting private sector development	

facing scandal or problems with their corporate image may proactively engage as a way to rebuild a firm's profits, but I argue this is only a partial explanation of firm behavior. In what follows, I further explain how environmental conditions encourage firms to build peace.

The Demand for Peacebuilding: Firms Fill the Gaps

Since acting to build peace entails investing in a community beyond what is necessary for economic exchange, corporations must have interests involved. Their choice is not as stark as that of traditional conflict managers, as third parties can avoid involvement altogether (Beardsley 2010; Melin and Svensson 2009). We are most likely to observe firms investing in peacebuilding when there is a gap in state capacity, as this creates a demand for engagement that directly affects corporations. State capacity is critical for economic system performance, and states with a high capacity are able to provide public goods such as infrastructure, security, and education. A state's capacity reflects how likely a state is to provide goods and services. These goods and services are necessary for commerce to operate smoothly. Weak state capacity increases the costs of business operations. For example, the firm must account for security costs when the state does not provide it (Deitelhoff 2009). Similarly, poor infrastructure and an untrained workforce increase the costs of conducting business. Weak governance means corporations are operating in circumstances where the infrastructure is out-dated, contract enforcement is poor, and policies are either not formulated or not enforced in a way that is supportive of the private sector. When the government has low capacity (but not a complete inability) to form and en-force policies, firms are likely to step in to fill the need because it is in their interest to do.

The private sector's skills and resources can help contribute to govern-ance, peace, and security in the context of weak states (Deitelhoff et al. 2010). This has created a new type of global governance, putting firms at the frontline of peace and stability in fragile and conflict-affected areas (Schouten and Miklian 2017). Case studies have shown corporations have contributed to governance during the conflict in Rwanda, the Democratic Republic of Congo, Northern Ireland, and Israel (Deitelhoff and Wolf 2010).

Firms are least likely to invest in peacebuilding at high and extremely low levels of state capacity. When the state completely lacks the ability to enforce the rule of law (or has extremely low capacity), there is unlikely to be private sector involvement due to a lack of large companies with the resources and willingness to risk engagement. For example, Bloomberg reports sixteen pri-vately held companies operating in Syria in 2018 compared to the eighty-four headquartered in (somewhat capable) Colombia. State failure suggests a lack of stable government institutions, which prevents secure property rights, wealth protection, and elimination of confiscatory government, thereby suppressing economic exchange and growth (North and Weingast 1989). On the other end of the governance spectrum, firms have less incentive to en-gage when the government is completely capable of providing stability and services since the risk of violence is much lower (Hegre and Nygård 2015). Corporations can influence political and social stability in low-capacity states, where there is a need for firm engagement but firm investments are not at risk of seizure.

The Supply of Peacebuilding: Peace Begets Peacebuilding

Domestic peace is stable, promoting investment and innovation. Companies operating in volatile environments face the challenge of conducting busi-ness with an unpredictable future, a condition that dampens investment and profits. While transnational corporations may offshore a business process to a more stable country, domestically headquartered firms often face higher exit costs and often operate in less mobile sectors (such as energy and agriculture). While transnational actors can influence conflict dynamics (Banfield, Haufler, and Lilly 2005b), they also have greater mobility, as they are already familiar with the challenges of operating in multiple nations. Locally headquartered corporations have fewer exit options and must close shop when operations are no longer viable.[2]

Companies operating in a volatile environment face uncertainty that depresses growth and investment. Violence and volatility in effect shrink the corporate pie, focusing corporate attention on staying afloat rather than innovative community engagement. When violence occurs, security costs and uncertainty increase the costs of doing business (Wolf, Deitelhoff, and Engert 2007). The company's investments are threatened, as conflict can damage production assets, infrastructure, local markets, and labor (Wenger and Möckli 2003). Similarly, political changes create uncertainty about the future rule of law, adding risk. Institutional change can have consequences on economic performance (North 1990), and it is likely that corporations are especially sensitive to these changes since they create the incentive structures of the economy. Political changes, especially those that strip rights and open processes, increase uncertainty. Such uncertainty can depress investments and scare away mobile assets.

Operating in a high-risk environment involves challenges and opportunities. Altruism alone cannot motivate peacebuilding, as there must be a positive business case for investing.[3] For example, Nespresso worked with local farmers in South Sudan to offer training, technical assistance, and support that both helped develop a coffee export market and contributed to the company's bottom line. The conflict management literature shows that third parties behave similarly, with strategic interests motivating mediation while helping create peace agreements (Terris and Maoz 2005; Melin 2011, 2013). Active conflict, violence, and political changes dampen investment and reduce the ability for firms to supply peacebuilding. Stability allows firms to grow, innovate, and adopt a business case for engaging in peacebuilding.

The alternative argument is that instability prompts firms to action. However, instability undermines growth and private investment (Feng 2001). Instead of investing in innovative ways to build peace, those firms that can weather storms of instability are likely focused on maintaining daily operations.

Alternative Explanation: Peacebuilding as Reputation-Building

Despite the spread of corporate responsibility norms, there are many examples of corporate negligence and misbehavior, especially during wartime (King 2001). Spoils of war can discourage peaceful settlement, and companies often operate outside the law. Business is often part of the problem for countries embroiled in conflict, particularly in those with natural resources (Switzer 2002). Shifting conflict dynamics change the payoffs for corporations, encouraging firms to consider how to profit under greater stability.

Technology increases corporate accountability as the potential for negative consequences from unethical behavior encourages responsible behaviors. Modern communication enables communities and activists to mobilize support and pressure corporations to take restorative measures (Andrews et al. 2017). Through peacebuilding, companies that have been called out for "bad" behavior can proactively work to rebuild their brand. As an alternative explanation of firm behavior, I explore the idea that corporate engagement is simply a public relations effort that can help a company rebuild its reputation following scandal, rather than a response to conditions in their operating environment.

Peacebuilding Outcomes

How does corporate peacebuilding affect peace and conflict? When a country has an active private sector, what is the effect on the levels of peace and violence the country experiences? I argue active corporations can prevent violence from occurring, but prolong the conflicts that do occur by adding additional veto players to negotiations. To understand the peacebuilding outcomes of corporate engagement, I build on rational choice approaches to civil war onset and termination. Engaged corporations can change the incentives to pursue violence, increasing or decreasing the likelihood of civil war occurrence. At the same time, engaged corporations can complicate negotiations to settle ongoing conflict, adding additional interests to the bargaining table. While corporate peacebuilding has important implications for conflict prevention, an engaged private sector creates challenges for peacefully resolving ongoing conflict.

Violence Prevention

Civil wars occur when the expected utility of war outweighs the expected utility of peace (Collier and Hoeffler 2002a; Walter 2004; Fearon and Laitin 2003; Collier and Hoeffler 1998). While the specific motivations for pursuing violence are complex and varied, the rational choice framework offers a useful way to organize such complexities theoretically. For example, opportunity costs for potential rebel recruits help us understand the motives for rebelling (Walter 2004; Collier and Hoeffler 2000), which can be seen as changing the payoffs of violence. Poverty can motivate belligerence, since the opportunity costs of war are outweighed by the private gains of conflict.

A corporation's involvement in peacebuilding can prevent violence by altering the payoffs each party expects from engaging in conflict. One approach is to reduce the incentives for rebellion, which is the product of the probability of victory and its consequences. Another approach is to raise the costs of rebellion, through loss of income and the costs of coordination. Thus, corporations can successfully build peace through (1) raising the cost of rebellion or (2) reducing the benefits of rebellion (Table 3.2).

Improving living conditions (Walter 2004), increasing average incomes or decreasing inequality (Collier, Hoeffler, and Söderbom 2004), and providing access to employment (Hegre 2004) are all ways the private sector can alter the incentives to turn to violence. Each of these approaches increases the opportunity cost of rebelling, since rebelling may no longer offer the possibility of a better quality of life. This means that corporate engagement efforts that reduce potential benefits from joining a rebel group can help prevent violence. Thus, countries with a private sector that actively engages communities are less likely to experience violent conflict.

Table 3.2 Causal Paths and Definitions in Peacebuilding Outcomes

Increased Conflict Prevention	Decreased Conflict Resolution
Peacebuilding Changes the Costs and Benefits of Conflict	Peacebuilding Increases the Veto Players in Negotiations
Higher proportions of engaged firms increase the quality of life, making conflict less attractive	Higher proportions of engaged firms increase influence over negotiations, making agreement more difficult

Conflict Resolution

Peacefully resolving violence requires the conflicting parties find an agreement that is acceptable to all involved actors. The more groups that must approve a settlement, the harder it will be to create an agreement that everyone will accept. This means that conflicts with multiple actors that must approve a settlement, or veto players, will be more difficult to resolve and will last longer than those with bilateral negotiations (Cunningham 2006a; Table 3.2).

When the business community is engaged, they become another veto player that must approve the terms of settlement. Since peace agreements often dictate the rules of post-conflict exchange, the business community will want to ensure these terms protect their interests. While peace increases economic exchange and can lead to economic growth, referred to as a peace dividend, the private sector is not always a supporter of peace negotiations. For example, the Guatemalan civil war was geographically contained and low intensity, keeping the economic costs of the conflict low and even providing some indirect advantages to certain business sectors (Joras 2007). In fact, the potential threats to economic interests posed by a peace process seeking to tackle the root causes of conflict can alienate the private sector. In other cases, such as Colombia and Northern Ireland, the private sector was a strong proponent of peace negotiations, but the terms of the agreement still had to account for their interests. Thus, both supporters and skeptics of peace negotiations can prolong conflict and make it more difficult to form an acceptable agreement.

Measuring Corporate Peacebuilding Actions

The preceding arguments suggest that creating a complete understanding of the causes of peace and conflict requires we consider the role of the for-profit sector. For instance, if we want to understand which conflicts end with successful peace agreements and which only end once one side reaches a military victory, it is worthwhile to consider not only the conflict and disputant characteristics but also the role firms play in supporting the peace process or instigating violence. The same limitation exists with scholarship on the initiation of conflict and duration of peace. How does the business community exacerbate tensions or promote peaceful interactions? The composition of these efforts may be important as well. Which firms contribute to peacebuilding and which ones engage in harmful actions? What are their mechanisms of engaging society? How consequential are these activities for building peaceful societies? These are important questions for scholars of peace and conflict to address. Our ability to consider the role of private firms is limited, however, by an absence of data (Wolf, Deitelhoff, and Engert 2007). Quantitative scholars have no information on firm activities in conflict processes. This limits our ability to generate a complete picture of peace and conflict processes and make meaningful contributions to the policy community.

The data presented here seek to remedy these limitations and enable the empirical testing of the preceding arguments. The Company of Peace and Conflict data (COPC) code new data on corporate peacebuilding activities. The data are coded in two formats, enabling this book to examine variation across countries and across companies. The *country-year* data contain aggregate information on the activities of the private sector across countries. The *company-year* data include information about each company and the nature of its activities. Both formats are collected for the period after the creation of the United Nations Global Compact, from 2000 to 2018. In what follows, I detail the coding process and present trends in the data.

Data Collection and Coding Process

The backbone of the disaggregated data is made up of large corporations and their defining characteristics. I then add information on their actions in the country where they are headquartered. I include all companies with over $100 million US in 2015 revenue.[4] While this is not to say that smaller companies do not have a role to play in the peace process (and research suggests they do play an important role in fostering peaceful communities, see Iff and Alluri 2016; Banfield, Gündüz, and Killick 2006), this limits the large number of businesses operating to a feasible number. While findings based on the activities of large corporations may not accurately reflect the activities of all businesses (especially as smaller businesses do not have access to the same resources or the same interests), they offer insights into a relatively new actor in the processes of peace and conflict.

The data include 925 large corporations based in Central and South America, the Caribbean, Africa, and the Middle East from 2000 to 2018. The spatial and temporal domains of the data are chosen for both theoretical and feasibility reasons. Business scholars show that firms engage in different ways across different societies. While there are over 14,000 corporations that might be included were we to code firms globally, these regions offer a subset of areas where instability has been common and government oversight of the private sector has been low. The data include 144 companies in Central America and the Caribbean, 162 companies in South America, 306 African based firms, and 162 Middle Eastern firms. The temporal domain of the data includes years after the creation of the United Nations Global Compact.[5] The availability of some of the firm-level indicators is limited by the fact that business data is generally forward focused, including current information but not historic data. Unless otherwise noted, information on the firms and their characteristics are coded using the Marketline Advantage program, a common source among business scholars.

Proactive Engagement

The data offer an overview of the positive contributions the private sector makes toward peace through value creation, as well as the societal damage the corporations cause. Actions are coded to reflect actively engaging the United Nations' Business for Peace (B4P) indicators: economic (strengthening equitable economies, shareholder dividends, and loan interest), social (building human capital, provision of infrastructure, healthcare, or educational benefits to society), and environmental (protecting the environment, investing in renewable energy, land stewardship, recycling). In addition, corporations are reported to have created negative externalities in the same realms: economic negative (avoiding taxes, corruption), social negative (low wages, negative health and safety effects, damage to societal health through pollution), and environmental negative (greenhouse gases and energy, water, and raw materials misuse) (Table 3.3). Getz and Oetzel (2009) show these types of activities offer ways companies can actively reduce conflict. Information on corporate engagement is coded from Lexis-Nexis and Google News searches. Both search engines offer ample local and international news coverage, although we were limited to English- and Spanish-language sources. One limitation of collecting reports of peacebuilding activities is that news coverage is dependent on an active press. Another approach to collecting information is to rely on company webpages, but these may overstate the company's engagement levels and do not enable coding information about the timing of engagement. Search terms focused on the company name to ensure capture

Table 3.3 Corporate Activities Can Be Coded in Line with the UN's B4P Performance Indicators

Mechanism	Indicator	Sample Headline
Economic	Strengthening equitable economies, shareholder dividends, and loan interest	"Arab Potash Company contributes to Jordan's national development," "Borusan, Supporting Women's Entrepreneurship"
Social	Building human capital, Supporting social cohesion and human rights, provision of infrastructure, healthcare, or educational benefits to society	"British Council, GraceKennedy partner for Boy Mentoring Group," "BBVA invertirá unos $7.900 millones en educación en 2016."
Environmental	Protecting the environment, investing in renewable energy, land stewardship, recycling	"Banco Pine S.A.: PINE is considered 'The Most Green Bank in Latin America and the Caribbean,'" "Environmental Science: New life for the Dead Sea?"

of both positive and negative reports. While the definition of engagement might be overly broad (including paying taxes, for example), events will only be covered in newsworthy cases (such as paying a large sum of back taxes). Thus, peacebuilding-related activities must be sizable and notable enough to garner news coverage to be included in the data.

Each corporate activity is coded as an event in a given year. Information about the timing of activities is based on the article publication date. Relying on press reports allows for consistency across engagement events. Publication dates were used because reports only rarely listed other dates for corporate actions, which often continue once implemented, adding additional coding challenges. This is certainly a simplification of corporate engagement. Programs may have been ongoing prior to news coverage, continue for years into the future, or be a one-time contribution. For example, BBVA Colombia made a one-time contribution to financing education that was reported on in January of 2016 and is coded as occurring that year. Since the contribution was spread over the year, this was likely properly captured. Its 2019 award for financial inclusion, however, would not capture the company's long-time commitment to serving lower-income populations and would only be coded for the year of news coverage. The same challenge is a concern for negative reports, as news coverage of a corporation being fined reflects prior behavior but is coded for the year the behavior is punished. What this means substantively is that the data bias solitary events over long-term commitments.

The measures code the presence or absence of reports of the three mechanisms of engagement in a given year. Each measure is coded both dichotomously for the presence or absence of each mechanism and as a count of the number of events per company in the company-year data and per country in the country-year data. This creates eight variables to measure peacebuilding-related events: six constituted of each type (dichotomous and count) and two composite measures of peacebuilding occurrence and number of total peacebuilding events. I present trends in these data in the pages that follow, but it should be noted that these trends do not control for other likely causal factors, such as the size of the country's economy or whether there is significant ongoing violence in the country. They do, however, give the reader a sense of the data and corporate engagement. I engage in a similar coding scheme for harmful activities, as described in Table 3.4.

Figure 3.1 presents the occurrence of corporate engagement in peacebuilding-related activities across time.[6] Several trends are clear. Mostly striking is the increase in the occurrence of all mechanisms of engagement since 2000. The first recorded economic, social, and environmental activity

Table 3.4 Harmful Corporate Activities

Mechanism	Indicator	Sample Headline
Economic	Avoiding taxes, corruption	"Eletropaulo buys electricity at the equivalent of \$31 per MW/h and charges customers \$60. Yet, thanks to inefficiency, corruption and high financing charges, the company has lost money every year since 1990"
Social	Low wages, negative health and safety effects, damage to societal health through pollution	"A firm owned by Brazil's vice-president will be investigated by congress for its possible involvement in an illegal campaign financing scheme."
Environmental	Greenhouse gases, energy waste, ecosystem damage, wasteful use of water and raw materials	"Dams built by Copel are claimed to be harmful to waterfalls"

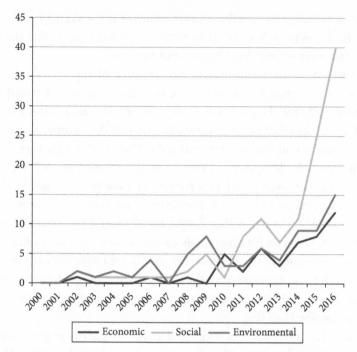

Figure 3.1 The Number of Firm-Led Peacebuilding-Related Activities across Time

is in 2002, with no more than five of any peacebuilding mechanisms occurring in any given year until 2009. While there may have been higher levels of engagement than the data capture, these are the events reported on by the news media. There is some concern about bias in reporting, however, as the media covers some sustainability topics more heavily than others and has increasingly reported on sustainability as it has shifted from being a fringe topic to headline news (Barkemeyer, Givry, and Figge 2018). After 2009, economic and environmental programs hover between three and fifteen activities per year, while social programs explode. The rapid rise in programs likely stems from shifting expectations about corporate behavior, where corporate engagement has become a mainstream global movement (Kell 2018).

Despite the growth in peacebuilding-related corporate engagement, it remains true that a very small percentage of companies are involved in these activities. In 2016, the year with the most reported events, only 5 percent of companies engaged in social mechanisms of peacebuilding, 1.5 percent

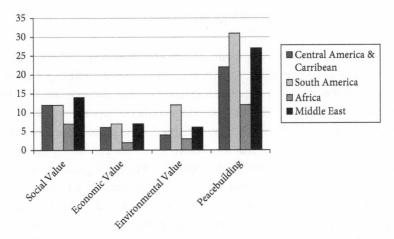

Figure 3.2 The Percent of Companies Engaged in Peacebuilding-Related Activities

engaged in mechanisms benefiting the environment, and only 1.3 percent engaged in economically beneficial mechanisms. Many of the same companies build peace with multiple mechanisms in a given year, meaning that only 6 percent are engaged in any way during the height of corporate peacebuilding-related activity. Could this lack of engagement by the world's most powerful companies help us understand the continuation of violent conflict?

Figure 3.2 graphs the occurrence of each peacebuilding mechanism across regions, revealing several notable trends. Comparing the different mechanisms of engagement, we see that companies are generally most likely to create social value, followed by environmental value and economic value. This trend was also present in Figure 3.1. The last group of columns, labeled "Peacebuilding," depicts the composite measure of all mechanisms and shows that Africa has by far the lowest percentage of companies engaged in peacebuilding (12 percent), whereas South America has the most active private sector, with 31 percent of companies engaged in some form of peacebuilding. While these trends may be biased by news media coverage of Africa compared to other regions (Golan 2008), the press can also serve to pressure policy changes (Norris 2000). This means that while peacebuilding-related behavior in Africa may be less likely to receive the attention of the press, the press is also putting less pressure on African corporations to invest in peace.

"Bad" Behavior

The data include information about reports of negative corporate actions that are harmful to communities. As with the proactive peacebuilding measure, I include information on activities that harm society, the economy, and the environment. Each variable is a sum of the number of reports of each type of harmful action, as well as a dummy variable for the presence or absence of a harmful event in a given year for each company (or country in the aggregate country-year data). This creates eight measures of negative actions: six of each sector that is harmed and two compiled measures of negative actions. The data show over 12 percent of companies are reported for having a negative economic, social, or environmental affect. Figure 3.3 presents the variation in the occurrence of harmful activities across the sector that is harmed and region.

As with peacebuilding activities, South American companies are most likely and African companies are the least likely to engage in harmful activities. The composite percentages show 24 percent of South American companies, 22 percent of Middle Eastern companies, 18 percent of Central American and Caribbean companies, and 5 percent of African companies engage in harmful actions. In Central America and the Caribbean, many of the same companies are reported for different types of harmful actions. Six companies in Mexico have been reported for engaging in all three types of

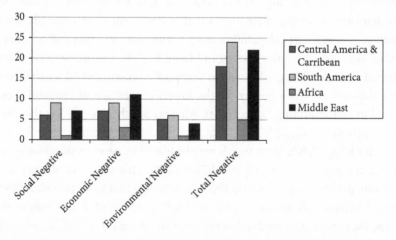

Figure 3.3 The Percent of Companies Engaged in Harmful Activities

harmful activities.[7] No other countries have multiple companies that have engaged in all harmful activity types.

At least some of this variation is due to regional biases in press coverage (Scott 2009; Golan 2008). That is, not all companies face the same risk of "getting caught" being bad actors. Variation may reflect different regional capacity for and interest in news media oversight. Media with greater "watchdog" capacity and press freedom are more likely to report on harmful actions. There are additional possible explanations of the variation in peacebuilding and harmful activities, such as differences in industrial sectors across regions. For example, the majority of African companies are headquartered in South Africa, which has a large financial industry. This industry has strong standards of operation, which should prevent them from poor conduct if followed. In Latin America, however, almost 60 percent of companies are headquartered in Brazil, with most corporations in a problematic energy and utility sector and a press that does a poor job of serving as watchdog (Vivarta and Canela 2006).

Figure 3.4 shows the rates of peacebuilding and harmful activities across time, based on the two aggregate measures. The two rates mirror each other fairly closely, likely reflecting new technology that increases watchdog capacity, as well as increased press coverage of corporate behavior. That said,

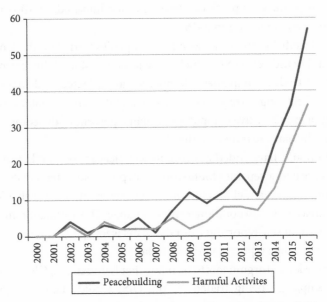

Figure 3.4 Temporal Trends in Peacebuilding-Related and Harmful Activities

after 2005, positive engagement occurs more frequently than harmful activities do. The split offers encouraging evidence that firms are less likely to harm the communities where they operate and more likely to positively contribute to them. Whether this results from shifts in watchdog capacity, shareholder pressure, or global norms is unclear but explored in chapter 4.

External Indicators

In addition to coding activities based on media coverage, the data include information available from reputable third-party reports. Increasingly, nongovernmental organizations (NGOs) and intergovernmental organizations (IGOs) are collecting information about and reporting on corporate activities. The United Nation's Global Compact (UNGC) is an example of one such organization. The UNGC was established to support companies in doing business responsibly in aligning their strategies and operations with the Global Compact's Ten Principals on human rights, labor, environment, and anticorruption. Membership requires corporations to operate responsibly, in alignment with the ten principals, and submit a report on their efforts annually. I code the number of years a company has been an active member of the Global Compact, which was created in 2000. Eight of the companies joined in the year of the Compact's creation, and one hundred, or 10 percent, of companies were members in 2016.

I include a dichotomous measure of companies traded on the Dow Jones Sustainability Indices (DJSI), which evaluates the sustainability performance of publicly traded companies. Companies are selected and incorporated based on their long-term economic, social, and environmental asset management plans. Only five companies, or half a percent of the companies, included in the data are traded on the DJSI.

In addition, I have coded a dichotomous measure of whether or not the firm has created a separate foundation. Corporations often create separate foundations as a channel for community engagement, often with a focus on specific areas of the corporation wants to change. The foundation measure is coded based on self-reporting from the firm's webpage. Just under 6 percent of firms in the data report having a foundation.[8]

There are logical arguments to be made that foundations, Global Compact membership, and being traded on the DJSI would encourage proactive peacebuilding, since firms must act according to certain standards, or could reflect a preexisting corporate culture that values engagement. Either way, we would expect these companies to engage at higher rates than other firms. Figure 3.5 shows variation in peacebuilding events for firms that are Global Compact members, are traded on the DJSI, and have established a foundation. Many engaged companies launch projects though their foundations, and Figure 3.5 shows that firms with foundations are likely to build peace using each of the three mechanisms. Three percent of firms with foundations engage in at least one mechanism of peacebuilding, whereas only 1 percent of those without engage. While few of the companies (around 5 percent) are members of the UNGC, many of those who do have membership do not actively engage in newsworthy peacebuilding activities. Global Compact Members do engage at rates higher than nonmembers, with 6 percent proactively peacebuilding compared to 1 percent of nonmembers. Only half a percent (or 6) of the large firms included in the data are on the Sustainability Index, but one of the six firms has been very active in peacebuilding. While these engagement trends do not account for other factors that may explain their peacebuilding action, they do suggest that these external indicators encourage corporate action. One possibility is that these organizations put peacebuilding on the corporate agenda, another is that they are validating preexisting projects. I further explore how each of these external indicators relates to a firm's peacebuilding engagement more thoroughly in the next chapter.

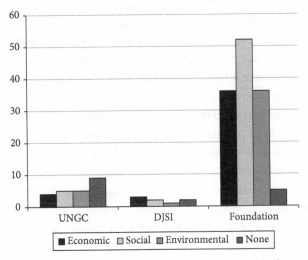

Figure 3.5 Peacebuilding-Related Activities across External Indicators

Industrial Sector

A company's propensity for peacebuilding is also linked to the sector in which it operates, as some sectors are more proactively engaging the communities where they operate than others (Haufler 2001b). A common mechanism of distinguishing among sectors is to differentiate among those corporations that operate in the extractive sector, which consists of any operations removing metals, minerals, and aggregates from the earth. While this industry has the potential to generate significant wealth and growth through generating revenue, countries with abundant natural resources often suffer from political turmoil and civil conflict. There is a large amount of scholarship on the link between natural resources and civil war (for a review, see Ross 2004). It is well established that countries with natural resources are more likely to be unstable (Dunning 2005), to experience civil war onset (De Soysa and Neumayer 2007; Fearon and Laitin 2003), and to have more severe civil wars (Lujala 2009). We also know that natural resource–dependent states tend to have slow economic growth (Sachs and Warner 2001), are poorer (Ross 2003a), have high corruption rates (Schloss 2008), and have authoritarian governments (De Soysa 2002).

To fully understand the underlying causal mechanism linking natural resources and war requires increased commodity specificity. Oil, for example has been linked to secessionist conflicts in Angola, Nigeria, and Sudan (Leary 2007; Sachs and Warner 2001; Ross 2004). The argument is that the rents available from oil and other minerals offer a financial incentive for conflict initiation, even if the actual value of the resource rents is exaggerated (Collier and Hoeffler 2002b). Civil wars are therefore more likely if the value of the resource is hard to estimate, as with oil and gas. Similarly, civil wars are found to be more likely if the resource is concentrated (Le Billon 2001), if they are extracted through a capital-intensive process, which offers few benefits to local populations, rather than labor-intensive process (Ross 2003b), and if they generate community-level grievances (Klare 2001). More "lootable" commodities, such as gemstones, timber, and drugs, have been found to increase the duration of conflict rather than its initiation, as rebel groups can use them to raise money (Le Billon 2001). Finally, agricultural commodities have not been shown to influence civil war (Collier and Hoeffler 2002b).

Such natural resources, along with the nature of the specific commodity type, change incentive structures for the actors that surround and work with them. While the majority of the civil war literature focuses on the actions of rebel groups and governments, it is logical to expect that firms dealing in natural resources may act differently than other firms. It is likely that firms operating in natural resource–focused industries are likely to have greater involvement in the events that are ongoing outside of the daily operations. One reason for this is the need to combat the negative externalities present in some sectors. For example, if corporations in the mining industry are causing environmental degradation, these corporate actors can potentially overcome such grievances through becoming more involved in the community. Additionally, the natural resource sector has very strong industry-led organizations that support the adoption and implementation of practices that go beyond minimum legal requirements. Known as Private Standard Initiatives (or PSIs), these voluntary standards and codes are developed and overseen by actors from the private and nongovernmental sectors. For example, GlobalG.A.P. certifies crops, livestock, and agriculture products according to industry standards and practices of food quality and safety. Finally, firms working with natural resources are often forced into conflict prevention activities because they cannot move to a new location should there be a breakdown in governance (Haufler 2010b). In contrast, firms operating in the manufacturing sector are shown to exit a country when armed conflict intensifies (Camacho and Rodriguez 2013). Immobility creates barriers to exit for firms, leaving them vulnerable to instability in the absence of the rule of law. For example, oil and gas companies operating in Colombia and Nigeria have been targets of rebel attacks. The immobility of assets also increases the perceived legitimacy of the firm and their ability to credibly commit to negotiations (Oetzel and Getz 2012).

Figure 3.6 shows the variation in peacebuilding-related activities across the sector of industry in which the firm operates. While finance has the most numerous firms that do not engage their community, they are also involved in the most economic and social programs. The extractive industry has also made strides, contributing to environmental programs. More broadly, the trends are similar across the different sectors, with most corporations not engaging. I examine variation in peacebuilding engagement across industrial sectors more thoroughly in subsequent chapters.

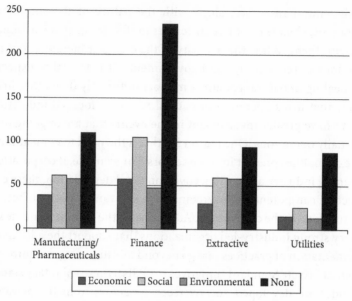

Figure 3.6 Contributions to Peacebuilding-Related Activities across Industrial Sectors

Case Selection and Analysis

In addition to the quantitative measures, I am comparing firm-led peacebuilding in the cases of Colombia, Northern Ireland, and Tunisia. I employ Gerring and McDermott's (2007) spatial comparison method. This method enables me to control for other possible causes of firm engagement and other possible explanations of the outcomes of firm engagement. The controls include characteristics that are present in each of the cases, such as income inequality, poverty, and colonial history. Because the cases share these commonalities, I can maintain stable assumptions across the cases and leverage the variation across space (across the cases) and time (within each of these cases). In this way, the case selection mimics experimental design and enables stronger causal inference.

Spatially, each of the selected cases varies in terms of the explanations of engagement (government capacity, violence levels, and corporate norms), the nature of corporate involvement (domestic versus international, direct talks versus third-party mediation, neutral versus one-sided engagement), and the outcomes of corporate involvement (violence prevention versus resolution). In Colombia, the government has moderate capacity that varies spatially by region, levels of violence differ across space and time as it urbanized, and norms of corporate-political links have become stronger over time. In Northern Ireland, British government capacity is strong but must be balanced against domestic concerns with home rule, violence has been clustered and targeted businesses, and there are not norms of corporate involvement. Tunisia has the lowest government capacity of the three cases, with very little violence and no corporate engagement norms. As a result, each case had different experiences with corporate peacebuilding. Since I do not expect firm-led peacebuilding to occur in cases of extreme under-development or state failure, I do not examine cases where the government is extremely weak or unstable.

Conclusion

Violence, rebellion, and war can all be understood as part of a rational decision process, although they are suboptimal. Corporations have the opportunity to change the expected payoffs from violence through raising actors' opportunity costs. Employment programs, donations to local education, and contributions to building infrastructure are examples of ways companies make peace an attractive alternative. Many companies have revenue larger than the economies of the states where they operate, suggesting there is an opportunity for these firms to substantially affect the lives of local populations.

The trends presented in this chapter offer evidence that some companies are actively working to build peace in communities. This supports theoretical arguments that the actors often viewed as exacerbating tensions are now participating in both commerce and peacemaking (Fort 2007). Given the high costs corporations face in the event of political violence, being proactive in facing these threats is imperative. The data discussed in this chapter are used in those that follow to examine the extent to which transnational corporations engage in preventing and resolving conflict.

The second question this book examines is how corporate peacebuilding changes the outcomes of peace and conflict. When these actors engage in preventative activities, what are the outcomes? Figure 3.7 uses the Uppsala Conflict Data Program Armed Conflict data to show trends in violence and civil war (twenty-five or more battle-related deaths a year) across levels of

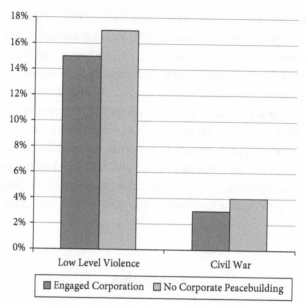

Figure 3.7 Trends in Corporate Engagement, Violence, and Civil War

corporate engagement. Countries that have at least one company engaging in conflict prevention and peacebuilding-related activities are less likely to experience both low-level violence and civil war. Civil war has complex causes, and I argue the relationship between corporate behavior and peace is not straightforward. While the trends suggest companies may offer hope for addressing the continued challenge of conflict, this book shows there is reason for cautious optimism. Indeed, none of the civil wars that did break out ended in a ceasefire or full agreement when there is corporate engagement. In chapter 4, I explore how corporate engagement has diverse effects on probability of civil war and its resolution.

Scholars are increasingly developing an understanding of state and international organization-led conflict management efforts; yet, they rarely address the role of the private sector in peace and conflict. This is partially due to the absence of data on the activities of corporate actors. This book seeks to highlight the significance of corporations in encouraging cooperation and peaceful interactions. While these actors are notably absent from international relations literature, research on corporate social responsibility, fair trade, human rights, and private security highlights the important role private companies can play in peace and conflict. It is likely that corporate engagement has implications for conflict prevention and long-term peace.

4

Supplying Peace

Which Corporations Build Peace?

In 2016, much[1] of Colombia was celebrating a peace agreement ending the longest civil war in the Western Hemisphere between the government and the Revolutionary Armed Forces of Colombia (FARC). Signs of the end to conflict were widespread and inescapable: government offices touted banners proclaiming their partnership with "paz"; cosmetic companies marketed nail polish colors "tolerant blue," "inclusive pink," and "glitter/ shine of trust";[2] beer ads encouraged drinkers to believe in peace;[3] and milk ads proclaimed, "Today, we are all milk from the same cup."[4] While the government's interest in supporting the deal they helped design is obvious, peace also has some less traditional champions. As the country transitions through the challenges of disarmament and reintegration of rebel troops, private companies are also helping to build peace—and not just with their marketing campaigns. Through hiring practices, infrastructure projects, and economic investments, the private sector often helps "fill the gaps" where governments are unwilling or unable to provide needed goods and services. These efforts can be especially salient in post-conflict societies where trust must be rebuilt. That said, the private sector has also been known to take advantage of the lawlessness resulting from a lack of government oversight, and several companies have been accused of hiring right-wing mercenaries in these same environments (Stel 2014). When do private companies champion peacebuilding? What conditions encourage firms to invest in conflict prevention and resolution?

Case-based evidence suggests corporate responses to conflict are shifting such that actors often viewed as exacerbating tensions due to gaps in accountability (Koenig-Archibugi 2004) are now engaging in both commerce and peacemaking (Fort 2007, 2015; Bais and Huijser 2005). Given the costs of political violence, firms have an incentive to

The Building and Breaking of Peace. Molly M. Melin, Oxford University Press. © Oxford University Press 2021.
DOI: 10.1093/oso/9780197579367.003.0004

be proactive in facing these threats. Creating value, encouraging development, building community, promoting the rule of law, and engaging in unofficial (track two) diplomacy are ways the private sector can help build peaceful societies and reduce conflict (Deitelhoff and Wolf 2010; Oetzel et al. 2009).

International organizations are increasingly calling on firms to proactively engage in collaborative and practical action to advance peace, such as with the United Nations (UN) Global Compact's "Business for Peace" program. Advice and practical guides, such as the Organization for Economic Cooperation and Development's (OECD) Guidelines for Multinational Enterprises (2008), as well as stakeholder- and industry-led initiatives, such as the Extractive Industries Transparency Initiative (EITI), are commonplace. These suggest that corporations have the desire and capability for action if given the knowhow (Ganson 2011). While theoretical work and case studies suggest firms are building peace in innovative ways (Deitelhoff and Wolf 2010; Jackson and Nelson 2004; Wenger and Möckli 2003), a more systematic analysis is warranted.

Despite the many examples of private sector contributions to peace, we do not understand the conditions that encourage them to do so. I argue corporations engage in peacebuilding when the operating environment creates the demand for action while enabling its supply. More specifically, firms are likely to engage in peacebuilding when there is a gap in governance (demand) and when domestic conditions foster innovation and economic growth (supply). These variations in a corporation's operating environment offer insights into how corporations respond to local dynamics and governance, as well as threats to their own ability to conduct business. I also examine an alternative explanation that corporate peacebuilding behavior is exclusively a public relations campaign in effort to build their reputation.

This chapter tackles a question of increasing relevance: under what conditions do firms engage communities beyond traditional economic exchange? This understudied topic is generally approached through frameworks for action and best practices and has yet to be a part of broad conversations on peace and conflict. As existing scholarship is either theoretical or based on single case studies, the empirical results I present offer initial quantitative evidence of the conditions that encourage peacebuilding cross-nationally.[5]

The Puzzle of Conflict Resolution and Corporations

Scholars in fields as varied as business, sociology, anthropology, and geography have noted that private firms can contribute to governance and public goods provision, and often take on responsibilities beyond those required by legal and profit-making concerns. Conflict and conflict resolution scholars, however, rarely address these actors, and this research has failed to break into dominant conversations in international relations. Conflict resolution scholars typically account for more "political" actors in peacebuilding (Melin 2013; Greig, Owsiak, and Diehl 2019): international organizations (e.g., the United Nations), regional governmental organizations (e.g., the Arab League), individuals (e.g., former US President Jimmy Carter), and states (e.g., New Zealand). We have a strong understanding of how each of these actors builds peace through activities like peacekeeping (Henke 2016; Hultman, Kathman, and Shannon 2013) and mediation (Beardsley 2011) as well as their motives for doing so (Melin 2011; Regan 2000; Terris and Maoz 2005). Can we extend these lessons to understand corporate peacebuilding activities? Or do private firms have different motives for involvement?

The failure to account for corporate peacebuilding efforts when studying the causes of peace and conflict likely leads us to biased results and inaccurate conclusions about peace processes. For example, scholars highlight that international mediators help generate peace agreements in civil wars. As disputants have shown variation in their willingness to work with an outside mediator (Greig and Regan 2008; Melin, Gartner, and Bercovitch 2013), the presence of engaged firms might both encourage outside offers to mediate and disputants' willingness to work with them through offering legitimacy to negotiations. Work attributing successful mediation to the activities of international organizations (Hansen, Mitchell, and Nemeth 2008) or major powers (Favretto 2009) is likely biased if it ignores ongoing peacebuilding activities of firms, which may directly support the mediation process (Iff and Alluri 2016). Accounting for how firms can contribute to peacebuilding will allow scholars to develop a more accurate understanding of how peace is created, reflecting a reality where private and political actors increasingly overlap.

Business scholars and increasingly political scientists reveal significant opportunities for private actors to strengthen preventive diplomacy (Eskandarpour and Wennmann 2011; Iff et al. 2010), support emerging economies (Hoskisson et al. 2000), and minimize negative company impacts (Ganson 2011). Companies promote economic development, the rule of law, and principles of external valuation, contribute to a sense of community, and engage in track two diplomacy and conflict-sensitive practices (Deitelhoff and Wolf 2010; Oetzel et al. 2009). There is also evidence that businesses contribute to the mediation process (Iff et al. 2010; Iff and Alluri 2016). Much of this research is based on analysis of cases without scientific selection criteria. For example, Nelson (2000) uses various examples of business engagement to develop five principals of corporate engagement in conflict prevention and resolution. Nelson and Jackson (2004) expand on this research to show how businesses can offer value and simultaneously profit. Similarly, policy-oriented research focuses on how governments and institutions (Banfield, Haufler, and Lilly 2005b), as well as nongovernmental organizations (Kolk and Lenfant 2012; Schepers 2006) and industry-led initiatives (Haufler 2001b) can encourage firms to contribute to peacebuilding. Evidence from multinational mining companies in the Democratic Republic of Congo, South Africa, Europe, and North America suggests contemporary companies are committing to norms of corporate social and security responsibility (Hönke 2013). Research on business–NGO partnerships in the Democratic Republic of Congo reveals corporations can help build trust and capacity in addressing governance problems (Kolk and Lenfant 2012). The tourism industry in post-conflict Rwanda suggests businesses contribute to economic growth and physical reconstruction as well as reconciliation and justice (Alluri 2009). Research on Azerbaijan, Bosnia, and Rwanda shows how the host governments, international agencies, and international companies worked together for successful post-conflict reconstruction processes (Davis 2012). These case studies suggest the role of corporations in conflict prevention merits further examination.

Other related research explores the broader relationship between trade and peace. There is significant evidence that trade partners are less likely to go to war. Trade offers nonmilitary ways of communicating resolve (Gartzke et al. 2001) and forces leaders to choose between economic stability and political goals (Gartzke and Li 2003). The logic of this trade-off might apply to firms, as these actors also suffer under instability. Investing in peace can foster a more predictable economic climate for investors and increase profits (Klapper, Richmond, and Tran 2013). Thus, while trading partners avoid jeopardizing their economy with war, firms operating in volatile environments have the incentive to invest in stabilizing activities to avoid the high costs of political violence.

There is a need to connect the largely quantitative conflict processes scholarship to understand how businesses contribute to mediation, intervention, and peacebuilding. This chapter uses cross-national data to explore when firms engage in activities that help prevent violence, offering an additional step toward creating a broader understanding of peace processes. If firms do contribute to peace processes, then research ignoring their role is likely biased (Wolf, Deitelhoff, and Engert 2007). This chapter endeavors to bring a very influential actor into our understanding of conflict processes through addressing the lack of attention by security scholars to the role of the private sector, as well as contributing the first large-N empirical analysis to an area of research dominated by case studies.

Why Invest in Peace as a Corporation?

While private companies have a long history of acting beyond the limits of economic exchange (consider the British East India Company, which came to rule and administer large portions of India in the mid-1700s, see Robbins 2006), private engagement is increasingly considered both acceptable and preferable (Avant and Haufler 2018). This is not to say all forms of private engagement are for the betterment of society, but we are observing a shift in corporate norms and standards of behavior; the merging of conflict prevention, development, and environmental agendas; and changes in when intervention in domestic affairs is deemed acceptable (Ballentine and Haufler 2005). Firms are operating in the complex social, market, and political environments that demand concerns beyond short-term profit maximization (Wolf, Deitelhoff, and Engert 2007). The complexities of market rationality require firms to consider reputational costs and normative expectations in their cost-benefit calculations of investment programs and corporate policies.

As a company's internal motives for peacebuilding, such as its culture, profitability, industry, and size, tend to be constant across time, I focus on external motives for peacebuilding. External dynamics can create an operating environment that requires company actions, such as when the government fails to provide security and law enforcement. Such factors define the setting in which the corporation operates: does that environment demand active peacebuilding involvement or not? In addition, environmental conditions can help foster innovation and investment, thereby encouraging the supply of peacebuilding. Variations in a corporation's operating environment offer insights into how corporations respond to local dynamics and shifts in political capacity, which can threaten their ability to conduct business.

I begin from the premise that corporate behavior is dominated by the desire to protect their investment. While a relatively straightforward assumption, examining corporate choices from this lens helps simplify the complexities of decision-making. Since engaging in peacebuilding is not costless, corporations must have sufficient interests at stake to engage proactively. Domestic companies do not face a choice as stark as that of traditional conflict managers who can completely avoid involvement (Beardsley 2010; Melin and Svensson 2009). Corporations are likely already in the conflict zone or would not consider involvement.[6] While transnational corporations may withdraw from a country (Haufler 2005), they do not always have the choice of investment locations, and exiting a market involves costs. Transnational actors have clear opportunities to influence conflict dynamics (Banfield, Haufler, and Lilly 2005b).[7] Local corporations have fewer exit options and are more likely to shutter their business or move into the informal economy.[8] Operating in high-risk environments is a strategic choice, involving challenges and opportunities. Altruism alone cannot motivate operating in such challenging environments, as there must be a positive business case for investing.[9] For example, Starbucks pledged to hire 10,000 refugees globally, but this will also help them overcome the barista shortage expected from Brexit (Oetzel and Miklian 2017). Similarly, third parties' strategic interests motivate mediation while helping to create peace agreements (Terris and Maoz 2005; Melin 2011, 2013). Peacebuilding enables firms to reduce risk at its source (Oetzel and Miklian 2017), thereby protecting their investment.

The Demand Side: Filling "Gaps" in Governance

State capacity is critical for political and economic system performance, as capable governments can provide public goods such as infrastructure, security, and education. The state's capacity, or the "degree of control that state agents exercise over persons, activities, and resources within their government's territorial jurisdiction" (McAdam, Tarrow, and Tilly 2003, 78), reflects how likely a state is to provide goods and services. Weak government, lack of transparency, and corruption can cause distrust that fuels conflict (Andrews et al. 2017). At the same time, conflict can inhibit the state's ability to levy taxes and formalize property rights (Ch et al. 2018). In the context of weak states, the private sector's skills and resources can help contribute to governance, peace, and security (Deitelhoff et al. 2010). When the state fails to provide security, the firm must account for security costs (Deitelhoff 2009), and firms are more likely to engage in the provision of security through their activities (Wolf, Deitelhoff, and Engert 2007). The political environment directly influences the types of goals a company pursues (Pauly and Reich 1997), since gaps in governance create a demand for other actors to fill in.

I expect corporate peacebuilding activities diminish as government functioning increases, since the demand for corporate peacebuilding goes down. Firms have less incentive to engage when the government is able to provide stability and services. Good governance means making investments in public goods and quality institutions, in which policymaking and implementation benefit the population at large and decrease the risk of conflict and violence (Hegre and Nygård 2015; Fjelde and De Soysa 2009). In less capable, but not yet failed, states, corporations can most influence political and social stability.

When the state cannot enforce the rule of law at all (or becomes a failed state), there is unlikely to be private sector involvement due to a lack of large companies with the resources and willingness to risk engagement. The lack of stable government institutions prevents secure property rights, wealth protection, and elimination of confiscatory government, which suppresses economic exchange and growth (North and Weingast 1989). In extremely low capacity states, where the government is unable to enforce the rule of law and hold actors accountable, firms may give profits precedence over people. The engagement of the private sector in political and public policy arenas is not always beneficial. Several large corporations, such as Talisman Energy in Sudan, adopted unethical business practices in failed states and conflict zones. Hiring private security forces can hurt community relations and cause conflict (Andrews et al. 2017).

For example, Colombia has a very active private sector, as outlined in the introduction. At the same time, it has one of the largest economies in South America, with untapped resources and human capital, while simultaneously facing governance challenges. The topographical challenges that the region poses have left remote areas with little, if any, national government presence. Rural development is one of the cornerstones of the peace accord, as the agrarian-based economy often lacks the basic infrastructure necessary to get goods to market. Over time, the private sector has worked to fill these gaps through programs like Promigas's expansion of gas lines to rural households and Alquería's investment in supplier development activities for small farmers. I expect to find:

> Hypothesis 1: Firms engage in peacebuilding activities in states that cannot fully govern.

It is important to distinguish government weakness, which is linked to the lack of good governance, the provision of goods, and the quality of institutions, from political instability and policy uncertainty (Kugler and Arbetman 2018; Feng 2001; Fjelde and De Soysa 2009; Hutchison and Johnson 2011). Governments can be consistently challenged in their capacity to provide goods, creating a gap that corporations can fill, while still creating trustworthy institutions and certainty about the future. Conversely, policy instability and uncertainty have more adverse effects on corporate willingness to engage, which I discuss further in what follows.

The Supply Side: When the Future Is Predictable

The private sector thrives in stability. The occurrence of violence, dramatic political events, and major changes in the rules of the game can negatively affect profits and suppress corporate investment. Conversely, years of peace and certainty allow for economic growth. As military spending is a significant drain on the economy (Ward and Davis 1992), scholarship on defense spending and economic growth shows that reductions in military spending have a so-called peace dividend: either directly promoting growth (Lindgren 1984; Huisken 1982) or promoting investment, which in turn promotes growth (Mintz and Huang 1990). Military spending impedes technological progress and innovation as well as limiting the capital stock in the economy (Mosley 1985). Civil wars have profound negative economic consequences on a state, due to the loss of human capital, destruction of infrastructure, and reductions in investments and trade (Murdoch and Sandler 2004). Companies may flee or shutter under such uncertainty, and companies are unlikely to invest in community engagement during tumultuous times. Thus, years of peace allow corporations to supply peacebuilding.

Political instability (Barro 1991), crime (Gaviria 2002), and policy uncertainty (Feng 2001) interrupt business activities and depress economic growth. The immediate relevance of conflict is the starting point for research on corporate security responsibility (CsecR). While traditional corporate social responsibility (CSR) research explores the role of firms in peaceful environments, the CSecR agenda deals with those operating in a violent environment (Wolf, Deitelhoff, and Engert 2007), looking to understand firms' contributions to addressing violence. When violence occurs, security costs increase the costs of doing business. The company's investments are threatened, as conflict can damage production assets, infrastructure, local markets, and labor (Wenger and Möckli 2003). Sri Lankan businesses were severely affected by the bombing of the Colombo international airport in 2001; and telecommunications companies in Somalia were faced with severe barriers to further development due to violence (Iff et al. 2010). This has created a new type of global governance, putting firms at the frontline of peace and stability in fragile and conflict-affected areas (Schouten and Miklian 2017). Case studies have shown corporations have contributed to governance during the conflict in Rwanda, the Democratic Republic of Congo, Northern Ireland, and Israel (Deitelhoff and Wolf 2010).

Long periods of conflict and violence create instability, whereas years of peace enable investment, innovation, and peacebuilding activity. For example, Colombia's economy took off as FARC rebels were pushed into more remote areas, although bombings continue to remain a challenge for the expanding mining and oil sectors (Murphy 2012). This armed conflict in Colombia has accumulated huge material costs, amounting to around 3 percent of GDP (Ibáñez and Jaramillo 2006), exacting burdens on the Colombian society and economy (Arias et al. 2014). These costs have pushed the business sector to be very supportive of peace negotiations both "as a solution to armed conflict and as a strategy to protect assets and operations" (Rettberg 2007, 465).[10] The large costs of conflict, such as kidnapping, violence, and pressure from leftist guerrillas, motivated firms to become involved in building peace (Rettberg 2004). As the conflict was pushed to more remote areas, corporations were able to make investments in peacebuilding. I therefore expect to find:

Hypothesis 2: Firms engage in peacebuilding activities during periods of peace.

Or Engaging to Protect Their Reputation?

There is significant evidence that firms often negatively affect the communities where they operate. As King shows, "There is a political economy to warfare that produces positive externalities for its perpetrators" (2001, 528). The wartime environment may have spoils that discourage peaceful settlement, as happened in Angola's diamond industry, Cambodia's timber industry, and coca in Colombia. In addition, companies may work outside the law to ensure the security of immobile investments. For example, several large companies operating in Colombia during its civil war have since been charged with crimes against humanity (teleSUR 2017). Multinational companies Del Monte, Dole, and Chiquita were named for voluntarily financing right-wing paramilitary groups that were a part of the so-called Bananero Block. Many researchers see business as part of the problem facing countries embroiled in conflict, particularly in those states with natural resources (Switzer 2002).

The cynic would argue that any investment in programs that are directly ties to economic exchange is implemented exclusively as a public relations campaign. Peacebuilding-related programs enable a firm to build "reputational capital" that allow it to suffer less harm to its image from negative publicity than a firm that does not have a good image (Decker 2012). While some companies may undertake programs as a proactive measure, this motive is likely especially valid for firms seeking to rebuild credibility following a public relations crisis. By targeting a broad range of stakeholders in their programs and messaging, firms can both rebuild their reputation and generate positive market returns (Chakravarthy, DeHaan, and Rajgopal 2014). When companies have been caught being bad actors, they must take steps to ensure their product remains competitive.

While having a poor engagement record is likely to stimulate a corporation to create programs that engage the community, it does not paint a full picture of motives for corporate peacebuilding. Yes, firms must protect their investment following a public relations scandal, but focusing on this motivation leaves us with an incomplete picture. Even these investments can have positive externalities; a road paved to get company products to market is still enjoyed by others on the same route. If we account for the operating environment of the firm, we can build a more complete understanding of corporate engagement that accounts for their strategic long-term choices rather than just putting out immediate fires. Thus, we might expect that:

Alternative Hypothesis: Firms engage in peacebuilding activities when they have been caught being "bad" actors.

Empirical Evidence

To understand the causes of variation in firm-led peacebuilding activities, I use the Company of Peace and Conflict (COPC) data discussed in chapter 3. The dataset includes 924 firms based in Latin America, the Caribbean, Africa, and the Middle East from 2000 to 2017. I select firms headquartered in these regions because their peacebuilding efforts tend to be localized, whereas firm-led peacebuilding in the United States, Europe, and Asia often focus on international peacebuilding. Because I want to explain which firms engage in peacebuilding-related activity, I examine the company-year, including all companies with over $100 million US in 2015 revenue. Since smaller companies also likely play a role in the peace process (see Iff and Alluri 2016; Banfield, Gündüz, and Killick 2006), I explore their contributions in the case studies of Colombia, Northern Ireland, and Tunisia. I am better able to access data on large firms, and focusing the quantitative analysis to larger firms offers one way of limiting the large number of global businesses to a manageable number. While findings based on the activities of large corporations may not accurately reflect the activities of all businesses (especially as smaller businesses do not have access to the same resources or the same interests), they offer insights about a relatively new actor in the processes of peace and conflict. Financial information about the companies headquartered within a country is gathered from Marketline Advantage, a market research program that uses an internal team of analysts to compile profiles on companies across the world.

Observing and Measuring Peacebuilding

Peacebuilding includes attempts to reduce, limit, or eliminate the level, scope, and intensity of violence in conflict and build a structure where the need to resort to violence in future conflicts is controlled (Deutsch 1973; Maoz 2004). For firms, peacebuilding often takes the form of social responsibility, "the commitment of business to contribute to sustainable economic development, working with employees, their families, the local community and society at large to improve their quality of life" (WBCSD 2002, 2). While the concept has been criticized for being vague (Sternberg 2009), I offer to add precision by quantitatively examining firm-led activities. While peacebuilding engagement may be less interesting than the corporate impact on the conflict environment in terms of immediate political relevance, peacebuilding has been highlighted as important because it sheds light on the intention to contribute to corporate security (Wolf, Deitelhoff, and Engert 2007).

I measure peacebuilding using the original COPC data discussed thoroughly in chapter 3. The outcome variable is coded 1 if there are any reports of each type of engagement involving the firm and 0 otherwise.[11] The data show over 35 percent of companies invests in economic, social, or environmental peacebuilding. To account for time-invariant factors and differences across companies, I run a random effects model.[12] This allows me to control for the effects of firm characteristics that are relatively stable across time and likely affect peacebuilding activities, such as corporate culture (Austin and Wennmann 2017; Dashwood 2012; Fort 2015), international norms (Haufler 2005; Banfield, Haufler, and Lilly 2005), industrial sector (Camacho and Rodriguez 2013; Haufler 2010a, Oetzel and Getz 2012), and firm size (Forrer, Fort, and Gilpin 2012; Russo and Perrini 2010; Tures and Hensel 2000). The models focus on variation in the operating environment of the firm.

Explanatory Variables

My theoretical argument suggests that corporate peacebuilding is more likely when there is a need to proactively protect firms' investment, such as when there are gaps in the government's ability to enforce the rule of law, but that periods of peace allow for such investment to occur. I use the World Bank's World Governance Indicators to account for *government effectiveness*, a dimension of governance that captures the "perception of the quality of public services, the quality of civil service, and the degree of its independence from political pressures, the quality of policy formulation and implementation, and the credibility of the government's commitment to such policies" (Thomas 2010, 4). This is one of two dimensions of governance that measure "the capacity of the state to effectively formulate and implement sound policies" (Thomas 2010, 4). The other dimension is *regulatory quality*, a similar scale "capturing perceptions of the ability of the government to formulate and implement sound policies and regulations that permit and promote private sector development" (Thomas 2010, 4). I also account for the country's *rule of law*, which captures the quality of contract enforcement, police, and courts. Each of these measures offers an indication of how well the government is doing its job: the lowest rankings (first to fifth percentiles, such as Sudan) indicate state failure, moderately low rankings (up to twentieth percentile, such as Nigeria) indicate substantial governance problems, and the highest rankings (above eightieth percentile, such as Chile) indicate strong governance.

To capture stability and instability in a firm's operating environment, I focus on periods of peace and violence. I use the Uppsala Conflict Data Project's Armed Conflict Dataset (Gleditsch 2002), which measures internal armed conflict that results in at least twenty-five battle-related deaths a year.[13] Since years of peace are shown to stimulate investment and economic growth, I account for the number of peace years a country has experienced.

I use the COPC data to test whether the company is acting to overcome *"bad" behavior*, thereby accounting for the alternative explanation that peacebuilding behavior is strictly a public relations campaign. The data include a dichotomous measure of media reports on firm activities that negatively impact society, the economy, or the environment in the previous year.

Control Variables

I also account for exposure to international investors and corporations, since these interactions are likely to connect firms with new ideas and innovative strategies of community engagement and peacebuilding. To capture this exposure, I use contact to international businesses through foreign investment and Global Compact membership. In foreign direct investment (FDI), an internationally based company owns a company in the country in question, which includes direct involvement with daily operations in another country. This investment is more than just money; it brings skills, knowledge, technology, and behavioral norms. I include the amount of foreign investment, which is commonly used to gauge general economic openness (Gilardi

2012), to measure how exposed companies in a given country are to international norms of business practices. In my analysis, *FDI* is the natural log of net inflows (balance of payments [BoP] in current US dollars), from the World Bank Data (2018b). While this measure does not allow me to test whether the investing companies have strong norms of engagement, several studies have shown that international investment can have a positive effect on domestic social and regulatory standards (Vogel 1997; Prakash and Potoski 2006).

I also examine membership in the UN Global Compact, which was established to support companies in doing business responsibly and aligning their strategies and operations with the Global Compact's Ten Principals on human rights, labor, environment, and anticorruption. To join, corporations must operate responsibly, in alignment with the ten principals, and report annually on their ongoing efforts. The spread of members offers evidence of the spread of the norm of good corporate behavior and peacebuilding (Berliner and Prakash 2012). I include a count of the years of *Global Compact Membership*. Each of the explanatory variables are lagged one year to account for reverse causality.

The analysis offers substantial evidence that a firm's operating environment can encourage or discourage its engagement in peacebuilding-related activities. Many of these situational circumstances, such as government effectiveness, years of peace, and rates of foreign investment, are beyond the control of the corporation. Interestingly, the results suggest that the government's effectiveness and ability to enforce the rule of law are more salient considerations than the immediate threat of violence. Generally, we can say that corporations engage in peacebuilding-related activities to fill gaps in governance, but do so under the peaceful conditions that foster investment and economic growth. This research offers three main lessons about the conditions that encourage corporations to invest in peace where they operate. Summary statistics, as well as robustness checks, are in the appendix. Table 4.1 presents the results from the random effects logit model.

The empirical findings suggest corporate engagement is a response to "gaps" in governance. First, each model specification supports my arguments about the relationship between the capacity of the state and peacebuilding activities. Firm-led peacebuilding is most likely when state capacity is low but decreases with increases in government effectiveness. The finding holds across different measures of governance: effectiveness, rule of law, and regulatory quality all decrease peacebuilding at high levels. This supports case

Table 4.1 Random Effects Models of Firm-Led Peacebuilding across Measures of Government Effectiveness, 1998–2018

	Model 1: Government Effectiveness	Model 2: Rule of Law	Model 3: Regulatory Quality
Variable			
Filling Governance "Gaps"			
Government Effectiveness	–0.0256**		
	(0.0092)		
Rule of Law		–0.0339***	
		(0.0091)	
Regulatory Quality			–0.0204*
			(0.0098)
Responding to Stability			
Years of Violence	0.0979	0.1170	0.0943
	(0.0677)	(0.0687)	(0.0670)
Years of Peace	0.1803***	0.1956***	0.1784***
	(0.0412)	(0.0420)	(0.0411)
Protecting Reputation			
"Bad" Behavior	1.7579*	1.7277*	1.7879*
	(0.8348)	(0.8474)	(0.8393)
Controls			
Global Compact Member	0.0619	0.0486	0.0588
	(0.0554)	(0.0568)	(0.0561)
Foreign Investment	0.0000*	0.0000**	0.0000*
	(0.0000)	(0.0000)	(0.0000)
Constant	–6.5120***	–6.5580***	–6.8470***
	(0.8123)	(0.7127)	(0.8424)
N	11,044	11,044	11,044
N (groups)	850	850	850
LR test	9.65***	10.99***	10.31***

Robust standard error in parentheses; Two-tailed test *$p \leq .05$; **$p \leq .01$; ***$p \leq .001$
[1] This model was used to create the "Government Effectiveness Percentile" portion of Figure 4.1, and Figures 4.2 and 4.3.
[2] This model was used to create the "Rule of Law Percentile" portion of Figure 4.1.
[3] This model was used to create the "Regulatory Quality Percentile" portion of Figure 4.1.

studies showing firms help contribute to governance, peace, and security in the context of weak states (Deitelhoff et al. 2010).

The models show that corporations adapt to years of peace rather than responding to violence. Increases in the years a country has experienced peace significantly increase the probability of peacebuilding. While years of violence also has a positive relationship with peacebuilding, it is not a finding we can be confident is not from chance. Peace years allow a corporation time to adopt to their operating environment, creating policies that help bring additional stability to communities.

The control variables included in the model perform as expected: foreign investment and longer membership in the UN Global Compact both increase peacebuilding, although Global Compact membership is not significant. These results suggest that exposure to international trade matters, as corporations operating in countries with higher levels of foreign investment are more likely to engage in peacebuilding. I also tested the size of the country's economy using its per capita gross domestic product (*GDPPC*) (Gleditsch 2002). Although stronger economies have more large companies operating in them, they are no more likely to have actively engaged firms. Even when controlling for size of the economy, firms are protecting their investments from reputational damage following negative news reports and filling in gaps in governance.

Lesson 1: Firms Fill the Gaps
I argue that firms are likely to engage in peacebuilding-related behavior as a way to fill gaps in governance. The results support this logic: corporations are more likely to invest in peacebuilding-related behavior when the government is ineffective, lacks the ability to enforce the rule of law, and has low regulatory quality. Figure 4.1, which only examines countries that have corporations with at least $100 million USD in annual revenue (thereby excluding so-called failed states that have no government capacity), shows the strong relationship between poor governance and corporate peacebuilding. Each of the governance measures captures a state's percentile rank in the category, such that a higher ranking corresponds with stronger governance capabilities. The results account for other environmental conditions (years of peace and violence, UN involvement, foreign investment) and firm characteristics (past behavior, Global Compact membership). The probability of peacebuilding decreases by 2.8 percent for every percentile increase in the state's government effectiveness ranking. Corporations are less likely to invest in peacebuilding efforts as the government's quality of public services, civil services, policy formulations and implementation, and credibility increase. The probability that a company invests in peacebuilding in a given year decreases by 3.3 percent for each percent jump in the government's rule

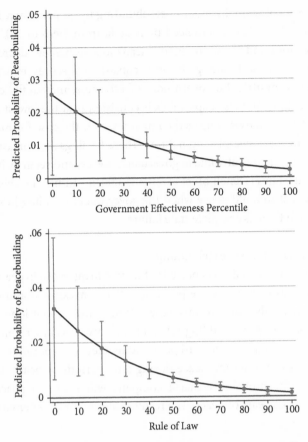

Figure 4.1 Probability of Firm-Led Peacebuilding across Gaps in Governance

of law ranking. Thus, the higher the quality of contract enforcement, police, and the courts, the less likely corporations are to invest in building peace. Similarly, the probability of peacebuilding decreases by 2.2 percent for each percentile increase in the state's regulatory quality ranking. Corporations are less likely to invest in peacebuilding when the state is highly capable of developing and implementing sound policies and regulations promoting private sector development. Each finding suggests that corporations are stepping in to fill gaps left by the government.

While the changes in probability seem small, the cumulative effects of shifts in governance are substantial, especially when we consider the effects over time. A ten-percentage point decrease in government effectiveness (such as that experienced by Venezuela from 2000 to 2006) increases the probability a company invests in peacebuilding by 28 percent; a 10 percent increase (such as that experienced by Angola from 1998 to 2015, or comparing Ecuador and Brazil in 2016),[14] leads to a 28 percent decrease in the probability of peacebuilding. Nigeria consistently scores in the bottom 20 percent of countries for government effectiveness, and has five companies that have helped fill these gaps. Libya is consistently at the lowest end of the data and has no actively engaged companies, as is the case for many of the high-scoring Caribbean Island nations. These findings support case studies showing firms help contribute to governance, peace, and security in the context of weak states (Deitelhoff et al. 2010), offering additional evidence that companies act to build peace when the government is failing in some way, but not when there is complete state failure.

Lesson 2: Peace Begets Peacebuilding

Firms respond to stability. I expected to find that firms invest in peacebuilding during periods of peace, since peace stimulates investment and economic growth. The results confirm this expectation, showing that longer periods of peace increase peacebuilding-related firm activity. While recent violence may instigate discussions toward policy adjustments, corporations are more likely to invest in building peace during long periods of peace. Figure 4.2 shows how the probability that a company will invest in peacebuilding increases across years of peace. The results account for other environmental

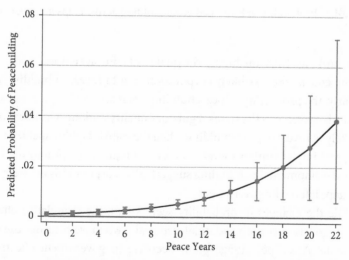

Figure 4.2 Probability of Firm-Led Peacebuilding across Years of Peace

conditions (government effectiveness, UN involvement, foreign investment) and firm characteristics (past behavior, Global Compact membership). Years of peace have an important effect on investments in peacebuilding, whereas the measures of violence and instability are insignificant (see appendix), meaning we cannot conclude there to be a causal relationship. Each additional year of peace increases the probability of investment in peacebuilding by 16.9 percent. The cumulative effects of peace are substantial: five years of peace increases the probability of corporate peacebuilding by 84.5, and ten years by 169 percent. Recent violence and years of violence have no discernable effect on corporate peacebuilding. The effect of peace is multiplied over time and across companies. By considering the proportion of companies that engage in peacebuilding within a state, the substantial effect of peace years is clear. Each additional year of peace increases the proportion of companies engaged in peacebuilding by 32 percent.

What do these findings tell us about the environments that encourage corporations to invest in peacebuilding? That corporate engagement is more likely in longer periods of peace suggests these actors invest and innovate during prolonged periods of peace. Companies adopt policies that invest in communities where the future is predictable. Companies are less responsive to recent shifts in governance and violence. Companies act to protect their investment when they operate in a predictably peaceful environment. In other words, peace begets peacebuilding.

The empirical results are not supportive of research showing firms respond when recent violence threatens the company's investments (Wenger and Möckli 2003). Firms do not appear to engage in peacebuilding in response to immediate threats of armed events but learn to operate in peaceful conditions over time. Case studies have shown violence motivates firms to actively build peace (Rettberg 2004) and positively contribute to governance and security (Deitelhoff and Wolf 2010).[15] A possible explanation of this result is the use of national-level violence data, as firms may be responsive to immediate threats that occur closer to their areas of operation. Violence is shown to attract mediation offers (Melin, Gartner, and Bercovitch 2013) and create domestic and international political pressure for resolution (Beardsley 2010). We need further study of the effect of firm-led peacebuilding on local levels of violence and consider how such efforts may affect other efforts to create peace, as mediation and peacekeeping are shown to interact in a way that enhances reductions in violence (Beardsley, Cunningham, and White 2018).

That firms are more likely to adopt programs that build peace in countries that have experienced more years of peace suggests that the places that most need firm engagement are unlikely to attract this type of investment. Corporations are most likely to invest in innovation and implement new strategies when the conditions foster economic growth: low levels of military spending (Ward and Davis 1992; Mintz and Huang 1990) and lack of domestic violent conflict (Murdoch and Sandler 2004). Evidence that firms engage in peacebuilding in places that have longer periods of peace helps shed light on the puzzle of continued conflict presented in chapter 1: some of the actors that have the greatest financial capabilities to invest in peacebuilding are unlikely to make this investment in places that are violent and unstable.

The findings that the governance measures and peace years have opposing effects on peacebuilding may initially seem contradictory, as states with lower capacity may be less likely to experience long periods of peace. Research on the connection between state capacity and civil war suggests, however, than lower state capacity does not affect civil war onset but civil war does reduce state capacity (Thies 2010). Indeed, "governing capacity" is a broad term that can be further specified to distinguish public goods spending from state coercive capacities, as the former can produce civil peace (Fjelde and De Soysa 2009). The tests here provide initial evidence that firms act when states do not have fully developed ability to enforce the rule of law, which is in line with this finding. Future research should work to further understand the links between governance and peacebuilding, especially at the local level.

Lesson 3: Firms Invest in Their Reputation
Firms are concerned with ensuring the future marketability of their products. Firms that hope to withstand the fallout of public relations scandals must be proactive in cleaning up their image. The results suggest that corporations are engaging in peacebuilding as a response to negative news surrounding the company. The probability that a corporation engages in peacebuilding-related behavior increases by 175 percent when the firm has previously received negative media attention. Negative media creates the largest change in the likelihood of corporate engagement, increasing the benefits of investing in peace that makes such an investment in the interest of the firm. While this offers some evidence of "brandwashing" after a crisis, the other results show reputational motives are only part of the story.

While corporations do respond to negative media coverage of the company, they also account for their operating environment. When a government

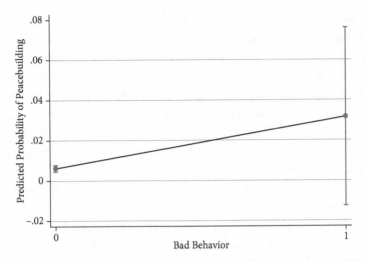

Figure 4.3 Probability of Firm-Led Peacebuilding Following Negative Media Coverage

fails to enforce the rule of law, to regulate policy, and to provide public services, these conditions pressure the private sector to act. Additional years of peace and stability encourage peacebuilding, as the environment encourages investment and innovation. Ten and a half years of peace have the same effect as negative media coverage in terms of encouraging corporate engagement; the same is true of a 50 percent drop for a country's rule of law percentile ranking. Thus, focusing on corporate effects at reputation-building misses interesting variation in the external motives for peacebuilding: the role of the state and peace in creating the demand for and supply of firm engagement.

Conclusion

What conditions encourage private firms to engage in their communities to prevent violence and build peace? The findings here contribute to a burgeoning literature suggesting firms are engaging in both commerce and peacemaking (Fort 2007). Given the high costs corporations face in the event of violence, being proactive in facing these threats is imperative. In this chapter, I explain variation in corporate peacebuilding behavior. I show that peacebuilding is more than just reputation building; firms invest in their communities as a way to fill holes left by ineffective governments.

While international relations scholars are increasingly developing an understanding of the conflict management practices of states and international organizations, this research rarely considers a role for private firms. This is due to a focus on traditional government actors in the conflict processes literature and the lack of data. Research on corporate social responsibility, fair trade, human rights, and private security suggests firms can play an important role in peacebuilding. This chapter offers an initial step in bridging this gap and offering quantitative evidence of the environmental circumstances that encourage investments in peace.

The focus of this chapter has been on understanding how different political environments can encourage or discourage firm-led peacebuilding efforts. The models suggest much of the variation being explained is across countries, rather than within countries, and across rather than within companies (see appendix). Future research should explore how changing conditions in a country and within firms prompt shifts in corporate approaches to peacebuilding. The conditions found to promote peacebuilding tend to be long-term and slow to reform, but it would be useful to understand more immediate solutions to engaging the business sector as an active partner in building peace for policy purposes, if that is indeed desirable.

Corporations engage in peacebuilding when their reputation is threatened, but also when they have experienced long periods of peace or there is an unfilled gap in the state's capacity to enforce laws. These variations in a corporation's environment offer insights into how corporations respond to local dynamics and shifts in government capacity. Through programs that invest in educational opportunities, provide new access to economic resources, and protect environmental integrity, these firms are investing in the long-term stability of the places where they operate.

5

The Building and Breaking of Peace

Understanding Corporate Effects on Conflict Prevention
and Resolution

In 2011, the world watched in awe as much of the Arab world overthrew
oppressive governments in effort to win additional rights and freedoms.
Massive crowds gathered to demand political change in Tunisia, Morocco,
Syria, Libya, Egypt, Yemen, and Bahrain. And yet, despite these efforts, many
of the citizens of these states do not have any more freedom than they began
with. In some cases, such as Libya, Syria, and Yemen, the situation deterio-
rated into horrifically violent civil wars. Peaceful protests in Bahrain were
violently suppressed. In Egypt, the ousting of President Hosni Mubarak
gave many observers hope, but authoritarian rule has since returned. Only
Tunisia, which is often celebrated as the Arab Spring's lone successful transition to democracy, was able to avoid violence and adopt political change.

How can we understand such drastic variation in the results of domestic
unrest? Why are some countries able to peacefully resolve domestic disputes
while others experience prolonged civil wars? In this chapter, I argue some
of this variation is explained by the private sector's role in society. Countries
that have an actively engaged domestic private sector are better equipped
to peacefully resolve disputes because these actors see it in their interests to
maintain peace and stability. When local firms are engaged in communities,
they have established networks through which they can work to prevent violence. I argue that private sector engagement affects local level factors that
can change individuals' incentives to join a rebellion, making traditional
forms of commerce more attractive. Investing in community programs,
providing training opportunities, and providing a desirable workplace encourage would-be rebels to pursue peaceful business rather than violence.

The relationship between corporate peacebuilding and peace is not
straightforward, however. Corporations can serve as reluctant champions
of peace, motivated to action out of frustration with warring groups' inability to come to agreement. When the private sector engages during ongoing

The Building and Breaking of Peace. Molly M. Melin, Oxford University Press. © Oxford University Press 2021.
DOI: 10.1093/oso/9780197579367.003.0005

conflict, they add their own preferences to the bargaining table and make it more difficult to reach an agreement. Thus, business engagement during ongoing violence prolongs civil conflict. This chapter argues that corporate engagement can have contradicting effects on generating peace, depending on when engagement occurs.

Chapter 4 highlighted that certain conditions, namely gaps in governance, foster firm-led peacebuilding. This chapter explores the implications of such engagement in terms of peace and conflict. Does corporate peacebuilding generate peace? Are countries with an active private sector less likely to experience violence? Can firm engagement help warring parties come to agreement? The answers to these questions have important implications for scholars looking to understand the causes of civil war and peace, as well as practitioners and policymakers working in these fields.

I begin with an overview of the literature on poverty as one of the causes of civil war, and then build off of this literature to explain how firm engagement changes the incentives for violence. I go on to explore the implications of firm engagement during active violence and civil war. I then present empirical results that support my arguments about inverse effects of firm engagement on violence prevention and resolution. I show that violence is less likely in countries with active private sectors, but that the same conditions produce civil wars that last longer and are less likely to end. The chapter concludes with a discussion of the results and implications for policymakers.

Economic Causes of Civil War

Since the end of World War II, the number of intrastate wars has vastly outnumbered the number of interstate conflicts (Pettersson and Wallensteen 2015). The increase in domestic conflict has been met with an increase in scholarship on this topic. One of the most agreed upon causes of civil war is based on economic explanations (Collier and Hoeffler 2004). Since companies are fundamentally economic institutions, it is the economic causes of civil war that they are most able to affect. In this section, I discuss economic causes of civil war at the national and individual levels and explore how the private sector may address these causes.

Early research on civil war focused on understanding why some states are more likely to experience civil war than others. Civil wars are unlikely to occur in established democracies with high per capita income. According to Collier (Collier et al. 2003, 53), "the key root cause of conflict is the failure of economic development." At the national level, states with low economic development are generally weaker both financially and militarily (Fearon and Laitin 2003). Rebels are more likely to be successful in fighting a weaker state, making civil war more likely under these circumstances. This suggests that efforts to strengthen state functioning decrease the likelihood of armed conflict.

Sambanis (2002, 216) writes that "civil war is a problem of the poor." The causal link, according to Collier and Hoeffler (2002a), is that rebel groups are better able to recruit fighters when the benefits of joining outweigh those of conventional economic activities. Thus, the incentive structure makes civil war more likely in impoverished societies. While the vast majority of the poverty and conflict scholarship focuses on national-level measures of income, the causal mechanisms of incentives and opportunities rely on a logic that varies subnationally. Disaggregated measures of the location where conflict breaks out and per capita income suggest that civil war is more likely to occur in impoverished locations (Buhaug et al. 2011). These findings suggest that programs increasing individuals' access to income and financial stability will decrease the risk of armed conflict.

While individuals might be motivated to join a rebellion by financial opportunity, others have pointed to the motivations of grievances related to political or economic inequality (Gurr 2015). Poverty may cause or increase the grievances that drive rebellion. Inequality among group lines allows for successful mobilization that results in violence (Cederman, Gleditsch, and Buhaug 2013). Local levels of exclusion and poverty increase the risk of civil conflict (Aas Rustad et al. 2011). These studies suggest that efforts to promote inclusion and equal access will decrease the probability of armed conflict.

In addition, civil conflict stagnates economic development, increasing the likelihood of further conflict. This cycle of conflict and underdevelopment experienced by some states is termed the "conflict trap" (Collier et al. 2003). That is, armed conflict creates conditions that make future conflict more likely. Conflict polarizes societies, undermines democratic institutions, and inflames the conditions that favor rebellion by increasing poverty, causing capital flight, and destabilizing neighboring states. There is substantial empirical evidence showing civil war causes economic decline due to the cost

Table 5.1 Economics of Civil War and Corporate Peacebuilding

Armed Conflict Cause	Implication for Decreasing Armed Conflict Risk	Relevant Peacebuilding Activity
Weak State →	State-Strengthening →	Lawful Operations
Poverty →	Financial Opportunities →	Employment Programs
Economic Inequality →	Equal Access →	Inclusion Programs
Prior Conflict →	All of the Above →	Investment in Post Conflict Economies

of military financing, the disruption of trade, the destruction of infrastructure, and the loss of life (Collier 1999; Staines 2004; Koubi 2005). Conflicts decrease average income, leading to civil war as described earlier. The economic instability created by civil war suggests that corporate investment in peacebuilding can be especially salient in post-conflict societies.

Private corporations have the opportunity to affect each of these economic causes of domestic armed conflict, as outlined in Table 5.1. At the state level, corporations can create economic development through paying taxes, avoiding corruption, and operating lawfully. The peacebuilding activities help to strengthen state capacity. Given the findings in chapter 4 showing gaps in state capacity incentivize corporate peacebuilding, such lawful operations that occur even in the context of a government that lacks the ability to enforce the law are likely to help prevent armed conflict in cases that need stronger governance. The challenge for corporations is that only the largest and most successful companies can have a strong impact on a state's overall development. It is also difficult to observe levels of corruption and illegal activity. In addition, investment is less likely to occur in those states faced with the highest threat of the conflict trap, since these are high-risk areas to operate. Individual financial and grievance-related incentives to rebel can be reduced with employment and inclusion programs, which are both most feasible for corporations to adopt and most likely change the risk of armed conflict. Programs that focus on training and skill development, along with those focused on hiring fairly, offer opportunities and access that reduce the incentive to rebel. I therefore build my theoretical argument on these individual incentives to rebel and then consider the effect of corporate engagement on the conflict resolution process.

Does Corporate Peacebuilding Create Peace?

Although civil wars now outnumber international conflicts, there has been a decrease in the number of civil conflicts and the battle-related deaths since the end of the Cold War (Pettersson and Wallensteen 2015).[1] At the same time, there has been an increase in the rates at which companies integrate environmental or social causes into their business practices. In 2017, over 90 percent of the 250 largest global companies published detailed annual reports of their corporate-responsibility practices (Blasco and King 2017). The rate of corporate engagement has drastically increased from 35 percent in 1999. These trends in corporate engagement and armed civil conflict suggest a possible correlation. The aim of this chapter is to go beyond that, however, and suggest that the activities of corporate responsibility initiatives often help address the underlying causes of civil war. Research has shown that private sector activity can play an important role in conflict prevention (Banfield, Haufler, and Lilly 2005a; Ballentine and Haufler 2005). In what follows, I develop a theoretical argument and hypotheses about how firms affect the probability of civil war in a state and their effects on the duration and end of violence.

The Positive Side: Reducing the Incentives to Rebel

The rational choice theory of civil war onset and termination is relevant to understanding the effect of firm engagement, as firms' peacebuilding actions can change the incentives to rebel. Civil wars occur when the expected utility of war outweighs the expected utility of peace. Conversely, these conflicts end when the expected utility of peace is greater than the expected utility of continued violence. This logic is the underpinning of much of the civil war scholarship (Collier and Hoeffler 1998, 2002a; Walter 2004; Fearon and Laitin 2003). While the specific motivations shaping belligerents' behavior are complex and varied, this framework offers a useful way to organize such complexities theoretically. The economic explanations of conflict discussed previously derive from this opportunity-cost framework. For example, scholars often cite the importance of opportunity costs for potential rebel recruits as a way to understand motives for rebelling (Walter 2004; Collier and Hoeffler 2000), which can be seen as changing the payoffs of war in comparison to peace. Low economic development and state capacity motivate belligerence, since the opportunity costs of war are low compared to the private gains of conflict. How groups perceive such preferences and opportunities can also help us understand when groups choose conflict (Hirshleifer 1995, 2001). In addition, each party has expectations about eventual outcomes, which inform their choice to either negotiate or fight for an anticipated victory (Mason and Fett 1996b). Governments can adopt redistributive policies as a means to defend against insurrections and maintain peace, since these measures change the expected benefits of rebelling (Azam 1995; Grossman 1992). I argue private corporations can also create policies that affect this calculus.

By engaging in peacebuilding, any actor has an ability to alter the disputants' or potential disputants' expected utility from fighting and thereby alter the likelihood of conflict. A firm's involvement in peacebuilding can enable a durable peace through altering the payoffs each party expects from engaging in conflict. One approach to this is to reduce the incentives for rebellion, which is the product of the probability of victory and its consequences. Another approach is to raise the costs of rebellion, through loss of income and the costs of coordination. In Colombia, companies like Coca-Cola, Electrolux, Coltabaco, and Exito[2] are training and hiring ex-combatants, thereby shifting opportunity costs for would-be rebels: individuals who might otherwise take up arms instead have peaceful means for bettering their lives and more to lose with violence. In post-conflict societies, reintegration programs add social ties and educational opportunities that decrease recidivism among ex-combatants (Kaplan and Nussio 2018). Similarly, increases in economic opportunities and security are shown to decrease the incentives to return to violence (Phayal, Khadka, and Thyne 2015).

Empirical studies show these payoffs manifest in several ways when examining the correlates of civil war. States are at a higher risk of civil war recurrence when living conditions are poor (Walter 2004) and when average income is low or inequality is high (Collier, Hoeffler, and Söderbom 2004). The incentives to join a rebellion increase when individuals have poor access to alternative employment (Hegre 2004) and when rebellion is economically viable (Collier and Hoeffler 2000).

It is important to acknowledge that many of the factors shown to decrease the probability of civil war, such as higher per capita income (Jakobsen, De Soysa, and Jakobsen 2013; Collier, Hoeffler, and Söderbom 2004), are tied to private sector behavior. Each of the correlates offers areas where private sector engagement can raise opportunity costs and dis-incentivize violence. For example, initiatives such as the Kimberly Process, which limits the access to funding for rebel organizations by shutting diamonds from conflict zones out of the market, can limit an individual's payoffs from joining a rebellion. As discussed previously, programs that offer job training, educational opportunities, and employment create incentives for would-be rebels to engage in legal forms of commerce.

Proactive corporate engagement needs to be distinguished from the mere possibility of employment opportunities that accompany corporate presence. While employment reduces the need to resort to crime and violence, individuals often lack the necessary training and skills to qualify for jobs (as has been the case in Northern Ireland). As outlined in chapter 3, proactive corporate peacebuilding involves engaging the community in a way that raises the opportunity-costs of violence: filling skill gaps through training and educational programs, investing in local school systems, working to address community needs. To be sure, many countries that experience civil war lack economic development (Collier et al. 2003). Proactive corporate peacebuilding takes the logic of economic development and peace one step further: addressing community and government shortfalls to empower communities with skills, technology, and infrastructure. Extending the rational choice logic to include the benefits a community gains from proactive corporate peacebuilding suggests that:

Hypothesis 1: States with an active private sector are less likely to experience violence.

The Negative Side: Complicating Negotiations with Additional Preferences

Firm engagement during ongoing conflict takes different forms in comparison to proactive corporate engagement during peacetime. When firms are engaging within the community during ongoing conflict, they inherently become political actors. That is, periods of violence blur already grey lines separating politics and business. Stepping into communities even with indirect, unilateral mechanisms such as training or philanthropic programs, paves the way for more direct and collaborative actions like negotiation and mediation (see typology developed in Oetzel, Getz, and Ladek 2007).

In many ways, particularly violent events can serve as an exogenous shock that prompts more direct engagement at the national level. Table 5.2 explores

Table 5.2 Violent Shocks and National Engagement

Event	Estimated Cost (in millions of USD)[1]	Coalition	Negotiations Begin	Ceasefire	End of Conflict
Sri Lanka					
Colombo Airport Bombing (July 2001)	534	Sri Lanka First formed, 2001	2002	2002	2009 (Government Victory)
Northern Ireland					
London Financial District Bombings (April 1992 and 1993)	1,212	Northern Ireland Confederation of British Industry publishes "Peace Dividend Paper," 1994	1996	1994	1998
Manchester Mall Bombing (June 1996)	996	Group of Seven formed, 1996			
Colombia					
Kidnapping & Conflict Urbanization	unknown	"Encounter for a National Consensus for Peace in Colombia" conference, 2000	March 2011	Various, 2012 initial in final agreement talks	2016

Source: Dillinger (2017).

how extreme violence pushed private firms to coordinate efforts in pushing for a national peace process. In each of these cases, conflict had been ongoing for many years before the private sector became engaged. However, events that directly affected the business community necessitated a response.

The civil war in Sri Lanka had been ongoing since 1983, without notable private sector involvement. This was the effect of the 2001 Colombo airport bombing, which drove home the economic consequences of the civil war and business vulnerability to it, prompting Sri Lankan businesses to work toward peace (Alert 2005). The bombing caused $534 million in damages (Dillinger 2017). One of the initiatives to come out of this event was Sri Lanka First, which harnessed the island's tourism, tea, garment, and freight sectors to mobilize a demand for peace. Sri Lanka First included a powerful group of business leaders advocating for peace, and later the Business for Peace Alliance acted as a working group from regional chambers of commerce fostering regional inclusion, reconciliation, and cross-business linkages (Alert 2005).

In Northern Ireland, the IRA mostly attacked economic targets, and this became increasingly costly for businesses as the group's capacity to cause damage increased. In 1992, the Baltic Exchange bombings involved the biggest bomb detonated on mainland Britain since World War II. The bombing caused an estimated $897 million in damages, and was followed with $1,212 million in damages from the 1993 London financial district bombing (Dillinger 2017). These are the costliest terrorist attacks in history besides the attacks of September 11, 2001. These events prompted the Northern Ireland Confederation of British Industry to publish a "peace dividend paper" laying out the economic costs of conflict in 1994. When the peace process was about to collapse following the 1996 Manchester bombings, major business organizations formed the Group of Seven to advocate for peace and revitalize the peace talks.

In Colombia, the shift toward more active and direct private sector participation was the result of a shift in conflict dynamics that directly affected business. Between 1996 and 2002, there were over 1,985 firm-related kidnappings reported (Pshisva and Suarez 2006). At the same time, the conflict was moving into more populated urban areas. While this shift reflected a change in FARC's strategy rather than a single event, it had the same effect in terms of involving private actors more directly in the conflict. The business community's reaction was also somewhat dispersed; jointly supporting conferences and exploratory meetings rather than creating a formal coalition. Each of these organizations represented a more collaborated effort across businesses to advocate for peace at the national level. While individual businesses were involved with indirect action building peace, these violent shocks served to coordinate efforts for more direct and collaborative action.

The second way we can distinguish private sector engagement during ongoing violence is that it is typically through coordinated efforts with other companies. While exceptionally violent events push the private sector toward national engagement in peace processes, they also motivate increased coordination among corporate actors. Rather than engaging as individual entities (as is frequently the case during peacetime), the business sector often works together to bring a peace agreement.

There are several benefits to engaging through coordinated efforts, and these benefits have implications for negotiation outcomes. First, coordinated lobbying increases the power of businesses vis-à-vis other actors, since groups of actors can present a united front and coordinate their efforts. While companies operating in extractive industries may have different concerns than those in finance or manufacturing, negotiating as a united front increases the bargaining power of the private sector. Second, coordinating with other businesses ensures the outcomes of negotiations produce an agreement that is beneficial (or at least not harmful) to businesses. Peace negotiations redefine the rules of the game, and the business community stands much to lose or gain depending on how those rules are specified. The private sector is therefore motivated to ensure their interests are protected during these discussions. Finally, coordinating efforts should, in theory, help generate peace. This last point, however, merits additional consideration.

In their most basic form, peace talks involve coordinating preferences among two warring parties. However, violent conflict increasingly involves actors beyond the initial disputants. Joiners, mediators, and even additional domestic actors are also likely to be party to the process of coming to an agreement. While many of the additional negotiators purport to be involved for the sole purpose of furthering the peace process, each actor has its own preferences on the agreement terms. Peace talks therefore often involve coordinating preferences across more than the initial disputants.

Additional preferences make it more difficult to come to agreement and prolong the peace process. When there are multiple actors that must approve a settlement (or veto players), there are fewer acceptable agreements, more acute information asymmetries, and shifting alliances that make negotiations more difficult and prolong civil wars (Cunningham 2006b). Civil wars that involve multiparty negotiations, such as in Colombia and Northern

Ireland, last longer and are more likely to fail due to spoilers. The logic of veto player theory is that when there are more actors with divergent preferences that must agree on and implement a new policy, it becomes harder to implement the policy and move from the status quo (Tsebelis 2002). In institutional arrangements that include more veto players, it is more difficult for these actors to come to agreement. At the negotiation table, veto player theory suggests that more preferences will prolong negotiations and make it more difficult to come to a resolution. In the context of civil war, more veto players make it harder to move from violence to peace, leading to longer civil wars. For example, external states that intervene in a civil war do so with their own preferences and agenda, thereby prolonging the conflict (Cunningham 2010).

When the business community engages during an ongoing conflict, they do so with their own preferences in mind, thereby acting as an additional veto player. We cannot assume private firms engage only to facilitate negotiations. Rather, the business community has its own interests, such as protecting investments and ensuring future profitability, and these interests are not always in line with others at the negotiation table.

While peace may be a priority for the private sector, business leaders will have their own vision of what the terms of a peace agreement should look like. The private sector therefore comes to the negotiating table with an agenda that is distinct from the goals of the combatants. It is therefore likely that the addition of the private sector to negotiations makes it more difficult to resolve civil wars. The involvement of the business community in peace processes can therefore prolong negotiations and increase the time to conflict resolution.

The forms of business engagement in negotiations can range from direct participation to indirect lobbying. Colombia offers an example of business representatives being physically present at the negotiation table. While technically part of the government's negotiating team, the business community had strong opinions over how past engagement with paramilitary groups would be prosecuted. Businesses in Northern Ireland played the role of outside lobbyist. The G7 publicly pressed politicians to come to an agreement, hosting events bringing together all negotiating parties and presenting the rationale for peace, and serving as lobbyists for the peace process. Even if firms are not immediately present at the negotiation table, their support (or lack thereof) of any agreement can be key for its implementation. I explore variation in the forms of business engagement more in the following case study chapters.

Private sector engagement can also complicate the actual fighting, prolonging violence by adding interests to the bargaining space. Armed conflict is a bargaining failure. That is, all involved parties should prefer the peaceful resolution of disputes to the costs of conflict. However, each of the parties have an incentive to misrepresent information to secure a better bargaining outcome, a problem that is compounded in a climate of mistrust (Fearon 1995). In civil conflicts, the challenges of bargaining are especially difficult since the incentives to renege on a deal can be especially high (Walter 2004, 2009). Third parties, such as mediators, can help overcome the problem of information asymmetries and strategic interaction (Kydd 2006), as well as serving as a trustee and decreasing the challenges of the commitment problem (Beardsley 2011). Private corporations that engage in political processes serve a more complex role, however, and can play mutually defeating roles in the bargaining process. On the one hand, businesses can agree to implement training and reintegration programs for ex-combatants who disarm, making a peaceful settlement more attractive to rebels. On the other hand, companies may condition such programs on tax reductions or other special treatment that can hurt the places where they operate, since decreased tax revenue affects education and infrastructure. While reductions in taxes are attractive to businesses, hiring unskilled labor with limited relevant experience is less likely to be. While businesses may increase their revenues during peacetime, business leaders likely have preferences over the conditions of peace that differ from those of government and rebel actors. The addition of interests adds to the complexities of the conflict environment, decreasing the likelihood that violence ends. This suggests the following expectation:

Hypothesis 2: States with an active private sector have longer periods of armed conflict.

Empirical Evidence

To understand whether private sector engagement helps prevent violence but also prolongs violence, I once again use the Company of Peace and Conflict (COPC) data discussed in chapter 3. Because this chapter is interested in variations in the private sector across countries and over time rather than the differences between companies, I test my theoretical argument using the aggregated country-year data. The dataset includes all countries in Latin America, the Caribbean, Africa, and the Middle East from 1998 to 2016. These data enable me to test the effects of private sector engagement on national level violence over time.

Observing and Measuring Violence

The focus of this analysis is to understand the effect of private sector engagement on peace and violence in a country. I am interested in two different outcomes related to armed conflict: the occurrence of violence and the end of violence. To measure these outcomes, I employ the Uppsala Conflict Data Project's (UCPD) Armed Conflict Dataset (Gleditsch 2002), which measures internal armed conflict that results in at least twenty-five battle-related deaths a year. I use two outcomes: *violence occurrence*, which captures whether a country experienced at least twenty-five battle deaths in a given year, and *violence end*, which measures whether the episode ended in a given year. I am agnostic to the ways by which the conflict ends, since corporate engagement can both prolong negotiations and enable each side to continue to fight. As many conflicts do not end with decisive outcomes like victory or a peace accord but with less clear outcomes where the violence has simply ended (Kreutz 2010), measuring the end of violence captures such complexities. Since both outcomes are dichotomous, I model them using a probit specification. However, as the end of violence is likely linked to the causes of violence, I also use a Heckman selection model to capture the independent effects of the explanatory variables on the end of violence. This allows me to test explanations of the end of violence while accounting for their effect on violence occurrence. The results are summarized in Table 5.3.

Explanatory Variables

There are several ways to capture the activity levels of a country's private sector. Drawing from the COPC data, I create three different measures of private sector activity. First, I create a raw count of the number of firms that have added value in a given country-year. The count variable *number of engaged*

Table 5.3 Probit Model of Violence, 1998–2012

	Proportion of Engaged Firms	Number of Engaged Firms	Engaged Firms (0/1)
Variable			
Value (Proportion)	−39.9411** (14.7354)		
Value (Number)		−0.3844** (0.1332)	
Value (0/1)			−0.4894 (0.2561)
Controls			
Prior Violence	2.5790*** (0.4877)	2.5776*** (0.4865)	2.5953*** (0.4919)
Population	0.2858** (0.0897)	0.2861** (0.0896)	0.2806** (0.0897)
Democracy	−0.0448 (0.4128)	−0.0446 (0.4119)	−0.0534 (0.4131)
GDP per capita	0.1883** (0.0701)	0.1859** (0.0700)	0.1908** (0.0696)
Number of Large Companies	0.0006 (0.0043)	0.0008 (0.0043)	0.0004 (0.0042)
Constant	−6.4061*** (1.2077)	−6.3917*** (1.2092)	−6.3735*** (1.1984)
N	1,305	1,305	1,305
Pseudo R²	.49	.49	.48
PRE/PPC	43.14/97.8	43.14/97.8	43.14/97.8
Log Likelihood	−110.85	−110.88	−111.31

Robust standard error in parentheses; Clustered by country; Two-tailed test *$p \leq .05$; **$p \leq .01$; ***$p \leq .001$

firms allows me to examine whether more firms actively working to build peace has a greater impact on the amount of violence a country experiences but creates challenges in reaching a solution that is agreeable to all parties. I also create a proportion of the number of firms that engaged to the total number of firms operating in the country. The *proportion of engaged firms* tests the amount of firm engagement while accounting for the number of firms that possibly engage (the number of large firms in a country divided by the number of engaged firms). Finally, I account for whether the presence or absence of firm engagement, measured dichotomously, is changing probabilities of violence and peace. *Any engaged firms* measures whether there is a firm working to build peace in any given year in the country. The presence of any active firms is likely to impact violence duration since even a single engaged firm can change the dynamics of negotiations.

In each specification of private sector engagement, I also include a count of the *number of large firms* operating in the country. This controls for many of the states that experience violence lack a strong private sector that might help prevent armed conflict. As cycles of violence reduce economic activity, the countries that might benefit the most from private sector peacebuilding are less likely to have a private sector from which to draw.

Control Variables

There is a vast literature on the causes of armed conflict and civil war. I control for the most common variables argued to increase the probability that a country experiences violence: previous violence, large population, regime type, and economic development. Given that violence creates a legacy of killing, destroys the economy, and creates conflict cycles (Collier et al. 2003; Walter 2004; Collier and Sambanis 2002), I create a lag for violence in the previous year, *prior violence*. Countries with large populations are also more likely to experience civil war (Fearon and Laitin 2003), so I include a logged measure of *population* (Gleditsch 2002). A *democracy* is more likely to settle their conflicts through peaceful means (Hegre et al. 2001), so I include a measure of whether or not the country has a polity score of 6 or higher (Marshall and Jaggers 2004). Because countries with higher economic development are less likely to experience civil war (Collier and Hoeffler 1998), I control for logged per capita gross domestic product (Gleditsch 2002). To account for economic hardship, which is shown to increase the incentive to rebel (Walter 2004), I account for *GDP per capita* (Gleditsch 2002). I use the UCDP data to control for the number of battle deaths. Unfortunately, many of these measures are not available through 2018 (as the COPC data are), so the temporal domain is limited to 1998–2012.

In the second stage of the model, which predicts the end of violence in a given year, I include additional controls that research suggests help encourage the end of domestic armed conflict. As cumulative causalities can lead to war weariness, I account for the *total deaths* in a conflict up to the previous year (Pettersson, Hogbladh, and Oberg 2019a). Recent deaths, however, suggest a remaining commitment to the cause, decreasing the probability that the conflict ends. I therefore include *recent deaths* that have occurred in the past year of conflict (Pettersson, Hogbladh, and Oberg 2019a). I also control for the effects of time using splines of the *duration* of the conflict. Each measure is lagged by one year to ensure the direction of causality.

Lesson 1: Engaged Firms Reduce the Occurrence of Violence

I argue that when firms proactively engage in peacebuilding-related behavior, their actions help foster a system where violence is a less attractive choice. This suggests that, at a national level, we should see less violence in countries that have firms engaged in peacebuilding. Countries with an active private sector are significantly less likely to experience violence (see Table 5.3). The temporal domain of these tests is limited by several of the control variables.

The data show that the presence of engaged firms, higher numbers of firms engaged in peacebuilding, and greater proportions of firms that are engaged reduce the probability that a country experiences violent conflict (see Figure 5.1). Of the seventy-five country-years that experienced violent conflict, only seven of them had a domestic company that was engaged in peacebuilding the year before conflict began, whereas seventy of the country-years had engaged corporations. This is a statistically significant difference (see appendix). The probability of violence decreases by 1.1 percent for each additional firm that is engaged in peacebuilding. Examining the proportion of firms that are engaged in peacebuilding also suggests these efforts deter violence, as the proportion of firms engaged in peacebuilding goes from zero to one, the probability of violence decreases by 112 percent. The probability of violence decreases by 1.5 percent when there is at least one firm engaged in peacebuilding. While this is a small change in the probability of violence, it suggests firm-led peacebuilding is having an effect on violence levels. Recall that these changes are for each country in a given year, meaning such effects accumulate over time and can make a substantial change in the probability that a country experiences violence.

The results suggest the effect of firm-led peacebuilding decreases in impact after the first firm, with the first firm having the largest effect on the probability of violence and additional firms creating smaller shifts in the probability of armed conflict. Countries with more engaged firms are less likely to experience violent conflict than those with only one or two firms actively building peace. There is a twelve percent probability of violence in a country with no firms working to build peace, a .4 percent probability of violence in

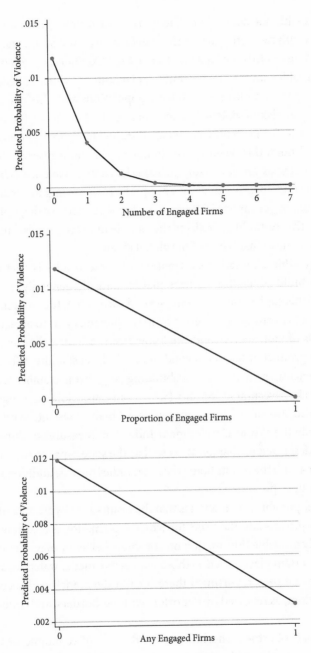

Figure 5.1 Probability That Violence Occurs, 1998–2012s

countries with one active firm, and a .01 percent probability of violence in countries with two active firms. This can be interpreted optimistically, as not every firm needs to be engaged to decrease the likelihood of violence.

The variables controlling for other explanations of violence generally perform as expected. Countries with large populations and a history of violence are at greater risk of violence. A previous conflict increases the probability of violence by 7.6 percent. Democracies are less likely to experience civil violence, although this result is not significant. Previous research has shown that democracies are less likely to experience civil violence (Hegre et al. 2001). The only measure that does not perform according to expectations is the measure of per capita GDP, which is shown to increase the probability of violence. This result likely reflects the sample of cases included in the data, which has a mean that is half of the global mean.[3]

One possible alternative explanation of these results is that firms are acting to build peace in countries that are already generally more stable. I rule out this explanation of events several ways. First, the analysis employs a country's firm engagement levels from the previous year to explain current year levels of violence. Second, we know from chapter 4 that firm engagement is a product of factors beyond domestic-level stability. While periods of peace encourage firm-led peacebuilding (suggesting stability is a factor), so do gaps in government capacity (which can cause violence, suggesting instability also encourages firm engagement). Finally, I test alternative models that include the World Development Indicators measures of domestic stability (as described in chapter 3), as well as the state capacity measures used in chapter 4, and the results hold. The case studies provide additional support for the findings presented here.

Another possible explanation is that the results are a byproduct of the data collection process and the firms for which information is available. Relying on publicly available information on corporate behavior may over count behavior in certain places, such as those with active media watchdogs or fewer restrictions on their reporting. I therefore test the models with a control for press freedom, as reported by Reporters without Borders, and generate similar results.

As a final robustness check, I test for the role of economic investments through foreign aid and foreign direct investment. Foreign interests in a state may decrease the probability of conflict resolution. Including these measures in the model does not significantly change the results, and only foreign investment (FDI) significantly decreases the probability of resolution.

This lesson does not suggest that firm engagement is a primary determinant of armed conflict. The purpose of this chapter is not to explain the causes of civil war, rather, it is to show the outcomes that result from corporate peacebuilding activities. I do not purport that the absence of firm-led peacebuilding is even a cause of armed conflict. Rather, I provide evidence that corporate activities that engage communities beyond standard economic exchange have a measurable and significant effect on the likelihood of violence. I argue this is because the efforts of private firms target the very sources of conflict: providing educational opportunities, training programs, and social ties that make conventional economic activities attractive. These programs help tip the opportunity costs in favor of peace, making a positive contribution to the communities where they occur.

Lesson 2: Engaged Firms Prolong Ongoing Violence

Countries experiencing ongoing violence are less likely to end the violence when firms are actively engaged in peacebuilding-related activities.

While corporate peacebuilding efforts decrease the probability of armed conflict, these efforts have an inverse effect on the probability that armed conflict ends (see Table 5.4). The data reveal a trend that ongoing conflicts are less likely to end both when there are more firms engaged in peacebuilding and when the proportion of engaged firms increases (see Figure 5.2). The probability of violence ending decreases by 5.4 percent for each additional firm that is engaged in peacebuilding. As the proportion of engaged firms moves from zero to one, the probability that violence ends decreases by 600 percent. Having at least one firm engaged in peacebuilding decreases the probability of violence ending in a given year by 5.4 percent. While the changes in probabilities may seem small, as with the models of armed conflict, they can accumulate over time to have a substantial effect on the duration of conflict.

This finding suggests that engaged firms complicate ongoing conflicts and make them less likely to end. One thing to note is that the data do not distinguish how the violence ends, as there is not enough information on each episode to know if the conflicted ended with a victory for one side or the other or in a negotiated settlement. The presence of an active private sector can prolong the negotiation process and make it harder for the parties to reach an agreement. It may also enable one or both sides to fight longer, also decreasing the likelihood that violence ends.

Table 5.4 Censored Probit Model of Violence Occurrence and End, 1998–2012

Variable	Proportion of Engaged Firms		Number of Engaged Firms		Any Engaged Firms	
	Selection: Violence Occurrence	Outcome: Violence End	Selection: Violence Occurrence	Outcome: Violence End	Selection: Violence Occurrence	Outcome: Violence End
Variable						
Value (Proportion)	-38.8481** (14.0765)	-6000*** (18.4512)				
Value (Number)			-0.4711 (0.2486)	-5.3957*** (0.1639)	-0.3742** (0.1285)	-5.3796*** (0.1641)
Controls						
Recent Deaths		-0.0013*** (0.0003)		-0.0013*** (0.0003)		-0.0013*** (0.0003)
Total Deaths		-0.0001 (0.0001)		-0.0001 (0.0001)		-0.0001 (0.0001)
Duration		0.0013* (0.0006)		0.0013* (0.0006)		0.0013* (0.0006)
Duration^2		-0.0000* (0.0000)		-0.0000* (0.0000)		-0.0000* (0.0000)
Duration^3		0.0000** (0.0000)	2.6467*** (0.4986)	0.0000** (0.0000)		0.0000** (0.0000)
Prior Violence	2.6304*** (0.4944)		0.2609** (0.0864)		2.6291*** (0.4932)	

	(1)	(2)	(3)
Population	0.2663** (0.0863)	0.2666** (0.0862)	0.0372 (0.4193)
Democracy	0.0456 (0.4194)	0.0458 (0.4187)	0.2092** (0.0750)
GDP per capita	0.2066** (0.0753)	0.2040** (0.0752)	0.0003 (0.0042)
Large Companies	0.0005 (0.0043)	0.0007 (0.0043)	
Constant	-6.4526*** (1.2697)	-6.4361*** (1.2703)	-6.4196*** (1.2601)
Large Companies	0.0009 (0.0084)	0.0009 (0.0084)	0.0009 (0.0084)
Constant	-3.0050 (2.1104)	-3.0050 (2.1117)	-2.9976 (2.1086)
Rho	0.3267 (0.3001)	0.3259 (0.2994)	0.3236 (0.2973)
N	1,303	1,303	1,303
N (Censored)	49	49	49
Log Likelihood	-119.129	-119.1554	-119.566

Robust standard error in parentheses; Clustered by country; Two-tailed test *$p \leq .05$; **$p \leq .01$; ***$p \leq .001$

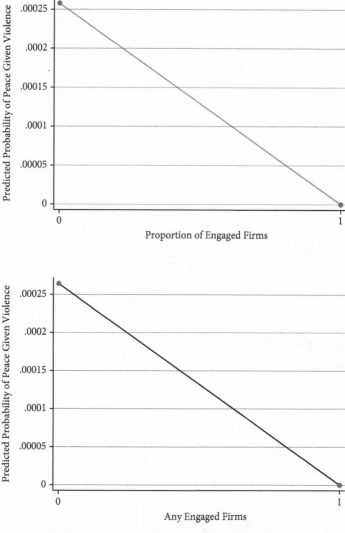

Figure 5.2 Probability That Violence Ends, 1997–2012

It is important to note that the findings here are not meant to explain why conflicts end but to understand the effects of corporate `ty engage-ment activities. There are certainly other factors with stronger implications for whether or not violence ends, as a large body of research highlights. In addition, many conflicts end without the presence of corporations engaged in peacebuilding activities. Rather, the findings presented here suggest that corporate engagement adds to the complexities of the conflict environment and prolong violence. I argue this is because the private sector has its own preferences that make it more difficult to reach a negotiated settlement or find a mutually agreeable end to violence.

Conclusion

This chapter has explored the peace and conflict outcomes of private sector engagement beyond traditional economic exchange. When private corporations engage in peacebuilding-related activities, do their efforts help create more peaceful societies? I argue the effects are not straightforward. While firm-led peacebuilding can reduce the opportunity-costs of rebelling, making peaceful forms of commerce more attractive, the same efforts during ongoing conflicts add an additional actor to the bargaining table. This further complicates an already difficult bargaining space and prolongs the violence. The chapter offers empirical evidence of these inverse outcomes, suggesting firm-led peacebuilding is best suited as a preventative measure for societies not experiencing ongoing conflict.

This chapter, however, only offers a first step toward understanding how corporate engagement changes the dynamics of peace and negotiations. The empirical findings use information on large, domestically headquartered companies that have engaged in a way that attracted media coverage. Variation in press freedom, access to information about and interest in corporate behavior, as well as shifting expectations about corporate behavior may be confounding the results reported here. To overcome these limitations, the next three chapters explore the role of corporate engagement in Colombia, Tunisia, and Northern Ireland.

6

Corporations, Conflict Prevention, and Resolution in Colombia

Introduction

The 2016 Colombian peace agreement ended the longest civil war in the Western Hemisphere between the government and the Revolutionary Armed Forces of Colombia (FARC). Private companies are playing an active role in the transition through the challenges of disarmament and reintegration of rebel troops. Firms' hiring practices, infrastructure projects, and economic investments are helping "fill the gaps" where governments are unwilling or unable to provide needed goods and services. Colombia's private sector was not always so actively engaged in peacebuilding, however, and their involvement has not always worked to further the peace negotiations.

This chapter explores the role of corporations in Colombia's peace process. I begin by considering the background of the conflict and the role of private businesses at both the local and national level. I then consider the circumstances that prompted firm engagement. Because Colombia is the only case being examined that experienced individual, domestic firm engagement, I discuss the nature of these firms in terms of size, sector, and profits. Finally, I discuss the results of Colombia's private sector peacebuilding activities.

The Background of Colombia's Conflict and Private Firms

As the longest civil war in the Western Hemisphere, Colombia's civil conflict left an estimated 220,000 dead, 25,000 missing, and 5.7 million displaced (Miroff 2016). The conflict began in May 1964, when the Colombian government attacked a small group of communists who had declared independence in the small village of Marquetalia. At the time, the FARC was one of several leftist guerrilla groups fighting the government. By the 1990s, however, the

The Building and Breaking of Peace. Molly M. Melin, Oxford University Press. © Oxford University Press 2021.
DOI: 10.1093/oso/9780197579367.003.0006

group had used the drug trade to expand their military power. Colombian elites began backing right-wing militias that were also competing in the drug trade. This resulted in decades of violence and atrocities that were especially hard on rural communities. Eventually, military setbacks pushed the group to the negotiations table, and a peace deal was agreed to in 2016. While the government still faces spoilers and gang violence, Colombia appears to be transitioning to a significantly more peaceful society (Maher and Thomson 2018).[1]

In the 1990s, some business leaders supported peace negotiations in the hopes of bringing a "peace dividend" to the country (Rettberg 2004), while others actively undermined negotiations for personal gain or from their allegiance to paramilitaries (Beittel 2015). Colombia's government has always had a close relationship with the business community (Rettberg 2003; Thorp and Durand 1997). Private sector factions have had privileged access to peace policy through Colombia's transition, either directly, through participation in the policymaking process or by being appointed to negotiator roles, or indirectly by frequent consultation with government officials (Miklian and Rettberg 2017). The business community also has more informal access to the government though shared elite networks. These close ties and trust have enabled Colombian businesses to be involved throughout the peace process.

Mechanisms of Peacebuilding in Colombia

Research has shown that private sector activity can play an important role in conflict prevention (Ballentine and Haufler 2005; Banfield, Haufler, and Lilly 2005b). How have Colombia's businesses worked to create a less violent society? What approaches have companies taken to reduce the incentives for individuals to join a rebellion? How have businesses contributed to the larger peace process? I first consider the role of business at the local level, and then at the national level.

Local Level: Investment and Development

Two of the major causes of civil war are poverty and inequality (Collier and Hoeffler 1998). Would-be recruits consider the opportunity costs of rebelling: what are the payoffs of peace compared to war (Walter 2004; Collier and

Hoeffler 2000)? Low economic development and state capacity motivate belligerence, since the opportunity costs of war are low compared to the private gains of conflict. Efforts to provide economic opportunities offer one way to develop peace at the local level.

Many businesses have invested in regional and local projects to encourage economic growth in conflict-ridden areas. These projects are started, at least in part, with the belief that local investment will enable more rapid change than national level efforts (Miklian and Rettberg 2017). Projects often focus on investment and development in rural areas where the government has less presence and capacity. The rural regions of Colombia are especially challenging for conducting business, as poor or nonexistent infrastructure makes it difficult for these communities to get their goods to a larger market. Villagers often must hike their goods to market due to the poor conditions of roads and absence of bridges. These were also the communities most affected by violence and illegal commerce. Rural areas have endured persistent conflict with violence, illegal crops, drug trafficking, land concentration, and displacements. Poverty consistently is higher in these areas despite Colombia's national economic growth and poverty reduction, leading the World Bank to recommend modernization in rural regions (Bank 2014). The economic underperformance in rural areas results from the absence of institutions, poor agricultural policies, and ineffective public investment. Both the government and private companies are increasingly investing in projects to modernize and expand Colombia's transportation infrastructure. One example is the Fourth Generation road construction program, an ambitious initiative that includes thirty-two projects and about 8,000 kilometers of road (Bauza 2017). The $25 billion, seven-year project is funded in part by the World Bank, with investment by both domestic and international actors (Bell and Schipani 2015).

Companies are also helping modernize production in rural areas through training programs and technical assistance. As agriculture employs one-fifth of all Colombians, reforms in this area would impact a significant population. Alquería, Colombia's third-largest dairy processor, has heavily invested in supplier development activities with a focus on increasing supply through increasing the quantity and quality of output from small farmers (World Bank 2018a). The result was increased supply without increased marginal costs, as well as higher quality milk that both commands a greater price and lasts longer. Siembraviva offers another important modernization example, as an ecommerce company delivering

organic produce. They work with small farmers using an ecommerce platform to connect them to an urban consumer base, eliminating inefficiencies in the supply chain and transportation costs. They help farmers switch
from growing commodities to organic produce, advising them when to
plant and harvest, and guaranteeing a produce purchase price. The company is allowing farmers to increase their wages and income stability while
reducing fertilizers.

While many of the local programs being adopted are not directly tied to
the peace process, they have implications for creating sustainable peace in
Colombia. Development programs are an important key to avoiding another civil war (Collier et al. 2003). The incentives to join a rebellion increase
when individuals have poor access to alternative employment (Hegre 2004),
poor living conditions (Walter 2004), and low income (Collier, Hoeffler, and
Söderbom 2004). Programs that offer job training, educational opportunities, and employment create incentives for potential rebel recruits to engage in legal forms of commerce. In Colombia, companies like Electrolux,
Coltabaco, and Exito[2] are training and hiring ex-combatants, thereby
shifting opportunity costs for would-be rebels: individuals who might otherwise take up arms instead have peaceful means for bettering their lives
and more to lose with violence. In post-conflict societies, reintegration
programs add social ties and educational opportunities that decrease recidivism among ex-combatants (Kaplan and Nussio 2018). This can also offer
the firm positive dividends later, as investing in training programs creates
a more skilled and efficient workforce that increases a firm's future productivity (Aw, Roberts, and Winston 2007). The Colombian government has
therefore made it a point to involve the private sector in peace-related tasks
such as former fighter reintegration, victims' social inclusion, and training
programs (Rettberg 2009).

National Level: Negotiations Team and
Supporting the Peace Process

Colombia's private sector has engaged in the national peace process as well.
As the costs of the conflict rose, the expected benefits of peace helped to promote pro-peace activism among the business community (Rettberg 2013).
The economic cost of the conflict has been estimated as around 3 percent
of the country's GDP (Arias et al. 2014). As guerrilla and paramilitary

attacks increased, so did firms exiting the Colombian market (Camacho and Rodriguez 2013). These costs, as well as the strong business–state relations that enabled access to peace policymaking, also pushed the business sector to support negotiations to protect their assets and operations (Rettberg 2007, 2019). At the national level, the private sector has helped to fund mediators, offered advice on the design of the agreement, and actively participated in negotiations as a form of local corporate peacemaking.

An early example of firm support for peace negotiations comes from the so-called telefono rojo (or red phone). In the 1980s, before the existence of cellular phones, Suramericana de Seguros, Colombia's largest insurance agency, and Bavaria, the largest beer company, paid $20,000 for a satellite phone that would allow the negotiating sides to remain in touch (Miklian and Rettberg 2017). The ability to communicate quickly enabled the sides to maintain communication, much as a similar phone line between the White House and Kremlin did during the Cold War. Businesses were beginning to see that peace was worth the investment.

Generally, however, the private sector was largely absent from peacebuilding prior to the 1990s, since they had little compelling reason to invest in peace (Guáqueta 2006). The conflict was then contained to rural areas and the economy was growing. This changed during the Samper administration (1994–1998), when a scandal linking the president with the Cali drug cartel led to a major political crisis and power struggles between the branches of government. The crisis both undermined the legitimacy of the government and lessened its ability to deal with growing violence. The vast rise in kidnappings, many of which targeted businesspeople, as well as an increased presence of armed groups in urban areas and an accompanying recession, pushed the private sector toward becoming more politically active (see appendix).

The business community's support in such communications helped lead to President Pastrana's talks with the guerrillas at the end of the 1990s. Business leaders were members of the negotiations team and helped with local peacebuilding initiatives (Rettberg 2009). For example, the president of Colombia's largest insurance firm, Suramericana de Seguros, gave speeches highlighting the costs of the Colombian conflict. Many firms were simultaneously involved in peacebuilding and philanthropic activities. While Pastrana's negotiations eventually failed following the hijacking of an aircraft, the fact that they occurred at all signaled a willingness of both sides to negotiate.

When President Santos came to office in 2010, his early years were marred by violence. In 2012, however, both FARC and ELN agreed to restart nego-tiations, which was also supported by Congress. Business leaders paid for foreign mediators to support the preliminary talks that eventually led to the 2016 peace accords. Angelika Rettberg, an academic who has extensively researched the role of Colombia's business community writes:

The government consulted candidly and frequently with the representatives of the largest companies and sectors. For example, when the public debate about rural land reform escalated amid rumors that the government was making concessions in 2015, a group of eight prominent business leaders traveled to Havana to discuss the issue first-hand with both negotiating teams. This served as a poignant reminder to both sides of the business community's veto power over the content of the peace agreements. In ad-dition, government has the power of appointment, putting visible business leaders in leading roles in the peace process. This was the case of Gonzalo Restrepo, the CEO of Éxito, the country's largest consumer goods com-pany, and most recently Juan Sebastián Betancur, the former leader of busi-ness think tank Proantioquia, who serve(d) as members of the negotiating teams with FARC. In this way, the government achieved three goals: buy-in by crucial factions of the business community, legitimacy by the opposite side (which saw the presence of their "class enemy" as a guarantee of com-mitment), and support by the general population, which trusts the business community more than it does politicians or the guerrillas. (2013, 18)

Having business leaders as a part of the negotiating team helps to provide the legitimacy and resources required to support the fledgling peace pro-cess. The dangers of the conflict became obvious to the private sectors, as bombings frequently disrupted production and the transportation of goods.

A business leader was also included as one of the six members of the government's team of representatives that met in Cuba and developed the final agreement (Murphy 2012). Luis Carlos Villegas held various positions within both the government and the private sector. He was head of the National Industrial Association (ANDI) and demonstrated an ability to maintain ties to both liberal and conservative sectors in Colombian poli-tics. His diplomatic skills and negotiation tactics were then used to repre-sent the private sector in the 2012 peace talks between the administration of President Santos and the FARC. The lawyer and socioeconomist is also president of Colombia's Business Association. He has participated in dialogue processes in the National Council of Peace and in conversations with the National Liberation Army (ELN) in Cuba and Costa Rica (Omari 2018).

When the negotiated peace deal failed to pass in a referendum, businesses remained actively involved in the process. The Colombian economy had been steadily growing with large amount of foreign investment even before a deal was in place (Flannery 2017). Business leaders were wary of truth commissions that would investigate parties linked to human rights violations outside of the disputants. The agreement was later modified to account for some of the critics' concerns, one of which was to reduce the emphasis on investigating the role of businesses in the conflict using an international tribunal (Board 2016).

The next challenge for Colombia is implementing the peace accord, a process that is also engaging business leaders. A committee of private sector leaders, called the Council for Sustainable Peace, was created with government approval to oversee the implementation of the peace accords (Jimenez 2017). While these national processes are important and necessary, peace must also be built from the bottom up, which is where businesses can have the greatest impact. The social projects in rural areas discussed earlier will play a major role in creating a peaceful future for Colombia, and these appear to be well underway. One example is Terpel, Colombia's third-largest oil and gas company, which is working to expand education to rural areas with work through their foundation and in coordination with Colombia's Ministry of Education. Projects like these offer new opportunities and help support national processes. While the implementation of this deal is yet to be fully realized, much of FARC is demobilizing, and private sector programs can offer important alternatives to violence.

What Conditions Increase Firm-Led Peacebuilding in Colombia?

As the example of Colombia's business community and its engagement in national negotiations shows, engaging in peacebuilding enables a firm to influence the political and social environments. Active involvement enables private firms to influence dynamics in a way that can be both self-serving and beneficial to the local community. As one of South America's biggest economies with untapped natural resources and human capital, many have

Table 6.1 Chapter 4 Results as Applied to the Case of Colombia

Lesson	Application	Outcome
Firms Fill the Gaps	Moderate Government Capacity & Rule of Law	Significant Firm-Led Peacebuilding Once Conflict Urbanizes
Peace Begets Peacebuilding	Predominantly Rural Violence Becomes Urban & Costly	
Firms Invest in Their Reputation	Strong CSR Norms	

predicted that peace will boost economic growth through investment as well as decreased security costs (Flannery 2017). Table 6.1 provides an overview of how the findings from chapter 4 apply to the Colombian case. Given Colombia's governance gaps and strong norms of corporate engagement, it is not surprising that Colombia has an actively involved private sector. However, Colombia's firms were pushed to involvement when the violence moved into urban areas, suggesting this pressure forced firms to become more direct peacebuilders. In what follows, I examine how the quantitative findings on firm peacebuilding apply to the Colombian case in greater detail, looking at how events promoted firm engagement, then I discuss the specific characteristics of the corporations that invest in peacebuilding.

Do Gaps in Governance Increase Colombian Firm Engagement in Peacebuilding Activities?

The quantitative analysis revealed evidence of a curvilinear relationship between state capacity and peacebuilding: firms increasingly engage in peacebuilding as state capacity rises, but this effect levels off at higher levels of capacity. As Colombia's government varies in capacity, how have firms reacted?

Colombia's national government can be considered moderately capable, as seen in Table 6.2. On each measure of governance, Colombia is consistently in the 40th–60th percentile. In terms of government effectiveness, these scores are in line with those of other upper-middle-income countries and the average for Latin America. Colombia's regulatory quality is slightly higher than other upper-middle-income countries and the average for

Table 6.2 Colombian Governance Indicators

Indicator	Country	Year	Percentile Rank (0 to 100)
Government Effectiveness	Colombia	2008	
		2013	
		2018	
Regulatory Quality	Colombia	2008	
		2013	
		2018	
Rule of Law	Colombia	2008	
		2013	
		2018	

Source: World Bank Worldwide Governance Indicators

Latin America, and its rule of law is slightly lower. These scores suggest that, broadly speaking, the Colombian government has moderate capacity.

The Colombian government's ability to enforce the rule of law drastically varies regionally, however. While the state has a significant presence in urban areas, much of the country is cut off from government resources and security due to the topographical challenges of the land. The Andes and Amazon both pose significant obstacles for building the infrastructure necessary to have a strong state presence. Many villages can only be reached by plane or boat, and this has often kept the government from making the necessary investments to have a significant presence in these regions. Thus, while the state might be considered moderately capable, in many areas its presence is extremely limited. In more isolated areas, the absence of the state has enabled rebel groups to flourish (Boudon 1996). Compañía Envasadora del Atlántico (CEA), which operates in the food and canning industry, is an example of a company that reacted to the security challenges facing their business. As CEA looked to expand to produce passion-fruit pulp to meet international demand, it faced challenges due to the absence of law enforcement and the presence of armed groups related to the drug trade in the coastal regions where passion fruit is grown. Many of the farmers in the region were growing cocoa, and those interested in growing passion fruit needed credit, training, and security. CEA began investing in peacebuilding through a partnership with the United Nations Development Programme (UNDP) that complemented its business interests (Guáqueta 2006). The UNDP was focused on encouraging legal economic development, decreasing conflict through creating a livelihood for farmers that would otherwise be a part of the drug trade. They had created a program that offered what CEA needed: business training, promoting social capital, and organization of associations. Partnering with UNDP also enabled CEA to build trust with local communities where it had eroded through decades of violence and the government's absence. This partnership enabled CEA to work with other international donors, including USAID, the EU, and the UN High Commissioner for Peace.

The difficulties in implementing the rule of law have important implications for the Colombian peace process moving forward. The government is well aware that the challenges it faces moving forward in the peace process vastly surpass its capacity and has enlisted the international public and private sectors as allies in the peacebuilding process. The Presidential Agency for International Cooperation of Colombia (APC-Colombia) seeks and manages public–private partnerships, international aid focused on peacebuilding, sustainable rural development, and conservation and environmental sustainability. Colombia's challenges are not limited to rural areas, however, especially as the vast majority of the internally displaces persons (IDPs) have fled to cities in search of opportunities and security (Atehortúa, Salcedo, and Vidal 2013). The municipal governments in the cities have served a major function in serving, protecting, and reintegrating these communities. The Japanese government provided funding administered by the World Bank for Strategic Regional Alliances (Allianzas Red) under which businesses worked with mayoral offices to ensure work for IDPs. The national government helped fund training and seed money, but businesses have played a critical role in creating stable solutions for these victims. Similar challenges involve demobilized FARC, ELN, and paramilitary members, who were often seen by the business community as lacking skills and predisposed to crime. The Ministry of the Interior has worked with agribusinesses and construction firms to create job opportunities, and the government has offered tax incentives to companies that hire combatants (Guáqueta 2006). Since 2003, the Colombian Agency for Reintegration (ACR) has worked to help former fighters prepare for the return to civilian life, assisting an estimated 47,944 people as of mid-2015 in a training program that can last up to six years (Aldwinckle 2015). Coca-Cola, Exito, and Electrolux, and Coltabaco have all hired ex-combatants through ACR. Other ex-combatants have used the government payment of approximately $2,500 to start their own businesses, but employment and reintegration continues to be a problem (Otis 2017). This is likely to be a challenge for a country that has struggled with poverty and inequality for so long.

Thus, many firms are adopting peacebuilding practices and working to offer new economic opportunities, and this is likely in part the result of the government's inability to create stability and enforce the rule of law alone. While many firms have a genuine interest in operating more ethically, many of the programs being implemented are a reflection of weak state institutions and their inability to provide basic services and security (Miklian and Rettberg 2017).

Does Peace Increase Colombian Firm Engagement in Peacebuilding Activities?

The quantitative results suggest stability enables firms to invest in peacebuilding. How have violent events affected firms in Colombia? Have firms operating in more violent areas responded differently compared to those operating in peaceful locations?

While firm-led peacebuilding cannot be attributed to a single factor, the location and impact of violence is a very strong factor engaging businesses (Guáqueta 2006). When the conflict was mostly rural and the economy was growing, businesses did not have a reason to become involved. During this period, business and the economy were able to grow. The strong private sector resulting from this peacetime built firms that had both the capacity and connections to act when the conflict shifted. When, in the 1990s, the number of kidnappings rose drastically, armed groups moved into urban areas, and a recession hit, business leaders became much more active in the national peace process (see appendix). Research also suggests that the higher the costs of violence to business, the more likely firms are to proactively support peace (Rettberg 2008).

Active conflict and violence create pressure for engagement and action to protect a firm's investments. For example, although Colombia's economy took off as FARC rebels were pushed into more remote areas, bombings remain a challenge for the expanding mining and oil sectors (Murphy 2012). In fact, many companies have faced attacks, including a bombing of the state-run oil company Ecopetrol (Murphy 2015) and a Blockbuster video store (Alsema 2009). Such attacks have happened as recently as September of 2018, with the bombing of the second-largest oil pipeline, the Cano-Limon Cavenas (Reuters

2018). This armed conflict in Colombia has accumulated huge material costs, amounting to around 3 percent of GDP (Ibáñez and Jaramillo 2006), exacting burdens on the Colombian society and economy (Arias et al. 2014). These costs have pushed the business sector to be very supportive of peace negotiations both "as a solution to armed conflict and as a strategy to protect assets and operations" (Rettberg 2007, 465).[3] The large costs of conflict, such as kidnapping, violence, and pressure from leftist guerrillas, motivated firms to become involved in building peace (Rettberg 2004). Firms are shown to invest less when kidnappings target firm managers or owners (Pshisva and Suarez 2010). As political instability (Barro 1991), crime (Gaviria 2002), and terrorism interrupt business activities and depress economic growth, promoting peace and stability is in the interest of these firms. In Colombia, when the conflict remained in rural areas, large firms were not engaged in peacebuilding. This shifted when business people became targets. As violence escalated and urbanized, firms and their inputs became direct targets of attacks, which prompted greater involvement in building peace.

Interconexión Eléctrica offers one example of how violence pushed the company to have greater community involvement. This is Colombia's largest transporter of electricity and suffered the many guerrilla attacks. Between 1999 and 2006, their energy pylons were bombed over 1,200 times, leading the company to think proactively about armed conflict and focus its social programs on long-term peace (Guáqueta 2006). It was clear that standard programs for addressing environmental and social issues were not sufficient and that their risk management must address the root causes of conflict. One result was the creation of Programma de Desarrollo para la Paz (Prodepaz), which focuses on regional peace and development. The program focuses on structural causes of conflict, providing technical assistance in entrepreneurship and financing and assisting business development projects. There are visible improvements in the lives of local populations by addressing the root causes of poverty and inequality.

Do Reports of Bad Corporate Behavior Increase Colombian Firm Engagement in Peacebuilding Activities?

The empirical results offer evidence that companies with reports of negative behavior are more likely to engage in peacebuilding. How have firms caught being "bad" corporate actors behaved in Colombia?

There is significant evidence that firms have often negatively impacted the communities where they operate. As King shows, "There is a political economy to warfare that produces positive externalities for its perpetrators" (2001, 528). The wartime environment may have spoils that discourage peaceful settlement, as happened in Angola's diamond industry, in Cambodia's timber industry, and with coca in Colombia. In addition, companies may work outside the law to ensure the security of immobile investments. For example, several large companies operating in Colombia during its civil war have since been charged with crimes against humanity (teleSUR 2017). Multinational companies Del Monte, Dole, and Chiquita were named for voluntarily financing right-wing paramilitary groups that were a part of the so-called Bananero Block. Many researchers see business as part of the problem facing countries embroiled in conflict, particularly in those states with natural resources (Switzer 2002). As the conflict environment shifts, however, so does the payoff structure for private firms. Those that may have benefited from conflict and instability can now think about how to strategically be a part of future stability.[4] As technology increases accountability, the potential for negative fallout from unethical behavior increasingly encourages behaviors that promote peace. The ease of communication enables communities and activists to mobilize support and pressure corporations to take restorative measures (Andrews et al. 2017). Engaging in peacebuilding can help companies that have been called out for "bad" behavior to brandwash.

There is also evidence that Colombian firms have learned from their experiences. Interconexión Eléctrica, discussed earlier as responding to increased and direct violence, has also learned to engage the communities where it operates in a way that promotes development and peace. During the construction of hydroelectric dams in its early years in the 1960s and 1970s, the company relocated entire villages and sparked deep social tensions (Guáqueta 2006). The company was not experienced in resettlement or impact prevention, and grassroots organizations began to demand compensation and lower water rates. This experience led the company to create better practices and protocols. When the FARC and paramilitaries escalated violence in their areas of operation, the firm was forced once again to revise its social programs to more directly build peace, as discussed previously.

Does Valuing Community Engagement Increase Colombian Firms' Peacebuilding Activities?

The quantitative analysis shows that members of the UN Global Compact are no more likely to engage in peacebuilding activities. And yet, Colombia has a strong culture of active corporate engagement. What can we learn from Colombian firms and their culture?

There are two main shifts in Colombia that pushed business culture to be more active in peacebuilding activities (Guáqueta 2006). First, in the late 1990s there was a large increase in the number of international actors involved in the peacebuilding process. International donations rose, tripling between 1998 and 2003 (Tierney et al. 2011). Much of the investment was for peacebuilding, including funds from states, NGOs, and the UNDP. These donors actively sought private firms as cosponsors and experts. One example of this is the donor-supported Peace Labs, which provides grants to youth-led organizations promoting peace.

The second shift was a move to be more in line with global corporate social responsibility (CSR) norms while accounting for the local context (Lindgreen et al. 2010). Firms began to invest both in their employees and their communities. Part of this shift resulted from the aforementioned presence of international actors, which was important given that CSR norms have generally been forged by US and European companies. Since the late 1990s, firms have increasingly integrated both ethical policies and CSR-related activities their practices (Guáqueta 2006).

These shifts are exemplified by comparing two of Colombia's largest energy firms, their cultures, and their peacebuilding activities. Promigas Colombia, a large energy company that has developed a strong culture of peacebuilding, offers an important example of the role corporate culture plays in its peacebuilding work. In 1999, Promigas established its own independent foundation, Fundacion Promigas, which focuses on developing educational opportunities. It has been an active member of the UN Global Compact, which requires companies submit annual reports on how they uphold the "10 Principals for Peace," since 2014 (the UN Global Compact started its local Colombian chapter, Pacto Global Red Colombia, in 2004). Finally, Promigas joined with the Global Partnership on Output-Based Aid (GPOBA) to make new natural gas connections to poor households (Mandri-Perrott 2010), as well as engaged in projects aimed at expanding credit to lower-income households that have traditionally faced financial exclusion in the country. As a part of this partnership, workshops were provided about home economics, self-care, hygiene, and productive entrepreneurship, including microeconomic credits (Management 2015).

Promigas is considered a major factor in helping build peace in Colombia through its creation of economic and social value. Moreover, it has been involved in the peacebuilding process through events like Forum Futuro Colombia, where the president of Promigas Foundation spoke on how corporate resources can generate social transformation (Suarez and Ferreira 2016). Promigas has also helped to create independent social institutions, including Entrepreneurs for Education, the Surtigas Foundation, the Gases del Caribe Foundation, Terpel Foundation, and Gases de Occidente Foundation. The World Business and Development Awards ceremony, which recognizes businesses for their efforts to improve the lives of some of the world's most disadvantaged communities, commended the company in 2010 (Poverty 2010).

We can contrast Promigas with Ecopetrol, Colombia's state-owned energy firm. It is engaged in the exploration and production of oil and gas, refining, transportation of crude oil and refined products, and the marketing and supply of refined and feedstock products. Ecopetrol primarily operates in Colombia, Peru, Brazil, Angola, and the US Gulf Coast. While the company lists numerous foundations to which it contributes financially, Ecopetrol has faced criticism for its attempt to drill in lands considered owned by local indigenous populations. Although the company gave up their plans due to delays and increasing costs of the litigation and conflict, they retain the permits for future drilling (Hill 2015). Another challenge for Ecopetrol is huge cost overruns related to fraud (Galvis 2016). While Ecopetrol joined the UN Global Compact in 2009, the company is only involved in peacebuilding through donations to third parties. While they report having created an internal Human Rights committee, they also report 116 leaks or spills in 2009 alone, comprising 7,533.1 barrels spilled (Ecopetrol 2009). Ecopetrol does not have as significant culture that generates value for proactive peacebuilding. This is likely the result of being state-owned and headquartered in Bogotá (as opposed to Baranquilla, where Promigas is headquartered, which has more violence and crime), although both Promigas and Ecopetrol have been the targets of bombings.

While there is variation, many of Colombia's firms promote this culture of civic engagement and peacebuilding. For example, BanColombia, Colombia's largest bank, has multiple ongoing social and environmental initiatives. It is a member of the UN Global Compact, the UN Environmental Financing

Program, the Equator Principles, the Business Council for Sustainable Development, the Carbon Disclosure Project, the Global Reporting Initiative, and the Green Protocol (BanColombia 2015). BanColombia has partnered with BanCO2 to preserve and restore forestland. Finally, their foundation, Fundación BanColombia, offers scholarships for vulnerable college students and supports early childhood education. There has been a shift in the expectations regarding corporate behavior, and majority of firms are engaged in some form of CSR activity (Lindgreen et al. 2010).

Characteristics of Colombia's Engaged Firms

The models used to explore variation in firm engagement control for variation in firm characteristics through a process called random effects. Given the active peacebuilding of many Colombian firms, however, the setting offers an opportunity to explore variation in firm engagement levels in greater detail. I do so by looking at how the firm characteristics argued to encourage firm engagement, size, sector, and profits, affect Colombian corporate activities (Wenger and Möckli 2003).

Does Firm Size Affect Colombian Firm Engagement in Peacebuilding Activities?

Several studies suggest that larger firms were more likely to engage in peacebuilding activities (Oetzel, Getz, and Ladek 2007; Oetzel 2005). Large firms are motivated by stakeholders to invest in social programs (Russo and Perrini 2010). Does this hold true in the Colombian case? Given that the data only include corporations with over $100M in revenue, have small and medium-sized enterprises (SMEs) contributed as well? Examining this case reveals several trends in how peacebuilding varies by business size.

In Colombia, violence affected large companies differently than SMEs due to differences in access to security and variations in how stakeholders are conceptualized. Large companies dealt with security issues by hiring private security and buying insurance. These companies also often made contributions to the local military and police to guarantee the protection of top personnel and company assets. Small and medium-sized enterprises rarely had the funds to enable such security and were more vulnerable to attacks, often facing extortion and kidnappings (Guáqueta 2006). Area paramilitary or rebels would demand monthly payments in exchange for security, requiring supplies once owners could not afford to give cash. In rural areas, sympathizers reported back to groups, eroding social trust.

As the conflict was pushed into more remote parts of the country, large corporations began to focus on peacebuilding rather than defense and survival. Many large companies began to think about ways to foster long-term peace and stability, both with the conduct of their daily operations and by being more actively involved in national political and social structures. As examples of this are explored extensively elsewhere throughout this chapter, it is worth discussing the role Colombia's SMEs play in peacebuilding.

As SMEs make up a majority of the world's economic activity and employment, they are also capable of making important contributions to building a peaceful society (Kechiche and Soparnot 2012). In Latin America, SME contributions tend to focus on ethical and religious factors, concern for employees and profits, and the need to foster a good relationship with clients, suppliers, and the community (Vives 2006). Survey and interview research of SME executives in Colombia reveals that the majority of these enterprises engaged in activities involving employee welfare, training, and development, as well as adopting charities (Pastrana and Sriramesh 2014). The same study showed these businesses were unlikely to engage in volunteering or cultural activities. As a result of such efforts, executives reported their businesses benefited from having an improved organizational culture, higher-quality employees, superior image, and stronger customer loyalty. These efforts are likely to be especially important as Colombia moves forward in the peace process, as they will help rebuild trust and a sense of community in the places where they do business.

In the case of Colombia, contributions to peacebuilding are not limited to large corporations. The quantitative evidence suggesting that large firms are more active peace builders likely reflects the availability of information on different businesses: SMEs are less likely to be covered by the media for their work or have webpages describing their contributions to peace. They are not a part of national peace talks or negotiations. These businesses still help to create more peaceful environments in the places where they operate, however. Their efforts focus on the people directly engaging with the business, either through employment or being a customer or supplier. Large firms often engage in activities that incorporate a broader definition of stakeholders. Both efforts will make important contributions in the process of moving

Colombia from war to peace. These findings support existing qualitative research that shows larger firms are more likely to engage in national level peacebuilding mechanisms, while other firms are focused on strategies that benefit their local communities (Lindgreen et al. 2010).

Does Firm Sector Affect Engagement in Peacebuilding Activities?

Finally, a company's utility for peacebuilding is also linked to the sector in which it operates, as some sectors are more engrained in the communities where they operate than others. A common mechanism of distinguishing among sectors is to differentiate among those corporations that operate in the extractive sector, which consists of any operations removing metals, minerals, and aggregates from the earth. While this industry has the potential to generate significant wealth and growth through generating revenue, countries with abundant natural resources often suffer from political turmoil and civil conflict. There is a large amount of scholarship on the link between natural resources and civil war (for a review, see Ross 2004). Given Colombia's large extractive sector, does Colombian firm engagement vary by sector? The extractive sector, in particular, is often highlighted as behaving differently during times of conflict due to immobility and its effects on the surrounding environment and populations. For example, research on the expansion of mining, oil, and gas in Latin America shows this expansion has also brought negative sociopolitical, environmental, and political economic consequences (Bebbington and Bury 2013). How is this reflected in Colombia's industry sectors?

Colombia has a large oil and gas industry, contributing significantly to its export revenues. While the oil industry makes up between 2 and 7 percent of the country's GDP each year, pipelines have been a regular target for rebel groups (Reuters 2017, 2018). As a nonlootable resource, the distribution systems themselves offer an attractive target for rebels as a way to create instability (Kathman and Shannon 2011). Colombia's less-known rebel group, ELN, has especially targeted Colombia's petroleum industry, demanding a change in the way oil and gas are managed and disrupting the flow of crude oil through pipelines leading to the coast (Boudon 1996). Since Colombia has few lootable resources, rebels instead have instead used illegal drugs, kidnapping, and extortion for funding (Hanson 2009).

Evidence suggests that, while the existence of a strong oil and gas industry might be contributing to the conflict, this does not distinguish which companies contribute to peace. As discussed further in what follows, there are some energy companies, such as Promigas, that have been very active in the peace process, and others, such as Ecopetrol, that have not. There has been speculation that the oil and gas sectors would benefit from the accord or even help to fund some of the reforms it requires (Boudon 1996), but there are also challenges to this idea (Cuéllar 2016). The story of Colombia's oil is complicated by the presence of local, national, and transnational actors, as foreign direct investment is heavily invested in this resource (Dunning and Wirpsa 2004). In addition, many actors in other industries, such as agriculture and manufacturing, have heavily invested in the peace process. The engagement of firms is much more linked to how affected they are by violence, as I discuss in the next section.

Do Profit Margins Affect Engagement Peacebuilding Activities?

Do profit margins affect firm activity in the Colombian case? One way to understand the role of profits is to look at variations in peacebuilding activity across firms with higher and lower profits. Do firms with lower profits do less to build peace? Another approach is to look at variations in profits across time within the same firm (Table 6.3). Do firms engage in fewer peacebuilding activities in years where profits are low? I now examine the links between profits and peacebuilding looking at both types of variation (across firms and within firms).

Many of these companies have been discussed earlier in the chapter, including Ecopetrol, Terpel, Interconexión Eléctrica, and Promigas, each of which engages in some form of peacebuilding. Ecopetrol is the least engaged in peacebuilding, only active through donations to third parties while others run their own programs. What about Grupo Argos, Empresa de Energia de Bogotá, Celsia, and Mineros?

Grupo Argos is a Global Compact member (joined in 2013), Empresa de Energia de Bogotá joined in 2005, Celsia joined in 2012. Of these companies, Mineros, a Colombian mining firm, is an active peacebuilder despite having the lowest average profits. It has been a member of the UN Global Compact since 2012 and created a separate foundation, Fundación Mineros, in 2010.

Table 6.3 Profit Margins across All Energy and Utility Firms Headquartered in Colombia[1]

Firm	2013	2014	2015	2016	2017	Mean
Ecopetrol	13,106,503	5,725,500	−3,987,726	1,564,709	6,620,412	4,605,880
Terpel	166,073	126,896	105,958	196,516	195,281	158,145
Grupo Argos	294,950	521,133	326,830	589,466	610,659	468,608
Inerconexion Electrica	433,048	509,713	701,548	2,136,629	1,437,936	1,043,775
Promigas	442,004	164,857	477,927	616,697	645,246	469,346
Empresa de Energia de Bogotà	843,560	816,349	1,013,867	1,288,984	1,500,121	1,092,576
Celsia	373,645	173,632	−166,414	32,997	149,147	112,601
Mineros	42,517	36,917	61,383	88,178	116,906	69,180

[1] Based on net income financial statements of energy and utility companies from Marketline Advantage. Detailed financial information was not available for Emesga, Isagen, Incauca, or smaller companies operating in this sector. Companies are listed by 2017 revenue in descending order.

The foundation's activities focus on supporting the communities where it operates through environmental protection and recovery, good governance, and social and economic development. The programs run through the foundation vary from beekeeping to business and technical assistance, running a chess program for local youth, and hosting sexual and reproductive health sessions. These programs have accompanied an increase in profits as well as shifts in global expectations about corporate behavior and Colombia's peace process.

Celsia, a renewable energy company that is a subsidiary of Grupo Argos, reports the lowest net income for multiple years (although Mineros has a lower average net income). It also has the worst record for peacebuilding. It is currently facing backlash for plans to build a hydroelectric dam on the Semana River, Colombia last free-flowing river. The river has been off-limits in the past, since paramilitaries inhabited one side of the river and guerrillas inhabited the other. That said, the company is focused on renewable energy, with hydroelectric-, thermal-, solar-, and wind-powered plants. Their foundation, Fundación Celsia, focuses on education through improving schools with electricity and water, as well as strengthening teaching skills. They also support Manos Visibles, which is helping build institutional capacity and local leadership. Thus, even the least profitable of Colombia's energy companies is engaged beyond standard business transactions. It is also likely that this company has fewer negative externalities and is less likely to have "bad" behavior to overcome compared to other energy companies.

Grupo Argos reports some of the highest profits across each year. The firm is a conglomerate with investments in cement and energy (including Celsia, as discussed earlier). As an infrastructure holding company, it has both worked to build peace and contributed to factors that undermine the rule of law. One subsidiary, Cementos Argos, was found guilty of price fixing between 2010 and 2012, and has been accused of land theft and financing death squads during the armed conflict (Alsema 2017). In 2014, they donated 16,000 acres of land to a charity for poor farmers as way to support peace given the uncertainty surrounding land reparations (Reuters 2014). The company is also a member of various sustainability institutions, such as the CEO Water Mandate, and is traded on the Dow Jones Sustainability Index (DJSI), which recognized them as the leading company in the materials sector, and the FTSE4Good Index Series. In December of 2018, the Colombian Federation of Human Management awarded Grupo Argos with the Sustainability Award for Good Labor Practices. It has a private foundation focusing on environmental conservation and has developed various initiatives on education and social development. While Grupo Argos may have been a "bad" corporate actor during the conflict, it seems to have embraced peacebuilding in its aftermath. Over time, and perhaps due to scandal, the company has grown to be a partner in the peace process. This may reflect events within Colombia itself, public scandals, or its growing profits. The dip in its 2015 profits did not seem to suppress this commitment, although they received multiple recognitions for their efforts in the following year.

Empresa de Energia de Bogotá works in the power and natural gas sector. The company was involved in the Macro-Round for Reconciliation in Calí in 2016, where they began "Energy for Peace," which focuses on energy transmission, demining, and vocational training. The project aspires to help consolidate peace in areas at high risk for land mines, while also improving access to services for remote communities. As with Mineros, it is difficult to separate the effects of growing profit margins on these peacebuilding activities from shifts in global trends and Colombia's peace process.

These examples of Colombian firms corroborate the empirical results that a firm's peacebuilding activities are not directly tied to its profits. These findings are true within the same firms, as their earnings rise and fall, and across firms with different average earnings. Even when a firm is operating at a net loss, it continues previous program and institutional commitments. Firms with lower profit margins are no less likely to engage in peacebuilding activities than those with higher profits. There are two significant things to note that likely also affect these examples of engagement: the global trend of increased corporate engagement in communities and the progress of Colombia's peace process.

Outcomes of Firm Engagement in Colombia

Has the active private sector helped create a more peaceful society in Colombia? What role have these actions played in resolving the conflict? The quantitative tests suggest that an active private sector can prevent violence, but that engagement during ongoing violence prolongs the peace process (see Table 6.4). The failure of firms to engage in peacebuilding allowed the conflict between FARC and government forces to become increasingly violent. However, firms became actively engaged in the peace process as violence moved into urban areas and the costs of violence increased. I find evidence that when firms engage after violence has begun, private corporations act as an additional veto player and prolong the negotiating process, as was the case in Colombia. Much of the previous discussion supports the large-N findings. In what follows, I further examine how post–peace accord engagement is likely to prevent further violence.

Are the post-2016 peace accord efforts of Colombian firms to build peace effectively doing so? Civil wars are the result of the expected utility of war outweighing that of peace (Collier and Hoeffler 2002a; Walter 2004; Fearon and Laitin 2003; Collier and Hoeffler 1998). When the expected utility of

Table 6.4 Chapter 5 Results as Applied to Colombia

Lesson	Application		Outcome
Firm Engagement Reduces Violence	Pre-2016 Peace Agreement	Lack of Firm Engagement Prior to 1990s	Violence
Engaged Firms Prolong Ongoing Violence			Late 1990s negotiations begin
Firm Engagement Reduces Violence	Post-2016 Peace Agreement	Firm Engagement	Limited Splinter-group Violence

peace is greater than that of continued war, these conflicts end. This framework offers a theoretical simplification to the complexities of actors' specific motivations. For example, scholars often cite the importance of opportunity costs for potential rebel recruits as a way to understand motives for rebelling (Walter 2004; Collier and Hoeffler 2000), which can be seen as changing the payoffs of war in comparison to peace. Low economic development and state capacity motivate belligerence since the opportunity costs of war are low compared to the private gains of conflict. How groups perceive such preferences and opportunities can also help us understand when groups choose conflict (Hirshleifer 1995, 2001). Each party also has expectations about eventual outcomes that informs their decision to negotiate or fight (Mason and Fett 1996b). Redistributive policies help governments to defend against insurrections and maintain peace, since these measures change the expected benefits of rebelling (Azam 1995; Grossman 1992).

When we consider the opportunity cost of joining a rebellion, it seems that Colombia's firms have positively contributed in ways that encourage potential rebels to choose peace. Through rural development projects, economic opportunities, and social programs, businesses in Colombia are making the life of a rebel less appealing. Individuals have access to training and opportunities that were absent for many years. When we consider peace at the level of individual choice, the role of the private sector has been and will be key in encouraging nonviolence.

Understanding peace at the national level is more complex. Certainly, peace has many causes and is the result of multiple actors and actions. While it is challenging to isolate correlates of Colombia's peace accord with FARC from the many other factors that played into its creation, Colombia's private firms clearly played an active role in encouraging the peace process and promoting its implementation. This engagement is unlikely to have been harmful and very likely had a positive effect.

Research suggests there are five main ways that businesses help build peace, and these pathways are all present in the Colombian case (Miklian 2017). Economic engagement helps create a peace dividend, since increased security allows for increases in productive contributions to society. Additionally, firms contribute to local development, which facilitates local capacity for peace. For example, Colombia's Coffee Federation (Federación National de Cafeteros) funded the Footprints of Peace project, which improved local societal and economic development (Miklian and Bickel 2020). Firms spread international norms, thereby improving democratic accountability. They can

also constrain the root causes of conflict. Finally, firms engaged in direct diplomatic efforts to build peace.

At both the national and local levels, evidence suggests firm-led
peacebuilding efforts are creating significant shifts in Colombia's society. As
the private sector's role in Colombia's armed conflict varies across firms, the
link between armed conflict and the private sector is the result of both national and subnational forces. While the nation was generally moving toward
peace, many firms were embracing this process as well. Company-specific
factors likely play a role in understanding these outcomes as well (Rettberg,
Leiteritz, and Nasi 2011). The private sector is likely to play an important role
in ensuring a peaceful Colombia moving forward. Effective peacebuilding
will require support beyond that of government policymakers to include a
wide range of social actors.

Conclusion

Colombia's violent history and shifts in firm-led peacebuilding offer an important case for examining the causes of firm engagement and explanations
of the outcomes of firm engagement. The government has moderate capacity
that varies widely by region, levels of violence differ across space and time as
it urbanized, and norms of corporate-political links have become stronger
over time. This case showed how shifting conflict dynamics can push firms to
more actively work towards peace, but it also suggests that these actions can
prolong peace processes. Since Colombia's firms were not actively engaged
prior to the start of violence and approached negotiations with their own
agenda, the evidence suggests not all corporate efforts to create peace are positive. At the same time, continued engagement in the post–peace agreement
era has helped bolster peace even when national leaders have failed to do so.

Peace in Colombia is far from cemented, especially considering the need
for a deal with ELN and the presence of FARC splinter groups. Despite these
challenges, much of the international community has celebrated the case as a
success story for peace. Given the international attention the peace deal has
received and the active nature of business communities in Colombia's peace
process, it is not a surprise that the 2018 Business for Peace Award went to a
Colombian (2018). Edgar Montenegro founded Corpocampo to provide a
source of legal and reliable income for farmers on Colombia's pacific coastline. The business promotes the sustainable use of forests through harvesting

hearts of palm and acai, providing technical assistance and buying crops at a fair price. Given the limited capacity of the Colombian government, grassroots efforts like these will be a necessary component of a peaceful Colombian future.

National policies provide the backbone for peace, however, and the business community continues to play an important role. Several large companies created the Ideas for Peace Foundation (Fundación Ideas para la Paz [FIP]) in 1999 as a think tank to advise government mediators on the design of a negotiation agenda and encourage a peaceful resolution of the conflict. In addition, FIP has developed a growingly sophisticated and policy-relevant research agenda that promotes peacebuilding, development, and security. Such partnership in the policymaking process can help fill the gaps where the government lacks capacity. For a successful transition to peace, the nation will need an active business community with a strong commitment to peacebuilding.

The case of post–peace agreement Colombia shows that when firms engage in peacebuilding and are partners in the peace process, a violent country can move forward to a more peaceful and inclusive future. In Colombia, all sizes of firms working in various sectors have contributed to peacebuilding. A part of this story is that many firms engaged in less-than-ideal behavior when the rule of law was absent. As international norms and Colombia's peace process shifted, however, the private sector has been able to adopt a culture of active peacebuilding. The violence and limited state capacity posed a challenge to business operations, and Colombia's firms are showing how important their role is in building the future.

7

Conflict Transformation and Prevention in Tunisia

Introduction

Tunisia's revolution in 2010 ended over five decades of authoritarian rule.

In 2014, Tunisia adopted a new constitution and held free democratic elections resulting in the peaceful transition of power to the secular Nidaa Tounes party. Tunisia is the only country to emerge from the Arab Spring with a functioning democratic government.[1] The Ben Ali regime had alienated many key civilian constituencies, setting the stage for mass demonstrations and protests. This chapter argues that a powerful private sector, acting through the organized structure of unions, prevented violence from erupting during the Jasmine Revolution and has helped maintain a peaceful transition process since. In the early days of revolution, activists in the main labor union, the Tunisian General Labor Union (or UGTT), played a leading role in spreading information and participation. Business leaders and their organizations have been important in Tunisia's continuing transition to democracy. Some scholars even suggest these actors were crucial in this transition. The awarding of the Nobel Peace Prize in 2015 to the "Tunisian Quartet" suggests this is indeed the case.

Tunisia's transition to a democratic state with strong institutions and government capacity is far from over, however. While Tunisia has been celebrated as the success story of the Arab Spring, the state remains very weak and requires fundamental reforms, especially in the security sector and economic policy. I argue a flip side to the strength of unions is a difficulty in building consensus around and implementing the reforms necessary to stimulate economic development and create stability. This chapter looks at firm engagement through active and powerful unions in Tunisia's democratic transition, the lack of individual private firm engagement, and the importance of both political reforms and firm-led programs that address the underlying causes of instability as the country moves forward.

The Building and Breaking of Peace. Molly M. Melin, Oxford University Press. © Oxford University Press 2021.
DOI: 10.1093/oso/9780197579367.003.0007

The Background of Tunisia's Regime, Economy, and Private Firms

Tunisia's history, governmental policies, and domestic institutions all played important roles in the peaceful nature of the Jasmine Revolution. The so-called twin tolerations of religious leaders toward the state (to make law) and of the state toward religious leaders (to practice religion) stem from a history of being a religiously neutral state (Stepan 2012). Tunisia also has an exceptionally small military (the smallest in the Arab world), on average spending less than 2 percent of its GDP in this way. Civilian rule and the lack of weapons in Tunisia also made civil war unlikely, despite the political unrest. Islamist moderation and the actions of unions during the unrest actively promoted a peaceful transition (Angrist 2013).

An important piece of the nature of the Tunisian transition during political instability is the strength of Tunisia's business organizations and unions. Activists in the UGTT played a leading role in spreading information and participating in the early responses to the Bouazizi self-immolation (Bowen 2013).[2]

Organized labor in Tunisia has a unique history and social dimension that enabled it to structure resistance and social contention (for more, see Omri 2015). Despite the relatively moderate nature of social contention in Tunisia (especially compared to neighboring Algeria and Libya), the ability of organized labor to communicate with and mobilize large segments of society is unique and helps explain the nature of the Jasmine Revolution. The power of UGTT enabled it to curtail many of the revolutionary ambitions.

UGTT has a long history of successful activism. The union was formed in 1946, before Tunisia's independence from France, and quickly gained widespread support and power. In the early days, UGTT was able to use its clout and strong international ties to pressure the French for social and political rights. It became a key player in the independence movement, consolidating the union's position as a major national political entity. Having roots in the struggle against French colonialism gave the union political involvement that it has maintained and guarded since, as seen in its charter, which declares its aims of:

building a socialist and nationalist economy, independent and free from all forms of dependency; calling for fair distribution of national wealth in a way which guarantees the aspirations of all workers and lower sections of society; defending individual and public liberties, and reinforcing democracy and human rights; supporting all people struggling to reclaim their sovereignty and determine their destiny and standing in solidarity with national liberation movements across the world. (as cited in Omri 2015, 19)

Thus, UGTT had interests that reflected those of the population at large. These interests, along with the credibility built during the independence movement, enabled UGTT to build a powerful network, power, and credibility nationwide. Leading up to the revolution, UGTT was considered a credible alternative to the ruling party and a key player in resisting its power. Unionists were considered to be opponents to the ruling party, allowing for and fostering an institutional space for dissent.

Additionally, UGTT emerged as a key power broker and mediator in the early days of the revolution. This ability to resolve disputes peacefully likely resulted from its position as government opposition. During the days that followed Bouazizi's self-immolation, UGTT played a key role in organizing the events that took place. They first passed the information about the event to the media and organized protests for the following day. They were able to quickly mobilize strike efforts, thereby taking a vanguard position in the protest efforts. UGTT filled a gap in power, helping to lead decision-making, steering debate, and offering a place for parties meet when they were in the early stages of formation.

Businesses and their organizations have played an important role in Tunisia's continuing transition to democracy. Some researchers even suggest these actors were crucial in this transition (Wennmann 2016). The awarding of the Nobel Peace Prize in 2015 to the "Tunisian Quartet," which consisted of UGTT as well as the Tunisian Federation of Industry, Trade, and Handicrafts (or UTICA), suggests this is indeed the case. That UGTT and UTICA worked together for national reconciliation in the years following the overthrow of Ali was key, since UTICA represents key employers and corporate interests across Tunisia. Despite the primarily peaceful nature of the transition, 2013 saw a marked uptick in violence as two key opposition political figures were assassinated. Through three separate national dialogues, the quartet was able to form an interim government, schedule legislative and presidential elections, and adopt a national constitution in 2014.

Ongoing Issues

Despite the impressive political changes that have occurred in Tunisia since 2011, the economy has been slow to recover. The lack of employment opportunities has created social dissatisfaction, which manifests in regular demonstrations and protests, as well as high levels of youth migration. Youth and women are particularly affected by the lack of employment opportunities and poor economy, especially inland. Tunisia is one of the few countries where higher education actually decreases employability. National unemployment levels hover around 15 percent, with significantly higher levels around 22 percent for women and 28 percent for graduates (World Bank 2020). Thus, policies must focus on attracting investment that can create new economic opportunities, especially inland and for women and youth.

These are issues that can be met with private sector investment, as long as such investments are encouraged through sound fiscal policy. Excluded members of society represent significant untapped market potential. As of 2017, women owned 17–20 percent of Tunisia's firms, yet their banking needs and access to credit goes largely unmet (International Finance Corporation 2017). Tunisia has some of the region's most progressive laws on women's rights, even recognizing the "equality between men and women" in the constitution. Women are also better educated, surpassing male participation in education. These rights have not translated to female economic empowerment, however, and women make up just a third of the workforce and are paid 15 percent less for equal work. Many lack access to financial services, and increasing access to this resource is likely to increase financial inclusion and greater economic stability nationwide. Firms that provide services to women and young people in the realm of banking, leasing, and insurance will both help support this underserved portion of the population, create economic growth from their untapped market potential, and help Tunisia's economy develop new wealth and job opportunities.

At the same time, there are barriers to expanding access and opportunities to the youth and women. A large portion of the economy is informal (an estimated 38 percent in 2013, according to UGTT), and the taxes from these businesses can help drive economic growth. Women are culturally more likely to approach friends or family for a small loan rather than a formal financial institution, and banks are also less focused on attracting new customers than serving existing ones.

The largest challenge, however, is that much of the work being done in Tunisia is either by government or nongovernmental actors, and does not include private firms. The Jasmine Revolution and Tunisia's successful political transition has attracted the attention of many different international actors, such as the European Union, the World Bank, and the United Nations and their subagencies. Many international actors are working to improve the economic conditions, but few domestic firms see this as a part of their role or responsibility. Some argue that one of the fallouts from the Arab Spring is a shift in the role of businesses as they incorporate new societal value and consumer spending patterns, but that these changes have yet to develop practices free of corruption (Avina 2013). While changes in corporate social responsibility (CSR) programs have led to more locally focused programs, as well as a focus on the challenges of democratization and underemployment, active corporate engagement in peacebuilding is far from the norm. Many of the programs that are in place are driven by transnational firms rather than local ones. For example, Microsoft equipped the Tunisian Commission for Investigation of Human Rights Abuses and Violations with an electronic case management system and supported dozens of new NGOs promoting democracy and economic opportunity. Manpower, Cisco, Intel, and Microsoft all run youth employability programs in the region. Total Petroleum, headquartered in France, has a foundation that focuses on road safety, environmental and cultural issues, and youth inclusion. One possible outcome of these internationally based firm activities is that they spread norms of corporate peacebuilding to Tunisian-based firms.

One of the goals of the quartet had been to open Tunisia up to foreign investment. Tunisia's economy has consistently been a key political issue. After the events of the Arab Spring, the international community significantly re-engaged with new lending arrangements and project initiatives (Hanieh 2015). The international community has made efforts to promote Tunisia's transition, focusing mostly on political and economic stabilization (Hinds 2014). In 2012, Tunisia received a total of 2.8 billion in external financial aid (Stiftung 2014), and levels of international aid have remained high. Table 7.1 summarizes amounts of official development assistance (or ODA) contributed to Tunisia in 2015, 2016, and 2017. Foreign aid contributions have remained high and even increased. As Tunisia's economy has suffered and aid has increased, aid is making up an increasing proportion of the economy. The World Bank, European Union, IMF, and African Development Bank have given substantial aid and contributed technical assistance.

Table 7.1 Official Development Assistance for Tunisia

	2015	2016	2017
Net ODA (USD million)	1,355.9	1,106.5	844.8
Net ODA/GNI (%)	0.5	0.4	0.3
Gross ODA (USD million)	1,420.5	1,167.4	928.0
Total net receipts (USD million)	5,593.6	1,052.5	2,991.1

Source: OECD Official Development Assistance Flows (OECD 2020).

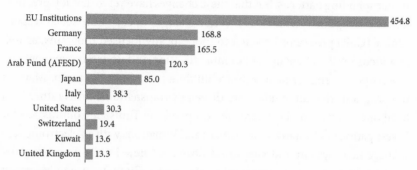

Figure 7.1 Top Ten Donors of Gross ODA for Tunisia, 2016–2017 Average, USD Million
Source: OECD Official Development Assistance Flows (OECD 2020).

Tunisia also received substantial bilateral support, especially from partner countries France, Italy, Germany, Qatar, and Saudi Arabia. Figure 7.1 summarizes the top donors to Tunisia in 2016 and 2017 with the European Union, Tunisia's largest trading partner, as the largest donor by far. The European Union and Tunisia have a "Privileged Partnership," which formalized the European Union's commitment to supporting Tunisia's transition and enabled access to higher levels of EU funding. Other European states also contribute aid outside the EU framework. The United States is the largest non-EU or Middle East and North Africa (MENA) donor. Much of this aid is tagged to help strengthen Tunisia's postrevolution challenges. The United States and the Center for Democratic Control of Armed Forces (DCAF) have given financing, training, and technical assistance to aid with security sector reform. The Tunisian American Enterprise Fund, run through USAID, offers small and medium-sized enterprise (SME) financing, with a special focus on women, youth, and the interior regions.

Foreign investment in Tunisia has yet to recover since the Jasmine Revolution, however (see Figure 7.2). Many of Tunisia's foreign investors fled the disarray of the postrevolutionary government, and terrorist incidents have also scared off investment (the tourism industry, which made up 7 percent of GDP collapsed to half its former levels following terrorist attacks in 2015) (Gall 2016). While economic growth stalled at around 1.5 percent following the revolution, government spending soared as the government invested in the military and new public sector jobs. Moody's has repeatedly downgraded Tunisia's credit ranking. Yet, being proximate to Europe and a gateway to Africa and with a highly educated workforce, Tunisia has much to offer. Attracting foreign investment, especially companies headquartered in countries with strong norms of corporate peacebuilding, is likely to help spread firm-led peacebuilding.

In addition to attract foreign investment, there needs to be a shift toward incorporating peacebuilding programs into the operations of domestic firms. Part of this puzzle relies on generally increasing the size of the private sector, as the largest employer is an overinflated public sector. Since the revolution, Tunisia's public sector has had the largest share of total employment of any MENA country (Assaad and Barsoum 2019). There is a cultural shift occurring, however, while previously working for the government was seen as a successful career path, startups are redefining success by showing

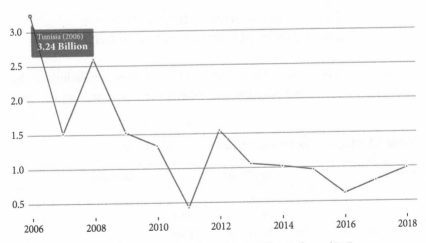

Figure 7.2 Foreign Direct Investment in Tunisia, Net Inflows (BoP, Current US$)

Source: International Monetary Fund, Balance of Payments Database (Bank 2018b).

young people they can work hard and make money (Aoudi 2019). A more educated workforce is less inclined to take a government job, preferring the opportunities that working in the private sector offers (Remili 2019). Growing the economy will depend on fostering entrepreneurial skills and ensuring a business-friendly environment, as bureaucracy and corruption stifle innovation.

What Conditions Increase Firm-Led Peacebuilding in Tunisia?

As Tunisia's business community and its engagement in national negotiations through unions shows, engaging in peacebuilding enables a firm to influence the dynamics of the political and social environments. Active involvement enables private firms to influence dynamics in a way that can be both self-serving and beneficial to the country at large. Table 7.2 provides an overview of how the findings from chapter 4 apply to the Tunisian case. The large-N results presented in chapter 4 suggest that several conditions prompt private corporations to engage in peacebuilding: gaps in governance, years of peace, and the need to reputation build. I explore how these factors prompted Tunisia's unions to prevent violence in during the Arab Spring.

Do Gaps in Governance Increase Tunisian Firm Engagement in Peacebuilding Activities?

Chapter 4 offers quantitative evidence of a curvilinear relationship between state capacity and peacebuilding wherein firms increasingly engage in

Table 7.2 Chapter 4 Results as Applied to the Case of Tunisia

Lesson	Application	Outcome
Firms Fill the Gaps	Moderate Government Capacity & Rule of Law	Union-Led Peacebuilding
Peace Begets Peacebuilding	Years of Instability and Low-Level Violence	
Firms Invest in Their Reputation	Lack of CSR Norms	

peacebuilding as state capacity rises, but this effect levels off at higher levels of capacity. How have the Tunisian government's capacity levels left room for firms to engage in peacebuilding?

Tunisia is a state with moderate government capacity and rule of law. In terms of government effectiveness, regulatory quality, and rule of law, the World Bank's Worldwide Governance Indicators depict Tunisia as ranging from 35th to 65th percentile (see Table 7.3). In years since the 2010 Jasmine Revolution, Tunisia has fallen in percentile rank. Only Tunisia's rule of law has recovered to prerevolutionary rankings. While these rankings are above the averages for the MENA countries, they suggest that the Tunisian government is in line with the averages for upper middle-income states.[3] These scores suggest the Tunisian government provides a moderate quality of public services, civil services, policy formulations and implementation, and credibility (the government effectiveness ranking), but that this is decreasing. Similarly, Tunisia's quality of contract enforcement, police, and courts (the regulatory quality ranking) is moderate but has decreased almost to the bottom third since the revolution. Finally, Tunisia is moderately capable of developing and implementing sound policies and regulations promoting private sector development (the rule of law ranking).

Given the political changes that have occurred in Tunisia between 2008 and 2018, the stability in government capacity is impressive. It has made important transitions toward a democratic system of governance, adopting a constitution and holding elections. Tunisia's government still faces challenges, however, to grow its economy and enable businesses to focus beyond the

Table 7.3 Tunisian Governance Indicators

Indicator	Country	Year	Percentile Rank (0 to 100)
Government Effectiveness	Tunisia	2008	
		2013	
		2018	
Regulatory Quality	Tunisia	2008	
		2013	
		2018	
Rule of Law	Tunisia	2008	
		2013	
		2018	

Source: World Bank Worldwide Governance Indicators.

requirements of daily operations. Political changes saw an increase in regulations and thereby the challenges involved in conducting business. In 2010, Tunisia was ranked number 40 out of 190 countries in the World Bank's Doing Business 2020 report (World Bank 2019). While the government is making changes to address shortcomings in the laws and regulations that impede investment, such as passing the Investment Law (#2016-71), Tunisia remains ranked number 78 out of 190 country (a two-spot increase in the rankings that reversed declining rankings between 2010 and 2017). The government has improved the ease of starting a business and dealing with construction permits, making impactful regulatory and administrative changes. The deep bureaucracy stifles reforms and the lengthy administrative procedures allow for bribery and corruption, which although still prevalent in postrevolution Tunisia, is now democratized (Lee-Jones 2019).

Businesses in Tunisia face significant gaps in governance, but are overburdened with the level of bureaucracy and lengthy administrative processes that make doing business difficult. Tunisia saw the departure of over 500 foreign companies following the revolution, with even domestically headquartered firms fleeing for Morocco because of Tunisia's political and social instability (Chebbi 2019). While there is a need to invest in infrastructure, the government is not providing for education, health, and safety. While businesses can help to invest in these areas, there is too great a gap for them to fill alone. This also helps explain the strength of unions in Tunisia, and why it is the unions rather than individual businesses that have acted as the primary actor in peacebuilding activities. Many of Tunisia's ongoing challenges, such as the push for women's rights and wage equality, are being advocated for through unions (Malek 2019). UTICA has even gone as far as to join the UN Global Compact in the fall of 2019, promising to uphold the Global Compact's values of sustainable development in its trade union activities and within its affiliated companies.

That said, many of the companies operating in the south of Tunisia must overcome the challenges of operating in a rural environment: getting workers to farms, poor road conditions, and bad safety environments (Malek 2019). While some firms operating in the agriculture industry have paid for vans to help overcome these challenges, larger projects have been undertaken by the World Bank through projects like the Road Transport Corridor. A vast majority of the Tunisia's wealth is on its coastline, with 85 percent of Tunisia's GDP being produced in Tunis, Sfax, and Sousse (Rivoal 2012). The inland faces widespread rural poverty, and rural urban migration has increased with lost interest in land-related occupations and insufficient opportunities in other sectors.

Do Firms Engage in More Peacebuilding Activities during Peacetime?

The quantitative results suggest peace enables firms to invest in peacebuilding, likely because stability promotes economic growth and reinvestment in community-oriented programs. How have violent events affected firms in Tunisia? Have firms operating in more violent areas responded differently compared to those operating in peaceful locations?

Since being granted independence in 1956, Tunisia has experienced various violent events, although none have been large-scale. One such event in 1980 involved the efforts of the Tunisian Armed Resistance (or Résistance Armée Tunisienne) to overthrow the authoritarian regime of Habib Bourguiba, who had been elected president for life in 1975. While there was a short intrastate conflict, the resistance group was defeated relatively quickly. Bourguiba was eventually replace by Zine el Abidine Ben Ali in a bloodless coup in 1987. Strikes and political turmoil were not uncommon in Tunisia, but the small size of the military and limited arms in the country never allowed for large-scale violence to occur.

Tunisia has faced some levels of violence as a result of the conflict and Islamic extremism in neighboring Libya and Algeria. There have been small-scale insurgencies within limited areas, due to the expansion of the Islamic State (IS) operations (Sundberg and Melander 2013). During 2015, the IS conducted two prominent attacks, one on the Bardo Museum in Tunis and another at a holiday resort in Sousse. Casualties met the Uppsala Conflict Data Project's (UCPD) twenty-five battle-related death threshold in 2016, when IS attempted to capture the town of Ben Guerdane on the border with Libya. The Tunisian government responded with increased border security and counterterrorism operations. In total, the UCDP has recorded 147 deaths, 86 of which were state-based violence between the Tunisian government and IS, and 61 of which were one-sided violence that IS directed at civilians.

Limited violence has occurred in Tunis and Sousse, which are home to many of Tunisia's major firms, whereas other violent events took place in less developed regions. It is unlikely that the threat of violence or these events are deterring Tunisian firms from engaging in peacebuilding activities, however, as Tunisia has a relatively peaceful history, especially by regional standards. Rather, it is likely the political climate that deters businesses from investing beyond their operations. Business thrives in stable environments where the future is predictable and rules and regulations are clear. Violence is certainly not the only type of instability that can prevent and hinder investment. The political and social instability, when combined with the antiquated infrastructure, made it difficult for private firms to invest in peacebuilding activities.

Political transition is inherently unstable. Tunisia has, however, held successful elections that were respected and is building a new republic. This success means the country is no longer as high a risk for investors. However, business investment has been hindered by high regulations and complex administrative processes, which encourage corruption, result in unpredictable taxation, and generally complicate business operations (OECD 2018). As Tunisia continues to stabilize and adopt additional reforms, firms are likely to increase their investment in programs that reach beyond daily operations.

Do Reports of Bad Corporate Behavior Increase Tunisian Firm Engagement in Peacebuilding Activities?

The empirical results offer evidence that companies with reports of negative behavior are more likely to engage in peacebuilding. However, the threat of negative fallout from being "bad" corporate actors depends on the presence of public pressure for corporate actors to behave differently. This pressure is simply absent in Tunisia. Rather, the public is largely focused on the responsibilities of the public sector and government to provide services and address the challenges facing Tunisia (Houry 2019; Remili 2019). The size of the public sector and its overtaking private companies is a significant problem (Assaad and Barsoum 2019). Any positive contributions that individuals make to building peace is due to the beliefs and actions of individuals and not government regulation or public pressure (Romdhane 2019). Business leaders adopt programs both as a way to enhance the image of their brand and to operate in congruence with their own leadership values (Gherib 2014).

To this day, Tunisia lacks strong norms of corporate engagement. This likely is the result of having a small and struggling economy, with few large companies that are domestically headquartered. The concept of corporate responsibility in Tunisia is still developing, with a focus on creating a positive employer–employee relationship and working environment, as well as creating an ethical image. There is an emphasis on workers' rights, quality of life, and human rights (Jrad 2019). For example, Knauer Instruments is a laboratory equipment manufacturer that has been recognized for best practices in corporate social responsibility. The company's programs focus on ensuring worker productivity and talent retention: offering two months of parental leave, onsite daycare, and flexible hours. Few corporations proactively work to build peace beyond their walls.

Survey research offers evidence that Tunisian firms are limited in their efforts to proactively build peace, and that most efforts related to corporate social responsibility are focused on preserving product quality and employee health and safety (Rekik 2016). Of the eighty-two survey respondents, selected based on a convenience sample, most focus their efforts on the primary stakeholders of clients and employees. Very few programs seek to incorporate environmentally responsible behavior, such as adopting a green supply chain. Additionally, most respondents, while claiming to have some form of CSR program, do not have an official CSR position (only 23.5 percent have a formal position fully dedicated to CSR) or a budget for these activities (only 32.1 percent have a dedicated CSR budget). Given that the results are from a convenience sample, they are likely biased toward overrepresenting corporations with active programs, suggesting national levels of CSR programs are even weaker. However, the results also suggest a majority of Tunisian-based firms are at least moderately engaged in some form of stakeholder engagement activity. That the broader concept of CSR is still developing in Tunisia suggests proactive peacebuilding is even further behind in becoming a behavioral norm.

One of the largest challenges to developing strong norms of firm-led peacebuilding is the size of the informal economy. Especially during the regime of Ben Ali, there was a large informal sector that did not pay taxes and spread corruption. After the revolution, as state capacity decreased, there was an increase in the proportion of the population employed in the informal economy (OECD 2018). Informal employment likely accounts for between 30 percent and 45 percent of Tunisia's economy. The informal economy tends to generate and exacerbate inequalities, as the sector offers lower earnings, insecure working conditions, and little access to the financial system. Bringing SMEs into the formal economy will help develop and spread best practices.

Norms of engagement have also been slow to develop because many Tunisian companies began as family businesses. That many of Tunisia's companies remain small and family owned means there is less concern for the well-being of stakeholders outside company operations (Gherib 2014). Humble beginnings leave a corporate legacy of never feeling like a public company with obligations to society at large, even if the firm grows into one (Baghdadi 2019). This corporate structure is common in the MENA region, and leads to little shareholder engagement and passive investors who fail to push forward the conversation on the role of the corporation (Amico 2014). There are few examples of successful foundations, and corporate leaders are threatened by an insecure future making them less willing to invest in such endeavors. Rather, corporate governance developments have been largely regulation driven.

That is not to say Tunisia's approach to corporate engagement is not changing. Several avant-garde corporations are pushing forward thinking about the role of the firm and opportunities to build peace. This is especially true of the banking industry, several of which have programs working to improve Tunisia's struggling economy. BIAT, the largest private-sector bank in Tunisia, has a long history of responsible behavior and created a separate foundation following the revolution. The BIAT Foundation has ten full-time employees and runs multiple programs that range from providing backpacks and supplies to children in impoverished interior communities (the "1 Backpack 1 Future" program), to running the "In Design" boot camp for art students to learn how to make money, to several entrepreneurship programs promoting social innovation (Baghdadi 2019). The vast majority of the existing firm-led program focus on promoting economic development due to the struggling economy. However, some programs, such as the Gorgi Painting Collection in Medina and Foundation Reume, are cultural. As of 2020, there were forty-eight listings for Tunisian participants in the UN Global Compact, forty-one of which were corporations or SMEs.

Civil society actors are also thinking about this challenge. Tunisia's Chamber of Commerce established the Tunisian Confederation of Citizen Enterprises (or CONECT) in September 2011. The organization is working with several Tunisian companies and the three largest unions to provide a benchmark for companies that want to adhere to socially responsible practices. They are also working on the challenges of regional investment, as well as environmental and sustainability issues, which are largely ignored by Tunisian industries. In reality, however, CONECT is another employers' organization and may not be able to push business engagement forward any more than UTICA has.

Finally, as a focal point for social unrest, Tunisia's youth are beginning to tackle some of the countries challenges through creative startups. Frustrated with the government's inability to reform and create economic opportunities, they are acting independently and innovatively. One such startup, Cogite, is a creative coworking space in Tunis that provides a platform for young entrepreneurs to collaborate. Cogite's CEO, Houssem Aoudi, noted, "As entrepreneurs, we share a communal sense as we believe it is our duty to construct Tunisia. For me, entrepreneurship is a kind of resistance against an unfriendly banking system and our old-fashioned government" (cited in Williams 2016, 106).

Given that social and governance challenges, such as social and economic disparities and unemployment, were at the heart of Tunisia's revolution, firm-led programs aimed at tackling these challenges are likely to expand. The state-centered development model adopted in Tunisia relied on significant government intervention in the economy depressed economic potential (Bouslah 2015). The favoritism, corruption, and weak governance are all challenges that can be mitigated through a combination of active firm-led social engagement and accompanying political reforms. While Tunisia's unions have been successful at negotiating with government actors to transition to democracy peacefully, their activism is likely to continue to be government- and regulation-focused. Programs adopted by individual firms, in contrast, are more likely to address ongoing challenges head-on, as with those lead by internationally headquartered firms. If Tunisia is able to adopt the necessary reforms to attract foreign investment, encourage entrepreneurship, and expand the private sector, individual firm-led peacebuilding activities are likely to become more common.

Outcomes of Firm Engagement in Tunisia

What affect has the active private sector had in creating a more peaceful society in Tunisia? What role have these actions played in preventing violence and civil war? The quantitative tests suggest that an active private sector can prevent violence, but engagement during ongoing violence prolongs the peace process (see Table 7.4). As discussed earlier, Tunisia has only experienced limited amounts of violence, but rather faces political, economic, and

Table 7.4 Chapter 4 Results as Applied to Tunisia

Lesson	Application	Outcome
Firm Engagement Reduces Violence	Active Union-Led Engagement; Fleeing Foreign Investment	Peaceful Revolution
Engaged Firms Prolong Ongoing Violence (Instability)	Active Union Involvement in Policymaking	Prolonged Reform Process

social instability. I consider how the engagement of unions in Tunisia has helped to prevent violence during the Jasmine Revolution but has prolonged the political and economic reform process.

Have Tunisian Firms Reduced Violence?

Although it is impossible to prove the cause of an event that never occurred, Tunisia was arguably at the highest risk of violence during the early days of the Jasmine Revolution. In fact, almost all of the other states that experienced popular uprisings during the Arab Spring had some level of violence associated with the demands for change. In the most extreme cases, Syria, Yemen, and Libya were ravaged by conflicts since 2012 related to the Arab Spring (Allanson, Sollenberg, and Themnér 2013). Tunisia's recent history has been fraught with political crisis, and yet has managed to avoid major violence. For example, in 1987, President Bourgiba was force to resigned during a peaceful, so-called constitutional coup. During the political turmoil of the 1980's as during the Jasmine Revolution, it is likely the alternative channels of political participation that existed through the labor movement, enabling protest against and dialogue with the government, that prevented the development of a violence situation (Hauge 2010).

The strength of Tunisia's business organizations and unions is an important piece of the nature of the Tunisian transitions during political instability. The history of organized labor in Tunisia and its strong social dimension have enabled it to structure resistance and social contention (Omri 2015). Organized labor has the unique ability to communicate with and mobilize large segments of society. Following the Bouazizi self-immolation, UGTT activists in the main labor union helped spread information and participation in early responses (Bowen 2013), emerging as a key power broker and mediator in the early days of revolution. They passed information to the media and organized protests, quickly mobilizing strike efforts and taking a vanguard position in the protests. When Tunisia lacked leadership, UGTT filled the gap in power by helping to lead decision-making and steer debate.

UGTT and UTICA worked together for national reconciliation in the years following the overthrow of Ali. As UTICA represents key employers and corporate interests across Tunisia, joining forces with the main labor union enabled a unity in structuring the transition. These unions, along with the Tunisian Human Rights League and the Tunisian Order of Lawyers, formed what is referred to as the Tunisian National Dialogue Quartet. The Quartet served as the central mediators working to consolidate the democratic transition following the revolution. The group initiated three separate national dialogues, and helped form an interim government, schedule legislative and presidential elections, and adopt a national constitution in 2014. In 2015, their efforts and success in leading negotiations and producing the historic constitution were recognized with a Nobel Peace Prize.

Rather than individual firms acting to prevent violence, many domestic and foreign firms fled Tunisia during and after the revolution. Instead, civil society elites collaborated to avoid violence and demobilize public unrest. While these actors may normally have divergent policy views, they were able to work together during the period of Tunisia's democratic transition. It is likely that the power of the unions to reach and coordinate large portions of the population enabled these actors to have a greater impact on preventing violence than individual or groups of private firms possibly could have had. While individual firms can adopt programs that address the underlying causes of violence, and perhaps even the underlying causes of Tunisia's revolution, states are particularly prone to violence during transitions to democracy (Mansfield and Snyder 2009). As is evidenced by the violence that erupted following the Arab Spring in other nations, there was a need for strong domestic institutions to help structure the course of the changes that took place. Organized labor and business were uniquely situated to serve this role in Tunisia's democratic transition.

Have Tunisian Firms Prolonged Instability?

While Tunisia has experienced limited amounts of violence and firms are most strongly engaged through unions, it is possible that the active engagement of organized labor and businesses have prolonged the instability that has followed the Jasmine Revolution. I explore this possibility in greater detail, considering the processes and actors involved in political decision-making.

As discussed earlier, part of the continued instability in Tunisia is due to the need to adopt political reforms that enable greater economic growth. Poverty, inequality, and unemployment have been sources of social and political unrest for years. There was a major effort to build consensus around the political changes being adopted. Evidence suggests such deliberations and citizen involvement are important for increasing the post-promulgation levels of democracy (Eisenstadt, LeVan, and Maboudi 2015, 2017). Successful constitutional reform needs to generate public "buy-in," and engaging a range of civil society actors helps to ensure public involvement during the deliberation phase. Tunisia's transition and constitutional reform focused on consensus building and inclusive decision-making through using national dialogue, coalition governments, and legislative institutions (Karray 2019; Thornton 2014). Civil society organizations, most notably UGTT, were key in ensuring a broad basis for decision-making, compromise, and consensus-building.

The active involvement of civil society actors in policymaking is not unique to Tunisia. While Egypt, Algeria, Morocco, and Libya also saw civil society involvement flourish during the Arab Spring, this active input on policymaking has continued only in the Tunisian case (Lynn Dobbs and Schraeder 2019). Women's, labor, and human rights organizations have taken a role in forming and debating policies and reforms. Such inclusive decision-making is likely to help build support for government policies, weaken the power of special interests, and decrease the risk of reform reversals (Gehlbach and Malesky 2010).

Veto players, those actors with a veto over policy choices, also have a negative affect through the role they play in creating policy stability. The flip side of avoiding policy reversal is that veto players preserve the stability of the status quo (Tsebelis 2003). Veto players can therefore make reform difficult and limit policy change (König, Tsebelis, and Debus 2010). For Tunisia, policy stability means continuation of policies in place during the prior regime: a large public sector, significant bureaucracy, and ample opportunities for corruption.

While active involvement of unions during the revolution helped to demobilize the population and find a joint path for democratic reforms, the involvement of these same actors in ongoing political reforms works to complicate the decision-making process. In 2011, the creation of the additional employers' association CONECT, which is said to be closer to the government, likely further complicates the decision-making process by adding a new veto player. Unions have been able to take a more independent stance since the revolution, serving as a force for both proposing and opposing policy (Stiftung 2014). While UTICA was the only organization authorized to represent the private sector in public–private consultations prior to the revolution, this process has opened up to additional actors, such as CONECT and the Arab Institute of Business Managers (or IACE), during the political changes that followed the revolution (OECD 2014). Reform continues to stall due to political inconsistencies, the involvement of numerous institutions, and onerous bureaucracy and the need to build consensus around these reforms, including all relevant political parties, interest groups like unions, and civil society actors. The numerous actors required to create a consensus for policy change make it more difficult to change the status quo. While the process of consensus building is likely to prolong the reform process, it will also work to rebuild trust in the government and limit the likelihood of policy reversal.

The prolonged process of adopting economic reforms has worked to destabilize the business environment and create concerns about the future of economic policy. Institutions are weaker under the new regime, yet there remain high barriers to trade, inefficient regulations, and the domination of government-owned sectors. Reforms are necessary to modernize the economy and attract the investments necessary to address the underlying causes of social unrest. Tunisia still suffers from the institutional legacy of the former regime and easily capitulates to social demands, lacking budgetary discipline and running increasing deficits that will stifle investment (Stiftung 2014). There is a need to create democratic institutions and policies that focus beyond the short-term challenges of unemployment and infrastructure to promote long-term priorities of economic growth and institutional reform.

Because Tunisia's strong unions focus mostly on the urban worker, rural underdevelopment and inequality have yet to gain the attention of reformers. Much of the focus of the revolution and the reforms that followed were on the urban issues, ignoring the plight of small farmers and their opposition to state agricultural policy. The agricultural reforms adopted under the transitional government were largely symbolic, doing little to improve farm worker wages and working conditions (Ayeb and Bush 2014). Because the farmers' union UTAP (Tunisian Union of Agriculture and Industry) represents land-owners and investors with strong ties to the old regime, medium and larger farmers came together to form the Farmers' Union of Tunisia in 2012. The new union, however, still excludes small farmers, who make up 80 percent of the agricultural industry, from strong political representation. There has been no attempt to reform agricultural policy in a way that improves rural conditions for small farmers, instead focusing on large farms and outside investment (Ayeb and Bush 2019). The plight of the small farmer suggests those without strong union representation lack political access and cannot attain policy reforms.

Tunisia's transition to a democratic state with strong institutions and capacity is far from over. While Tunisia has been celebrated as the success story of the Arab Spring, the state remains very weak and requires fundamental reforms, especially in the economic and security sectors (Carothers 2018). Reports of security force abuses, the government's partial rollback of fundamental freedoms, incomplete judicial reforms, and a weak legislative branch are evidence of some democratic backsliding (Fassihian 2018). While Tunisia does not have any domestic or international spoilers looking to ruin the democratic transition, a predatory military, or territorial division that could fuel irredentism (Carothers 2018), its bloated public sector, strong civil society actors, and bureaucracy means the government faces an uphill battle in agreeing to and implementing reforms. The main challenges facing the transition include tension from the strong division between the secularists and Islamists, socioeconomic factors, Islamic radicalization, youth marginalization, and geographic economic disparities (Hinds 2014; Boukhars 2015). Many of these were the underlying causes to the Jasmine Revolution (Schraeder and Redissi 2011). These factors, unless successful tackled, are likely to flame social and political conflict and instability and limit Tunisia's ability to become a stable democracy with a strong economy.

Conclusion and Implications

Tunisia offers an important test of the findings in chapters 4 and 5. In a state experiencing domestic unrest in the transition from authoritarian rule to democracy, violence could easily have prevailed. Yet the private sector, though relatively small in comparison to the public sector, became a leader in organizing and shaping the political dialogue that occurred following the revolution. Activists in the main labor union, UGTT, helped ensure peaceful tactics were employed and there was direct communication across different segments of society. This proactive engagement allowed for a peaceful transition to democratic rule and the adoption of a new constitution. I have shown that while Tunisian firms do not have strong norms of corporate engagement, the actions of organized labor and business leaders helped diffuse the volatility of Tunisia's democratic transition. Their continued engagement, however, has prolonged the adoption of badly needed reforms. While consensus building is necessary for public support and trust, the many veto players involved in the negotiation process make it difficult to build consensus around any new laws or programs, serving instead to create policy stability. Without political change, Tunisia is likely to continue to experience economic decline and social instability.

Should changes be adopted to attract international investment and support domestic entrepreneurship, many of the challenges currently causing domestic unrest are likely to subside. That is especially likely if investment comes in the form of internationally headquartered firms with strong policies of social engagement and peacebuilding. Transnational firms can help to spread norms of corporate engagement and increase the number of actors working to address Tunisia's sources of instability. Such engagement would likely work to address women's issues, youth unemployment, and regional disparities in development, which, while not traditional peacebuilding, have been major sources of political and social instability in Tunisia. Successfully addressing these issues will help solidify the important democratic changes that have occurred and build a more stable future for Tunisia.

8

Transnational Corporations and Conflict Resolution in Northern Ireland

In the late sixties, the long-term conflict in Northern Ireland escalated into what is known as the Troubles. The violence was largely contained to bombings around Northern Ireland, but in 1992 and 1993, the Irish Republican Army (IRA) dramatically shifted its targets and tactics to create much larger scale destruction in London. While continuing a long-time focus on commercial targets, the bombings of the London financial district caused the most damage seen since the German Blitz campaign during World War II. Two bombings in April 1992 and 1993 each caused an estimated £1 billion in damages, killing four and injuring over a hundred people. Shifting to target the British mainland was intended to showcase the military strength in a way that made Northern Ireland too costly to hold onto and thus to push for negotiations. While backroom negotiations were occurring, this strategy also created a shift in the private sector's engagement. US-based companies began actively changing their operations in ways that would promote the peace process. Companies saw that they could no longer avoid involvement, as their bottom line was at stake.

This chapter examines the case of Northern Ireland and shows how engaged transnational corporations can help move a country from violence to peace when domestic firms lack either the capacity or the will to do so. The sectarian conflict, which dates back hundreds of years, has always had economic roots and consequences. It makes sense then that corporations, as the main drivers of modern economic exchange, would be a large part of the answer. I look at how the engagement of US business leaders used their investments to transform expectations of corporate behavior and create economic opportunities.

I begin with a background on the conflict, then explore how the results from chapters 4 and 5 apply to Northern Ireland at the national level. Given the economic roots of the conflict, I next examine unemployment and economic opportunities in Northern Ireland. I then look at domestically

The Building and Breaking of Peace. Molly M. Melin, Oxford University Press. © Oxford University Press 2021.
DOI: 10.1093/oso/9780197579367.003.0008

headquartered local companies, their engagement, and local trends in violence, comparing them to transnational corporations, their engagement, and local violence. The findings suggest that firm engagement can benefit peace processes and durability when done correctly, and that transnational firms can help move this process forward.

The Background of Northern Ireland's Violence, Peace Process, and Private Firms

Northern Ireland has a history fraught with violent conflict that can be traced to the 1600s or earlier, largely dependent on which history is read.[1] Northern Ireland's deeply divided society dates from the Reformation's mass violence events and wars on the island. As a result, when Britain finally achieved control in the very late 1600s it established a "Plantation" in the north populated by Protestant Scots and English settlers. Beginning in 1919 and following the partition of Northern Ireland in 1921, the Catholic minority of Northern Ireland considered themselves to be an oppressed minority, as Protestants had more civil liberties and political access. Catholic "Nationalists" or "Republicans" desired to join the independent Republic of Ireland, whereas Protestant "Unionists" or "Loyalists" wanted to remain part of the United Kingdom. The inability to find a political solution to the unequal access in politics, employment, housing, and schooling led to a push for greater civil rights and the violence known as "the Troubles" during the late twentieth century. This violent conflict lasted from the end of the 1960s through the signing of the Belfast (or Good Friday) Agreement in 1998.

The violence and political instability had major social and economic consequences (see Rowthorn and Wayne 1988). High male Catholic unemployment during the 1970s, as well as rising inflation, made Northern Ireland dependent on aid from the United Kingdom. Standards of living dropped, and the economy and private sector suffered. The negative impact of the conflict on the economy eventually motivated companies to act, but only in response to years of violence and instability.

The vast majority of the conflict occurred prior to the corporate social responsibility era. Rather than working to resolve tensions, many corporate policies, such as discriminatory hiring practices, actively flamed ongoing tensions (Gudgin 2019; Osborne 1980). One of the most famous incidents was the violent expulsion of Catholics from Belfast shipyards during the 1920s unrest accompanying partition. The public sector, which made up around 40 percent of employees in the 1970s was especially discriminatory. The 1976 Fair Employment Act enabled investigations into discriminatory practices, and found the Northern Ireland Civil Service had serious imbalances in its workforce, especially toward senior positions, in favor of Protestants (Osborne 2003). Despite the fair employment acts passed in 1976 and 1990, as well as the creation of a Fair Employment Commission, multigenerational unemployment and economic inactivity remains a challenge. As discussed further later, this challenge is not exclusively a Catholic one.

Peace in Northern Ireland has always been fragile, despite the Good Friday Agreement. Long periods of peace, the transfer of policing and justice powers to Northern Ireland, and local governance have been punctured by sporadic incidents of violence. For example, street riots broke out in December of 2012 following a Belfast City Council decision to limit the number of days the Union Jack flag can be flown above City Hall. The marching season of July, when the Orange Order commemorates King William of Orange's victory over King James II in 1690, is often contentious and has caused riots. Outstanding issues in dealing with the past still threaten ongoing peacebuilding efforts. These challenges highlight the important role "good actors" can play in upholding the tenuous peace. Political negotiations and agreements alone are unlikely to help build longterm peace and reconciliation or address the underlying causes of violence (Knox and Quirk 2000).

Present-day Northern Ireland remains a highly divided society. Segregated housing and education means many individuals do not have cross-religious relationships until they are eighteen, making it easier to dehumanize the other. This suggests adopting diverse hiring practices and hosting cross-community events are key to destigmatizing the other. In the sections that follow, I show how businesses failed to act to prevent violence during the late 1960s but later became integral to the peace process. I also show how internationally based multinational corporations have helped to build a society that is less likely to resort to violence. I conclude that corporate actors can help continue to move Northern Ireland toward a more "positive peace," through addressing the structural inequalities that lead to the initial violence.

What Conditions Increase Firm-Led Peacebuilding in Northern Ireland?

The concept of corporate social responsibility (CSR) is new relative to the centuries of conflict in Northern Ireland. Throughout much of the conflict, there was no social pressure on private firms to engage in the communities where they operate, and firms were not acting as proponents of peace. Returning to the lessons of chapter 4, the lack of corporate engagement is not surprising (see Table 8.1). The positive contribution that firms eventually made to push for peace in Northern Ireland suggests the results from chapter 4, which show firm engagement during ongoing violence prolongs conflict, merit further exploration.

The large-N results presented in chapter 4 suggest several conditions prompt private corporations to engage in peacebuilding: gaps in governance, years of peace, and the need to build their reputation. Each of these pressures was absent during the years leading to the start of the Troubles. In what follows, I examine why there was no need to fill gaps in governance, how violence kept businesses from investing in peacebuilding activities, and how the lack of CSR norms meant there was no public pressure for firms to proactively work to build peace.

Do Gaps in Governance Increase Northern Irish Firm Engagement in Peacebuilding Activities?

The quantitative analysis offered evidence of a curvilinear relationship between state capacity and peacebuilding: firms increasingly engage in peacebuilding as state capacity rises, but this effect levels off at higher levels of capacity. While the lack of the rule of law at the lowest state capacity levels

Table 8.1 Chapter 4 Results as Applied to the Case of Northern Ireland

Lesson	Application	Outcome
Firms Fill the Gaps	Strong Government Capacity & Rule of Law	Lack of Firm-Led Peacebuilding
Peace Begets Peacebuilding	Centuries of Violence	
Firms Invest in Their Reputation	Lack of CSR norms	

deters any investment, firms are able to contribute meaningfully when there is some government effectiveness. The United Kingdom as a whole is one of the most capable states in terms of governance, rule of law, and regulatory quality (see Table 8.2). This is well above the scores of the Latin American, African, and Middle Eastern countries included in the Company of Peace and Conflict (COPC) data. In the United Kingdom, there is no need for companies to assist in providing security, investing in infrastructure projects, or upholding rules and regulations. As such, there is no "gap" that corporations must fill in order to operate successfully.

The United Kingdom scores above the 90th percentile in each indicator of governance. The government has high-quality public service, civil service, and policy formulation and implementation (the government effectiveness measure). Similarly, the United Kingdom is able to develop sound regulations and policies that permit and promote private sector development (the regulatory quality measure). Finally, there are high rates of contract enforcement, strong property rights, and effective policing and courts (the rule of law measure). The strength of the United Kingdom in providing governance meant that private firms did not need to act beyond normal daily operations. Roads and ports of entry have always been kept in working condition, thereby enabling commerce to be conducted without major delay. Being a small region, only about 5,500 square miles, and with much of the commerce in a few locations, it not a significant challenge for businesses to get their products to market.

Table 8.2 The United Kingdom's Governance Indicators

Indicator	Country	Year	Percentile Rank (0 to 100)
Government Effectiveness	United Kingdom	2008	
		2013	
		2018	
Regulatory Quality	United Kingdom	2008	
		2013	
		2018	
Rule of Law	United Kingdom	2008	
		2013	
		2018	

Source: World Bank Worldwide Governance Indicators.

These measures, however, are nationally coded for the whole of the United Kingdom, with no comparable quantitative indicators at the subnational level. As Northern Ireland has a devolved government, the Parliament of Northern Ireland (and after 1973 the Northern Ireland Assembly) makes choices regarding major public services, such as healthcare, infrastructure, finance, justice, and education.[2] Since the devolved government up until 1972 always had an Ulster Unionist Party majority, it is claimed that policies created by the Parliament of Northern Ireland favored unionist areas. There was heavy investment in the business, industry, and infrastructure in the east, which was highly Protestant unionist, compared to the largely Catholic west. One such policy choice, which is said to have galvanized the civil rights movement, was to bypass Derry, the second-largest city with a majority nationalist population, to locate Northern Ireland's second university in unionist Colraine (Walsh 2000). Derry was the natural place for such an investment on demographic, commercial, historical, and cultural grounds, but the unionist government would not make such an investment in a nationalist city.

This lack of representation might have created governance gaps that mostly affected nationalists, which chapter 4 suggests would push firms to engage in peacebuilding-related activities to fill. However, given that the majority of firms were owned and operated by Protestant unionists, there would be little incentive for them to engage. The majority of industry and agricultural investment was in heavily Protestant areas, meaning the company owners and managers were unlikely to be negatively affected by gaps in governance. Rather than investing in peacebuilding measures, companies often engaged in discriminatory hiring practices, at the point of both recruitment and promotion (Walsh 2000). Thus, while there likely were gaps in the United Kingdom's governance in certain regions of Northern Ireland, firms did not engage in peacebuilding-related activities to fill them.

Does Peace Increase Northern Ireland's Firm Engagement in Peacebuilding Activities?

The quantitative results suggest longer periods of peace enable firms to invest in peacebuilding-related activities. How have violent events affected firms in Northern Ireland? Have firms operating in more violent areas responded differently compared to those operating in peaceful locations? Has Northern Ireland's violent history encouraged or discouraged firm engagement?

The corporate history of Northern Ireland suggests centuries of violence did not leave room for companies to invest in community engagement. Even before the start of the Troubles, violence flared at various periods, but especially following the end of World War I. The struggle for independence often turned violent, and the political instability created an unpredictable future that discouraged would-be investors. As discussed earlier, the conflict depressed economic growth and investment due to the human, social, political, and environmental costs of the conflict. The partition, as well as the political instability that resulted, meant businesses were often concerned with the security of their daily operations rather than investing in community engagement.

For businesses, what was more important than the national economic slowdown was the way violence often directly targeted businesses. Since most companies were Protestant-owned, businesses were often seen as a symbol of discrimination against Catholics and the legacy of imperial Britain. Businesses were therefore frequent targets for IRA bombings. The Provisional IRA, a splinter group that began in 1969, even stated this as a part of their tactics in their strategy and training manual, *The Green Book*: "A bombing campaign aimed at making the enemies financial interest in our country unprofitable, while at the same time curbing long term financial investment in our country" (cited in Coogan 1993, 420). As a way to undermine the government of Northern Ireland and maintain public support, attacks were aimed at causing economic damage while minimizing civilian casualties and were assessed in monetary terms (Jackson 2005). Targeting businesses and undermining investment helps to create both political pressure and publicity (Hearnden and Moore 1999). In the case of Northern Ireland, there were many small businesses that were targeted and, as a result, had to close. Even larger corporations had a hard time recovering from attacks. Those affected therefore put pressure on the government to provide greater security and compensation.

Thus, while the violence in Northern Ireland was nowhere near as catastrophic as that in Colombia, that the focus of bombings was financial districts and institutions made businesses focus on security rather than adopting policies that may have helped to build peace. The sectarian nature of business ownership, employment discrimination, and violence also had the effect of dissuading firms to invest in more community-oriented policies.

Do Reports of Bad Corporate Behavior Increase Northern Irish Firm Engagement in Peacebuilding Activities?

The empirical results offer evidence that companies that have reports of negative behavior are more likely to engage in peacebuilding. How have firms that were caught being "bad" corporate actors behaved in Northern Ireland? How does the public respond to those firms that adopt policies or practices that may be a source of conflict?

Poor private firm activity was commonplace in Northern Ireland prior to the Good Friday Agreement. Discriminatory hiring practices and promotion policies exacerbated the economic exclusion already felt by the Catholic community. Since Protestants owned most businesses, the business community was effectively on the unionist side of the conflict, however, and did not actively correct policies that may have worsened tensions. Employment in the public sector was no less discriminatory, serving as a major employer and hiring mostly Protestants. Since the Ulster Unionist Party had a majority in the government, there was no legal recourse for discrimination or government pressure to hire diversely. Not until the Northern Ireland Act of 1998 was an equality commission created to advance fair employment practices and offer legal recourse for those that are treated unfairly.

In addition to the absence of legal recourse was the absence of norms of socially responsible behavior and community engagement when it came to private businesses. Not only was there no expectation that corporations make positive contributions to society but also there were few public repercussions for misbehaver. Were companies to act poorly, as with the discriminatory hiring practices, there was unlikely to be any resulting negative public fallout. Thus, firms did not need to invest in "brand washing." As discussed further in what follows, much of the pressure for reform came from the Republic of Ireland and the United States. Northern Irish companies, especially the shipping giants like Harland and Wolff, in many ways mirrored the social divisions of Northern Ireland rather than working to erase them (Johnston 2008).

When Northern Irish firms did move to adopt more engaged policies, these actions were following the larger peace process spearheaded by the United States and Republic of Ireland. For example, the MacKie International factory spearheaded one of the most ambitious efforts to desegregate the economy after years of employing majority Protestants (Stevenson 1994). Over a three-year period from 1991 to 1994, MacKie went from employing

11 percent Catholics to 29 percent. Even Harland and Wolff shipyards have worked to reverse decades of anti-Catholic discrimination in the wake of the larger peace movement. Adopting fair employment policies offered an important step in correcting years of unfair treatment. However, as discussed later, the true effect of firm-led engagement was at the national policy level rather than reducing individual incentives to rebel.

Outcomes of Firm Engagement in Northern Ireland

I now turn to apply the results from chapter 5, which imply that firms can prevent violence but also prolong it, to the case of Northern Ireland (see Table 8.3). The lack of positive firm engagement failed to act as a preventative, and violence began in 1969. Throughout the Troubles, businesses and large corporations remained uninvolved, although they were frequently targeted with violence. As mentioned previously, businesses and shops were a preferred target of IRA bombs, since these were seen as the heart of British economic structure and strategically hampered the administration and governance of the country (Drake 1991). One of the most violent examples of the IRA's commercial bombing campaign would become known as "Bloody Friday," referring to the twenty-two bombs that were exploded in Belfast city center in 1972, killing nine and injuring 130. Although the IRA's goals were to destabilize British rule rather than causing casualties, the campaign was based on violence and caused significant damage, loss of life, and instability.

Eventually, the direct and indirect costs of the conflict compiled and compelled companies to push for peace. That action took the form of a

Table 8.3 Chapter 5 Results as Applied to Northern Ireland

Lesson	Application		Outcome
Firm Engagement Reduces Violence	Pre–Good Friday Agreement	Lack of Firm Engagement Prior to 1994	Violence
Engaged Firms Prolong Ongoing Violence		Neutral Firm Engagement Begins in 1994	1994 Ceasefire, 1996 Negotiations, and 1998 Agreement
Firm Engagement Reduces Violence	Post–Good Friday Agreement	Transnational Firm Engagement	Limited Splinter-Group Violence

neutral push for peace, argued on the basis of a peace dividend. In 1994, the Northern Ireland Confederation of Business Industry (CBI) published *Peace—A Challenging New Era.* This publication would become known as the "Peace Dividend Paper" because it argued that ongoing violence had depressed the economy and a peace deal would create economic growth. The CBI highlighted that "the loss of life, property destruction, and high security costs" led to divestment and economic decay (quoted in Reilly 2008, 74). Businesses, they argued, had an interest in building peace since political instability leads to economic stagnation. One avenue for economic recovery was to promote international investment through improving the country's image. The argument was widely promoted by the media and led to a 1994 investment conference. The CBI later worked with the Community Relations Council to publish antisectarian hiring guidelines for employers. Together with other trade and business organizations, they formed the Group of Seven (or G7) in 1996 to further make the case for peace.[3]

Throughout its involvement, CBI and the G7 remained a neutral, nonpolitical proponent of peace. The main goal of the G7 was to promote a single peace message through engaging the general population with grassroots movements and civil society campaigns (Democratic Progress Institute 2017). They encouraged businesses to push for peace as a part of their social responsibility. They hosted multiple meetings in Belfast that were open to all political parties, which enabled them to maintain an impartial image and gain credibility (Sweetman 2009). Such meetings were critical in building bridges between these competing groups striving for power. They also worked to promote investment through bringing US business leaders and the secretary of commerce to visit Northern Ireland in June of 1998. The G7 also released media statements that pressured politicians to come to an agreement. After the signing of the Good Friday Agreement, the G7 did not even lobby on behalf of the peace agreement that was voted on in a national referendum (Democratic Progress Institute 2017). The G7 group only used their influence to advance peace talks, and such a neutral stance enabled the business community to engage without prolonging negotiations.

Since the signing of the Good Friday Agreement, norms of corporate engagement have spread and become more commonplace. Still, many of Northern Ireland's domestically headquartered companies do little to actively engage existing local and national challenges. Even CBI has limited its peace and reconciliation efforts since the peace accords, with the exception of publishing various background papers such as its report on the "benefits of a diverse workforce" (CBI 2003, 3). While laws prevent discrimination in hiring, segregated schooling and housing persists. Many do not have a meaningful encounter with the "other" (a Protestant or Catholic, as the case may be), until they are an adult. While violence is limited, these communities remain exceptionally segregated, which could allow for renewed violence should a catalyst occur. Efforts to increase integration, like the One Small Step program that encourages people to form constructive relationships to assist in reconciliation, face challenges in sustaining public interest against the backdrop of community tensions and sectarianism (Cox, Guelke, and Stephen 2006). Both the Catholic and Protestant communities face the challenges of poverty and intergenerational unemployment, which is further explored in the next section. While some domestically headquartered companies are offering training and community engagement programs, transnational firms have more aggressively worked to better these challenges.

A Closer Look at the (Un)Employment Issue

Although Northern Ireland's conflict is built on identity, economic issues are a key underlying element. Unemployment is consistently one of the largest challenges in Northern Ireland and is often exacerbated by downturns in the global economy. While the economy has traditionally been largely focused on the manufacturing sector, structural weaknesses in this industry have persisted (Patterson 2016; Bryan 2019). In the early 1980s, the United Kingdom was experiencing a recession, along with the rest of the global economy. This recession served to confirm Northern Ireland's position as the poorest region in the United Kingdom and one of the poorest in the European Community, with unemployment rising from 10 percent to 17 percent from 1980 to 1983 (Econometrics 2000). Starting in 1983, however, the UK economy entered into a period of sustained growth that far outpaced a cyclical recovery from recession. Despite this national growth, Northern Ireland lagged behind, with unemployment rates decreasing only half a percent, compared to 4 percent in the United Kingdom (Gudgin and Roper 1990). This is likely due to large job losses in manufacturing and slow growth in financial services.

In the 1990s Northern Ireland's economy grew both as a result of the "peace dividend" and the rapid growth in the Republic of Ireland (dubbed the "Celtic Tiger"). There was an increase in international investment, especially around Belfast and Derry. The Northern Ireland Investment Bureau worked to bring international investors, and with it came business leaders without an interest in the conflict (Bryan 2019). Commercial centers became a place where diverse groups interact, and investment in industry helped create employment opportunities.

Northern Ireland has the smallest economy of any UK region, but this is in part due to its small population. Figure 8.1 compares the Northern Ireland GDP in purchasing power that of the UK average. While both the national average and Irish economies exhibit growth, that of Northern Ireland consistently is lower. Northern Ireland's unemployment was at a record high in 1986 at 17.2 percent, down to 6.2 percent by 2001 (Banfield, Gündüz, and

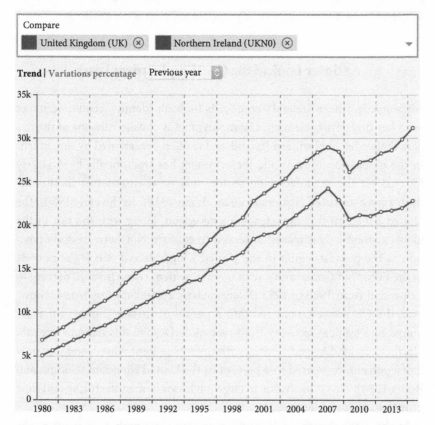

Figure 8.1 Gross Domestic Product (GDP) per Inhabitant in Purchasing Power Standard (PPS) per Head

Source: European Commission Urban Data Platform.

Killick 2006). Even when unemployment hit a ten-year low in 2017, the decrease was due to more people claiming economic inactivity (not claiming unemployment benefits but also not being paid for a job).

Over all, Northern Ireland consistently has an excess of labor supply over labor demand, a large amount of emigration, and some of the lowest participation rates in the labor market. Despite decades of public-sector support to both domestic and international firms, the local economy still struggles to generate sufficient jobs for its labor force, likely due to the weak productivity and inefficiencies of local firms (Roper 1996; Townroe and Martin 1992). Social enterprise and innovation programs, like the Resurgam Trust, are helping to build development from within the communities themselves, an integral part of transforming Northern Ireland's economy (Halliday 2019). In combination with programs promoting safe places for cross-community dialogue, like Derry Center City Initiative, businesses and communities are becoming more intertwined (Roddy 2019). The key is encouraging private investment and stimulating entrepreneurship, thereby generating sustained employment (Johnson 2019).

Domestic Firms and Local Violence

The empirical results suggest three cross-national trends with regard to peace and corporate peacebuilding: (1) firms headquartered in countries with longer periods of peace are more likely to invest in peacebuilding, (2) countries with more engaged private sectors experience less violence than those without private sector engagement; and (3) countries with ongoing violence have more difficulty resolving those conflicts when the private sector is engaged. While these results offer important findings on the national effects of peacebuilding, they don't offer a picture of local-level variation in violence prevention and resolution. Are communities with engaged corporations more peaceful? In addition, the findings suggest complexity in causation: does peace cause peacebuilding or peacebuilding cause peace? To further explore the effects of corporate engagement on violence and peace processes, I compare three cities in Northern Ireland.

Armagh, Dungannon, and Omagh are very similar in most respects: the demographics and the economies are strikingly alike. Each is near the border with the Republic of Ireland, a traditional hot spot for violence. The towns have economies heavily focused on meat processing and production, with

Moy Foods headquartered in Armagh and Dunbia Meats headquartered in Dungannon. Both are the major employers in nearby Omagh. I compare changes in these companies' approaches to community engagement and peacebuilding to understand whether these approaches affect the violence experienced in each town.

Dunbia is one of the largest employers in Dungannon, employing 7,000 in 2019. Throughout the Troubles, the company was expanding its facilities in Dungannon, opening new facilities in 1983, 1985, 1990, 1993, and 1996. Such efforts offer additional employment in a place where violence is often attributed to the lack of economic opportunity. The expansion of Dunbia's facilities in this area also correlates with a reduction in violence: only six of the casualties in Dungannon occurred after Dunbia began expanding.

Moy Park was owned by Courtaulds, a London-based textile company, during many of the violent years of the Troubles (from 1968 to 1984), at which time it was sold to the directors. Expansion for Moy Park then moved from a focus on international expansion to growth in Armagh, which became the new headquarters. Prior to this shift, Armagh had experienced years of violence. Armagh remains the headquarters of Moy Foods, currently employs 7,000 people, and has long been Northern Ireland's largest private sector employer. Despite this expansion, violence in Armagh remained high.

The implementation of the Good Friday Agreement has been accompanied by new expectations of corporate behavior. The late 1990s and early 2000s saw a shift in public expectations with regard to corporate responsibilities to society in developed countries. Programs like Business in the Community, which is a network for responsible business corporate engagement with over 260 current members, are spreading and becoming more commonplace (Harding 2020). This network is pushing both small and large businesses to be a force for good in tackling environmental and social issues.

In recent years, both Moy Park (now a subsidiary of Pilgrim's Pride) and Dunbia have moved to incorporate more active corporate social responsibility programs. Dunbia published its first corporate social responsibility report in 2017. In recent years, it has proactively engaged the community through numerous programs such as the Young Beef Farmer Sustainability program and Young Farmers Lamb Supply Program, which trains participants to adopt more efficient farming practices, and Project Daire, which helps improve children's knowledge of the food supply chain and dietary choices. In addition, Dunbia is proactively working toward the United Nations' Sustainable Development Goals. For example, in line with goal of ending poverty, Dunbia works with the Open Doors Project and Turas Nua, and also reaches out to marginalized groups to offer employment and training. Such efforts make violence a less attractive option for stakeholders. Dunbia has received numerous awards for its environmental standards.

Moy Park's current CSR program is both environment- and employee-focused. Moy Park published their first CSR report in 2010. Employees volunteer with a local education charity, Young Enterprise. In 2013, it was the first poultry company to be awarded in the Corporate Responsibility Index, and has received multiple third-party awards for its environmental programs and treatment of employees. Moy Park is a member of Business in the Community, while Dunbia is not.

Despite the recent active engagement of the two major employers in these areas, neither town was immune to violence during the Troubles (see Table 8.4). Trends in violence differ in each of these towns: Armagh experienced

Table 8.4 Demographic Trends and Violence in Armagh, Dungannon, and Omagh, Northern Ireland

	Armagh	Dungannon	Omagh	N.I. Total
Population (2001)[a]	14,590 (.86%)	47,735 (2.83%)	19,910 (1.18%)	1,685,267
Population (2011)[3]	30,286 (1.67%)	57,852 (3.19%)	19,659 (1.09%)	1,810,863
% Catholic (2011)[3]	70.11%	64.11%	71.32%	45.14%
% Protestant or Other Christian (2011)[3]	26.83%	33.03%	25.36%	48.36%
Unemployed (2011)[3]	6.15%	4.88%	5.36%	7.2%
Economically Inactive (2011)[3]	33.67%	32.52%	39.02%	4.6%
Total Deaths (1969–2001)[b]	150 (4.6%)	142 (4.3%)	76 (2.3%)	3,269
Post-Negotiation Deaths (1991–2011)[c]	17 (15%)	3 (2%)	29 (26.8%)	108
Post–Good Friday Agreement Deaths (199–2011)[b]	0	0	30 (93.7%)	32
Total Violent Events (1989–2011)[b]	28 (25%)	8 (7%)	31 (27.6%)	112

[a] From Northern Ireland Statistics and Data Agency (2011).

[b] From Sutton (2001).

[c] From Sundberg and Melander (2013).

many of its violent events throughout the Troubles, during the negotiations, and even after the agreement was signed; Dungannon experienced the majority of violence in the early stages of violence; Omagh experienced the deadliest violent event after the Good Friday agreement. Armagh earned the nickname the "Murderous Mile" due to the violence. Although Armagh and Dungannon have very similar casualty totals, considering the different population sizes makes the violence in Armagh more striking. The town has less than 1 percent of Northern Ireland's population and yet experienced a quarter of the violent events and almost 5 percent of the casualties. In Dungannon, much of the violence took place during the 1970s and early 1980s. Omagh was able to avoid violence throughout much of the Troubles but has had two of the three major violent events that followed the Good Friday Agreement. The Omagh bomb, which killed twenty-nine people and injured hundreds more in August of 1998, and a car bomb in 2011 that killed a police constable, both occurred after the signing of the Good Friday Agreement. The Omagh bomb is the single deadliest incident of the conflict. Thus, the towns had different experiences in violence across time (Figure 8.2). These differences are statistically significant (see Appendix).

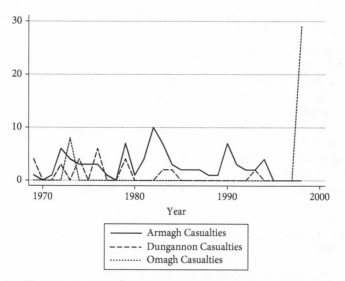

Figure 8.2 Variation in Casualties in Armagh, Dungannon, and Omagh, 1969–1998

Casualty data from McKittrich et al. (2001) and Sutton (2001).

The events in Armagh, Dungannon, and Omagh suggest that employment opportunities cannot resolve ongoing violence once it has begun. Had those opportunities been available before the conflict had turned violent, however, there may have been a different outcome. Each of these towns struggled with high unemployment throughout the 1970s and early 1980s, especially among Catholics. Catholics reported 13.9 percent unemployment in the 1971 census and 25.5 percent unemployment in 1981, rates that were 2.5 times those of Protestants (Osborne and Cormack 1986). In the 1981 census, Armagh had a Catholic unemployment rate of 24.2 percent and a Protestant unemployment rate of 10 percent; Dungannon had 32.6 percent and 12.4 percent respectively; Omagh had 23.4 percent and 10.8 percent. Those numbers fell in the 1990s, in part likely due to the Fair Employment Act (nationally, Catholics increased as a portion of the workforce from 34.9 percent in 1990 to 38.1 percent in 1997) (Statistics and Staff 2002). Moy Park employed 60 percent Protestants and 40 percent Catholics in 1997.

If we look at these shifts in being more actively engaged as peacebuilding in the post–Good Friday Agreement era, the increase in stability suggests that such efforts are having an impact in upholding the peace. According to Notre Dame's Peace Accord Matrix, 95 percent of the terms of the Good Friday Agreement were implemented after ten years (2019). That locally headquartered firms are hiring more diversely suggests the laws preventing discriminatory hiring practices are one factor helping create a durable peace. Employment practices can have both direct and indirect effects on violence levels. Offering fair employment opportunities gives would-be belligerents a way to better their lives through legal means, thereby making violence a less appealing alternative. Indirectly, a diverse workplace offers a space where opposing sides interact peacefully with the "other," breaking down stereotypes through promoting cross-community relationships. The Fair Employment Act, and the fact that it is largely followed, offers a national policy explanation for the durability of the peace accords.

In recent years, Dungannon has had exceptional growth in its immigrant population, and now the significant division is between recent arrivals and citizens rather than the Irish and Protestants. The shift is mirrored nationally, as Northern Ireland has become increasingly diverse over a short period of time. Many of the immigrants have come to work in the meat-packing industry. For example, Dunbia Meats reports a decrease in Domestic Irish and British employees from 51.7 percent in 2016 to 38.6 percent in 2018, as employees are increasingly from central Europe. Given reports of anti-immigrant attacks, employers may need to focus on worker- and community-relations. While working to make the production process more environmentally efficient is an important contribution, perhaps a more local focus that acknowledges the challenges inherent in changing demographics would enable long-term stability.

Have Transnational Firms Helped to Reduce Violence in Northern Ireland?

Throughout the United Kingdom's colonial history, the United States held a firm policy of noninterference in the internal affairs of another friendly power. The United States had a strong relationship with the United Kingdom, its strongest NATO ally, with a shared language and ideals. The presidencies of Carter, Reagan, Bush, and Clinton saw a fundamental shift in the American position toward Northern Ireland. With the end of the Cold War and growing power of Irish American politicians Tip O'Neill and Edward Kennedy, efforts seeking to draw attention to the conflict through legislation fell flat due to the close relationship with the United Kingdom. Only by looking outside the Washington, DC, establishment to Irish-Americans and finding a solution that did not involvement violence, could there be a push for a more active policy. The issue that united Irish Americans was religious discrimination in employment practices. The precedent of the Sullivan Principles, which used US subsidiary policies in South Africa to defeat apartheid, offered a useful model of corporate influence. The Irish American aim was to urge politicians to persuade US corporations operating in Northern Ireland to adopt nondiscriminatory employment policies.

At the time, discrimination was a fact of life for Catholics. The most famous examples are of Short Brothers and Harland and Wolff, companies that accounted for 10 percent of manufacturing employment and received a third of public resource for industrial support, yet had well over 90 percent Protestant employees. (McNamara 2009). US companies were a part of this problem due to both the geographic location of factories (23 of the 34 plants operating in 1978 were in unionist areas) and hiring practices of the management (managers frequently discriminated blatantly against Catholic during hiring). Such figures led to the introduction of House Bill 3465, which would impose tax penalties on companies operating in Northern Ireland that failed to implement fair employment practices. While the bill never left committee, seventeen states and multiple municipalities adopted what would later be known as the MacBride Principals, nine fair employment principles published in 1984. Signatories had to report annually on implementing the principles, but the repercussions of their publication were much further reaching, having lasting effects on foreign policy.

The active role that Irish and American firms played in the Northern Irish economy allowed the government of Ireland (through the Anglo-Irish agreement of 1985, which was also a product of American pressure) and US companies (through the MacBride campaign) to politically pressure the government for reform. These principals were modeled after the Sullivan principles for American investment in South Africa, linking the two issues and widening support in the US action in Northern Ireland. The MacBride Principals eventually became the standard for all US economic dealings with Northern Ireland (Cochrane 2007). As this effort gained momentum in the United States, the British government began to accept the case for reform (Osborne 2003), resulting in the Fair Employment Act of 1989. The MacBride campaign changed the climate of what was publicly acceptable, drawing attention to the cause of economically deprived Catholics. Irish Americans united around this cause, using the power of the dollar and the threat of lost business to achieve social and economic reform.

Many Irish Americans were frustrated by continued violence in Northern Ireland. The Irish American lobby in Washington was second in power only to the Israeli lobby, and the 1990s saw a period of moderating attitudes. At a time when direct political inaction was not forthcoming, Irish American business leaders took action, at one point taking out a full page ad in the *New York Times* in support of the peace process (Guelke 1996).

The Clinton administration's eventual active involvement reflects both the moderating attitudes of the Irish American lobby and a larger foreign policy of conflict resolution. The United States was an active part of the negotiations that created the Good Friday Agreement, mediated by Ambassador George Mitchell. The Clinton administration's interest in creating a stable and peaceful Ireland had a significant economic dimension (MacGinty 1997). The United States already had a significant investment in both the north and south of Ireland, and a peace deal would open up further investment opportunities. The Irish workforce is highly educated, English-speaking, and American-friendly, and the government offers tax incentives that create a probusiness environment. This economic partnership and investment plays a major role in the Irish economy, and American investment strategies include both economic and political considerations (Peyronel 2017). Between 1995 and 2015, the Republic of Ireland benefited from over $277 billion in US investment, and this rose to $387 billion in 2020, with 155,000 Irish employed by 700 US companies (MacGinty 1997).

Northern Ireland's economy has long been heavily dependent on foreign investment for employment. In 1996, 1 percent of companies operating in Northern Ireland were internationally owned but these companies employed about 9.5 percent of the workforce. This trend has only increased with globalization and the Good Friday Agreement. In 2015, 2.4 percent of businesses were internationally owned, but these employ almost a quarter of Northern Ireland employees (Agency 2015). The Republic of Ireland is the most heavily invested, followed by the United States. Both countries expanded their investments once the peace process was underway: Irish-owned businesses expanded from 100 to 123 from 1996 to 1998, and American-owned firms grew from 71 to 111. These investments have continued to expand as peace has taken hold (see Table 8.5). Such trends suggest the economy has overcome the challenges that instability and violence during the Troubles posed, as large violent incidents and conflict intensity are both shown to have reduced investments and employment opportunities in Northern Ireland (Fielding 2003).

The strong economic ties between the United States and Northern Ireland have continued since the Good Friday Agreement was signed. Table 8.5 shows that the United States is one of the strongest investors in Northern Ireland, second only to the Republic, when measured in terms of number of businesses. American-owned companies continually make up around 20 percent of foreign-owned companies. American companies, however, are the largest foreign-owned employer in Northern Ireland. Companies headquartered in the United States consistently employ around 27 percent of Northern Irish employees who work for a foreign-owned business, followed by the 23 percent of employees working for Irish companies.

Have Transnational Firms Prolonged Violence in Northern Ireland?

The United States has consistently supported both the peace process and economic growth through private investment. American companies Terex, Allstate, Seagate, Dupont, NYSE Technologies, Caterpillar, and Citi, as well

Table 8.5 Foreign-Owned (Defined as Non-UK) VAT and/or PAYE Registered Businesses Operating in Northern Ireland by Country of Ownership—Number and Employees, 2008–2019

Number of Businesses

Country	2008	2009	2010	2011	2012	2013	2014	2015	2016	2017	2018	2019
Total	665	715	710	740	805	830	840	885	895	910	1,025	1,100
Ireland	245	255	245	235	265	280	275	290	305	320	335	355
United States	140	145	140	150	165	185	175	175	190	185	200	210
Netherlands	30	40	40	35	40	45	40	50	45	40	50	55
France	45	45	45	50	50	45	45	45	40	35	35	40
Germany	35	30	45	45	40	45	45	45	40	40	40	40

Number of NI Employees

Country[1]	2008	2009	2010	2011	2012	2013	2014	2015	2016	2017	2018	2019
Total	70,970	79,810	82,190	83,335	88,615	94,100	94,455	99,855	99,470	99,530	99,955	99,295
Ireland	16,560	15,335	16,635	19,420	18,110	17,780	17,815	17,475	15,905	17,165	15,360	18,245
United States	19,215	19,550	21,270	18,995	18,825	22,825	23,895	24,225	25,700	26,870	25,605	26,565
Netherlands	1,435	3,175	3,235	2,655	3,835	4,415	3,060	5,820	6,755	4,660	6,855	5,725
France	4,845	5,275	5,455	6,420	6,355	6,225	6,300	6,150	6,695	5,795	5,315	4,855
Germany	2,535	2,605	2,765	2,690	3,080	2,995	3,160	3,150	2,015	2,050	1,775	1,840

Source: Northern Ireland Statistics Research Agency, Inter Department Business Register.

as television and film production companies, have invested in Northern Ireland. Despite this investment, the Northern Irish economy has had mixed success, with comparatively strong economic growth up until the 2008 recession. Many of the jobs remain in the public sector, and the instability of the eurozone has caused further economic challenges. The most violent communities have been hardest hit by downturns in the economy, with high suicide rates, low male life expectancy, and high crime all threatening a return to violence (Agency 2011).

That American-owned businesses are both strong investors in Northern Ireland and early proponents of fair employment practices means these economic ties are important actors in promoting changes in the underlying causes of social conflict. Their actions suggest that firm engagement can benefit peace processes and durability when done correctly, and that transnational firms can help move this process forward. While US firms brought new norms of employment and community engagement to Northern Ireland, the companies were not directly involved in the peace negotiations. Yet, the ties between American Companies and US-led mediation created a precedent of active peacebuilding that remains strong. Allstate, which opened operations in Northern Ireland the year the Good Friday Agreement was signed, offers one example of this engagement. It is consistently one of Northern Ireland's largest companies both in terms of employment and revenue. As of 2020, they have three sites in Belfast, Londonderry, and Strabane. The focus of its operations in Northern Ireland is software development, working as the largest IT company in Northern Ireland.

Allstate's operations offer multiple benefits to stakeholders in its areas of operation, in terms of the economic development and opportunities it provides, social investment, and environmental sustainability programs. Ongoing expansion has increased employment opportunities in locations with high intergenerational unemployment. It has worked to proactively engage communities as well, through a wide variety of programs. Allstate was a founding partner of Diversity Mark, a not-for-profit charter for diversity and inclusion, and operates several programs to integrate diversity into the organizational culture. Allstate also has various employee volunteerism programs and corporate giving plans, as well as programs working to mitigate the environmental impact of conducting business. Allstate has been awarded Green status by the Northern Ireland Benchmarking Survey. Finally, the company works closely with Business in the Community to align their business needs with the needs of broader society.

Since US companies were neutral proponents of peace and not involved in the peace negotiations, their engagement did not work to prolong violence. Rather, US firms brought new norms of employment and community engagement to Northern Ireland. US business leadership was essential to transforming employment practices in Northern Ireland, something that had long exacerbated sectarian tensions. In addition, the strong connection between American Companies and US-led mediation created a precedent of active peacebuilding that is still a part of US business operations in Northern Ireland.

Conclusion and Implications

While the Good Friday Agreement is generally seen as successfully ending the violence between Northern Ireland and the United Kingdom (DeRouen et al. 2010), challenges remain. Despite significant progress since the signing of the agreement, past economic inequality, discrimination, and segregation in housing and education have created a society that remains deeply divided. Northern Ireland still faces long-term challenges in building peace and reconciliation, and proper private firm engagement can help to further these processes. While businesses alone cannot create peace, they can complement the peace process and are essential to ensuring postagreement economic growth and stability.

This chapter applied and extended the quantitative findings in chapters 4 and 5 by examining corporate peacebuilding in Northern Ireland. Centuries of violence in this case create an especially challenging environment for would-be peacemakers. However, as the costs of conflict accumulated and Northern Ireland's economy lagged behind, private corporations began actively pushing for a negotiated peace agreement. The neutral approach taken prevented their engagement from prolonging negotiations. In the post–Good Friday Agreement setting, however, domestically headquartered firms do little to actively build peace. Transnational firms, which are also the largest employers, are more engaged in peacebuilding-related activities. They have expanded their investments and developed programs that helped create the economic opportunities necessary to help Northern Ireland sustain peace.

The policy implications of this chapter are notable, as they suggest that corporate peacebuilding during ongoing conflict does not always prolong violence. Rather, the case of Northern Ireland suggests that neutral engagement can encourage peace processes. Most notably, firms can help to build a "positive peace" by addressing some of the underlying structural factors that lead to the onset of violence.

9

Conclusion

As I write this, the world has shut down due to the health threat of COVID-19. Educational institutions from elementary schools to universities have canceled in-person classes while large gatherings are prohibited. Restaurants and bars are closed, and in some places governments are banning people from leaving their homes other than for groceries and medical care. There is a huge concern over how this will affect those at the bottom of the economy—those who rely on tips or have jobs that require their physical presence to be paid. The stock market had its worst day since Black Tuesday, kicking in mandatory pauses in trading. As the World Health Organization encourages "social distancing," there have been runs on necessities as people prepare to stay home for long periods of time.

There are also signs of our joint humanity with global efforts to protect the most vulnerable, research the virus, and care for the sick. Many corporations have promised large donations both to help fight the virus and to lessen the community and economic impact of the pandemic. In his March 13, 2020, press conference declaring a national emergency, President Trump was joined by the CEOs of Walmart, Target, CVS, and Walgreens, who are working to help defeat the spread of the virus by hosting drive-through testing centers in their parking lots. CEOs of laboratory, research, and medical device companies were also present, working to increase the availability of tests for COVID-19.

That is not to say that corporate competitors always collaborate to address global challenges. While the current pandemic has put global citizens and corporations in uncharted territory, other global challenges continue without a corporate response or even because of corporate maleficence. UNICEF estimates that one in four children in the world's poorest countries are engaged in child labor (UNICEF 2019). Ten percent of the world's population lives in poverty, surviving on less than $1.90 a day (World Bank 2015). While the number of fatalities from organized violence and one-sided violence have dropped, those resulting from nonstate violence have risen in number (Pettersson, Hogbladh, and Oberg 2019a). There has also

The Building and Breaking of Peace. Molly M. Melin, Oxford University Press. © Oxford University Press 2021.
DOI: 10.1093/oso/9780197579367.003.0009

been a global spike in the number of armed conflicts. Were corporations to focus their attentions to helping address these global challenges, which are very much linked to one another, it is likely there could be significant movement forward. For better or worse, this is unlikely to happen anytime soon. There are cases of firms instigating violence, escalating conflict, and reaping benefits from instability and conflict.

Profitability is at the very heart of business. Yet, even chief executives from the Business Roundtable, which includes the leaders of the world's largest companies like Apple and JP Morgan Chase, say companies must invest in employees and deliver value to customers (Benoit 2019). Profitability and progress on global challenges can go hand in hand, and even build off one another.

This book has not set forth to suggest that corporations can or will resolve the world's problems. It has endeavored to understand why, given the multitude of actors working to prevent and resolve conflict, violence persists, and how private firms might help solve this global challenge.

I have argued that generating an accurate answer to this question requires scholars to reconsider whose interest it serves to prevent and resolve violent conflict. While research on conflict processes identifies multiple actors, it ignores the role of private corporations. We know peace is in the interests of the disputants themselves, as war is costly, but that war still occurs due to private information, issue indivisibility, and commitment problems (Fearon 1995). There is also ample evidence showing actors outside the conflict have an interest in maintaining stability, such as states with strong ties to one of the disputants (Melin 2011) and organizations with relevant missions (Beardsley and Lo 2013; Gartner 2011). However, state actors often face tight constraints on financial policy (Zielinski 2016), and intergovernmental organizations also face budgetary and organizational constraints (Gaibulloev et al. 2015). Since each of these actors faces limitations on their ability to prevent and resolve instability, they must be strategic about where they become involved. Little is known about the role of private corporations in the dynamics of peace and conflict.

I suggest that, because it is often in their interest to engage in peacebuilding-related activities, corporations can act to prevent violent conflict. These firms are invested and lose financially from instability, since attacks often damage the infrastructure necessary to get goods to market or may target the companies themselves. Profits increase in stable, secure environments. In addition, firms increasingly face local and international stakeholder pressure to respond to violent conflict (Oetzel and Getz 2012). Business scholars are now discussing how firms can engage in both commerce and peacemaking (Fort 2007; Bausch 2015; Bais and Huijser 2005), helping to build peaceful societies through promoting economic development, the rule of law, and independent oversight, contributing to a sense of community, and engaging in unofficial, or track two, diplomacy and conflict-sensitive practices (Getz and Oetzel 2009). New technologies and shifts in corporate accountability mean many firms are thinking about stability where they operate. Much of this scholarship remains anecdotal or based on single case studies (Wolf, Deitelhoff, and Engert 2007). Conflict processes scholarship does not consider a role for corporate actors.

What Is the Nature of Firm-Led Peacebuilding?

Former UN Secretary-General Boutros Boutros-Ghali's 1992 report "An Agenda for Peace" offers a broad approach to creating peace. He introduced the concept of peacebuilding as "action to identify and support structures, which will tend to strengthen and solidify peace in order to avoid a relapse into conflict" (Boutros-Ghali 1992, 204). Reports and scholarship since then consider peacebuilding to be any activity meant to help create a less violent society (Doyle and Sambanis 2000), ranging from large-scale government reform (which often includes democratization, see Jarstad and Sisk 2008) to grassroots civil society programs (Lederach 1997). Although peacebuilding scholarship explores activities in the aftermath of conflict, many post-conflict challenges are not unique to this environment. Conflict prevention, preventative diplomacy, peacemaking, and conflict management offer a coherent approach to securing the peace envisioned by the UN Charter. I have therefore considered corporate engagement in the preventative, ongoing, and post-conflict settings.

I define firms' peacebuilding-related activities as *any activity attempting to raise the opportunity costs of violence, thereby preventing the occurrence, continuation, or recurrence of violence.* This definition draws from the rational choice approach to understanding the causes of violence and enables me to account for firm actions in both conflict-prone settings and peaceful ones.

Private firms can help create and sustain peaceful societies by altering the payoffs of conflict. By making violence a less attractive alternative, firms reduce the likelihood of conflict. One approach is to reduce the incentives for rebellion; another approach is to raise the costs of rebellion. Violence becomes an attractive choice when individuals have poor access to alternative employment (Hegre 2004), living conditions are poor (Walter 2004), and average income is low or inequality is high (Collier, Hoeffler, and Söderbom 2004).

In practice, firm-led peacebuilding can target individual incentives to rebel at the local or national level. It can take the form of job training, educational opportunities, or employment programs, which create incentives for would-be rebels to engage in legal forms of commerce. At the national level, firms can join forces to engage in dialogue and adopt policies that make conflict less attractive through more overtly political efforts to generate peace. Efforts like the MacBride Principals and the Kimberly Process brought multiple firms together to reduce the incentives to resort to violence. Sri Lanka's National Committee for Peace (see Keethaponcalan 2001), Northern Ireland's branch of the Confederation of Business Industry (see Aliyev 2017), and the negotiated agreement between the so-called National Dialogue Quartet in Tunisia (see Schraeder and Redissi 2014) included the business community in national peace processes.

Methodology

This book endeavored to fill the gap in our understanding of firm-led peacebuilding by presenting a strong theoretical approach supported by both qualitative and quantitative evidence of the conflicting roles corporations play in building and preventing peace. In first examining the corporate motives for peacebuilding then examining the implications of these activities for preventing violence and conflict resolution, I build a more holistic picture of the peace and conflict process. The findings help explain why armed civil conflicts persist despite the multitude of diverse actors working to end them.

I examine firm-led peacebuilding behavior using original cross-national data and three in-depth case analyses of corporate actions and outcomes. The Company of Peace and Conflict (COPC) data code firms' activities that span beyond traditional economic exchange in Latin America, the Middle East, and Africa, which are coded from 2000 to 2017. Chapter 3 provides a detailed overview of these data. Chapters 4 and 5 use these data to understand when firms contribute to peacebuilding and the outcomes of this engagement.

Then, based on in-country interviews, I show variation in the experiences of Colombia, Tunisia, and Northern Ireland. Colombia, having recently emerged from the longest ongoing civil war in the Western Hemisphere, offers evidence of the transformative effect that an emerging, active private sector had on encouraging negotiations, but also that firms' active engagement also prolonged the peace process. Tunisia was the only country to emerge from the Arab Spring with a functioning democratic government. While a powerful private sector prevented violence from erupting during the Jasmine Revolution, it has stifled the ability of the country to adopt badly needed reforms. Finally, the case of Northern Ireland shows how engaged transnational corporations can help move a country from violence to peace and push domestic firms toward greater engagement. The experience in Northern Ireland also suggests neutral firm engagement during ongoing violence can prevent their actions from prolonging the peace process, as occurred in Colombia, or preventing reform, as we are observing in Tunisia. I now turn to the findings and broader lessons.

When Do Firms Contribute to Peacebuilding?

I first examined the conditions that prompt private corporations to act beyond "business as usual" and proactively build peace. I argue that variations in corporate conflict prevention result from changing local dynamics, shifts in governmental capacity, and threats to the ability to conduct business. Corporations engage in peacebuilding when their investments are threatened, when there is a gap in the state's capacity to enforce laws, and when there is political stability. Below a certain threshold of stability and capacity, however, corporations are more likely to shutter or flee. This disengagement has an even more destabilizing effect on already volatile environments. What follow are the main lessons of which conditions encourage firms to engage in peacebuilding.

Lesson 1: Firms Fill the Gaps

I argued that corporate peacebuilding-related activities diminish as government functioning increases, since the demand for corporate peacebuilding is low. Firms have fewer incentives to engage when the government is able to provide stability and services. I hypothesized that firms engage in peacebuilding activities in states that cannot fully govern.

The quantitative results in chapter 4 suggest this is indeed the case and that corporations are stepping in to fill gaps left by the government. Corporations are more likely to invest in peacebuilding-related behavior when the government is ineffective, lacks the ability to enforce the rule of law, and has low regulatory quality. Corporations are less likely to invest in peacebuilding when the state is highly capable of developing and implementing sound policies and regulations promoting private sector development.

Colombia's experience with firm-led peacebuilding supports this finding. While the Colombian government has moderate capacity at the national level, its ability to enforce the rule of law drastically varies by region. The state has a significant presence in urban areas, but the country's topography cuts much of the country off from government resources and security. In Colombia's rural areas, the absence of a strong state has led to security issues, leading the companies operating in these areas to provide their own security and infrastructure. Many of the firms operating in rural areas engage in peacebuilding activities to protect their businesses. Colombia's limited state capacity creates a gap in governance for companies to fill in the areas where they operate.

Northern Ireland has faced similar challenges. While the United Kingdom as a whole is one of the most capable states in terms of governance, rule of law, and regulatory quality, these measures are national. Northern Ireland's devolved government makes choices regarding major public services, such as healthcare, infrastructure, finance, justice, and education. In the years before and during the Troubles, the Parliament of Northern Ireland had an Ulster Unionist Party majority that created policies favoring unionist areas. Such representation created governance gaps mostly affecting nationalists. These gaps suggest firms would engage in peacebuilding-related activities, but most firms were owned and operated by Protestant unionists and the majority of industry and agricultural investment was in heavily Protestant areas. This meant the company owners and managers were unlikely to be negatively affected by gaps in governance and there was little incentive for them to engage in peacebuilding activities. Rather than investing in peacebuilding measures, companies often engaged in discriminatory hiring practices, at the point of both recruitment and promotion (Walsh 2000). Engagement came only after years of violence threatened the economy and profitability. Thus, while there likely were gaps in the UK's governance in certain regions of Northern Ireland, firms did not act to fill them until conflict had been on-going for years.

In the case of Tunisia, businesses face significant gaps in governance. There is a need for investment in infrastructure, and the government is not pro-viding for education, health, or safety. Firms operating in the south of Tunisia especially face challenges given the rural environment: getting farmers to the farm, poor road conditions, and bad safety environments. Inland Tunisia faces widespread rural poverty, and rural urban migration has increased with lost interest in land-related occupations and insufficient opportunities in other sectors. Although businesses can invest to aid in these areas, there is too great a gap for them to fill alone. In addition, firms are overburdened with the level of bureaucracy and lengthy administrative processes that make doing business difficult. Peacebuilding therefore has occurred as a joint effort through unions rather than individual businesses. Many of Tunisia's ongoing challenges, such as the push for gender and wage equality, are being pushed for through unions.

Both the quantitative results and the case studies suggest that firms are responding to the demand for peacebuilding, engaging when the state cannot fully govern. Firms engage in peacebuilding when state capacity is limited and affects firms' abilities to operate. This suggests that firm-led peacebuilding is not the result of altruism but a need to fill gaps in govern-ance in order to conduct business.

This study has not examined countries with extremely low state capacity, where the government is completely unable to provide basic infrastructure or rule of law. I expect that in these extreme cases, there will not be large companies with the resources and willingness to risk engagement at present, meaning there is unlikely to be private sector involvement. It is likely that in extremely low capacity states, because the government is unable to enforce the rule of law and hold actors accountable, firms give profits precedence over people. The engagement of the private sector in political and public policy arenas is not always beneficial. Future research should explore how firms operate in these volatile environments.

Lesson 2: Peace Begets Peacebuilding

Years of peace offer stability and certainty, thereby enabling economic growth and allowing the private sector to prosper. Violence increases the cost of doing business. Long periods of conflict and violence create instability, whereas years of peace enable investment, innovation, and peacebuilding activity. I hypothesized that firms are more likely to engage in peacebuilding activities during periods of peace.

The quantitative results suggest this is indeed the case, showing that longer periods of peace increase peacebuilding-related firm activity. Years of peace significantly increase firm investments in peacebuilding, when the measures of violence and instability are insignificant. Companies are less responsive to the sudden emergence of violence. That corporate engagement is more likely in longer periods of peace suggests these actors invest and innovate during prolonged peace.

The case studies suggest another angle as to how peace and violence affect firm-led peacebuilding. In Colombia, evidence suggests the location and impact of violence are very strong factors in engaging businesses. For many years, conflict was mostly rural and the economy was growing, so businesses were largely insulated from the violence. In the 1990s, kidnappings increased, armed groups moved into urban areas, and a recession hit. This shift in the nature and location of violence, as well as its economic effect, pressured business leaders to become much more active in the national peace process. Large firms were not engaged in peacebuilding when the conflict remained in rural areas, but this shifted when business people became targets. Violence escalated and firms and their activities became direct targets of attacks, which pushed greater involvement in efforts to build peace.

Northern Ireland's history also suggests the location of violence was an important part of firms' decisions to invest. While the human, social, political, and environmental costs of the conflict depressed economic growth and investment, the use of violence to directly target business also made peace efforts relevant to the business community. Eventually, those firms affected put pressure on the government to provide greater security and compensation. Thus, it was prolonged violence and violence being directed at businesses that propelled the private sector into active peacebuilding.

Tunisia has a relatively peaceful history, especially by regional standards. While business leaders have engaged in peacebuilding collectively through unions, there are few individual businesses that are independently engaged. It is unlikely that the threat of violence is deterring Tunisian firms from engaging in peacebuilding activities. Rather, it is the political climate that deters businesses from investing. Business thrives in a stable environment with predictable futures, clear rules, and regulations. The political and

social instability in Tunisia, when combined with the antiquated infrastructure, made it difficult for private firms to invest in peacebuilding activities.
Business investment has been hindered by high regulations and complex administrative processes, which encourage corruption, result in unpredictable
taxation, and generally complicate business operations. Thus, Tunisia has
little firm-led peacebuilding despite years of peace.

Firms respond to stability. I expected to find that firms invest in
peacebuilding during periods of peace, since peace stimulates investment and economic growth. The large-N results suggest this is the case
and that companies adopt policies to invest in communities where the future is predictable. The case studies provide additional information about
the link between peace, violence, and firm-led peacebuilding. In Colombia
and Northern Ireland, firms did not engage until violence directly affected
them. In Tunisia, political unrest has depressed engagement despite the
lack of violence. To understand firm engagement, we need to understand
more than national trends in peace and violence. It is necessary to account
for how violence and political instability affect the economy and the ability
for firms to conduct daily business operations. Firms are willing to invest in
peacebuilding both when years of peace allow for investment and innovation
and when directly targeted violence forces firms to act.

Lesson 3: Firms Invest in Their Reputation

One might argue that firms invest in programs outside normal operations
in an effort to improve their image or as a public relations campaign. New
technology increases accountability and increases the potential for negative
fallout from unethical behavior. Communities and activists can easily communicate to mobilize support and pressure corporations to take restorative
measures. Community-oriented programs enable firms to build "reputational capital" and suffer less reputational harm from negative publicity than
a firm that does not work to maintain a positive image. Companies that have
been caught in a scandal must take steps to ensure their product remains
competitive in an effort to "brandwash." I therefore consider that firms may
engage in peacebuilding activities when they have been caught being "bad"
actors.

The quantitative results presented in chapter 4 suggest corporations are
engaging in peacebuilding as a response to negative news surrounding the

company. Negative media creates the largest substantive change in the probability that a corporation will engage in peacebuilding. Negative media coverage makes investing in peacebuilding in the interest of the firm. This finding offers some evidence of "brandwashing" after a crisis. Other results show reputation-related motives are only part of the story and that businesses also account for the nature of their operating environment.

In Colombia, there is evidence that firms have learned from their experiences. Multiple firms caused public outcry and even legal action around their activities during the civil war but have learned to engage the communities where it operates in a way that promotes development and peace. Experiences and public pressure have led companies to create better practices and protocols, revising programs to more directly build peace.

"Bad" behavior was commonplace in Northern Ireland prior to the Good Friday Agreement. Discriminatory hiring practices and promotion policies were routine, and there was no legal recourse for discrimination until the Northern Ireland Act of 1998 created an equality commission. Additionally, there were no norms of socially responsible behavior and community engagement and few public repercussions for misbehaver. The eventual adoption of more engaged policies followed US and Irish efforts working to reverse decades of anti-Catholic discrimination in the wake of the larger peace movement. While adopting fair employment policies offered an important step in correcting years of unfair treatment, the true effect of firm-led engagement was at the national policy level.

Tunisia still lacks strong norms of corporate engagement. The concept of corporate responsibility in Tunisia is still developing, with a focus on creating a positive employer-employee relationship and working environment, as well as creating an ethical image. This likely is the result of having a small and struggling economy, with few large domestically headquartered companies and a large informal economy. Norms of engagement have been slow to develop also because many Tunisian companies began as family businesses. Tunisia's approach to corporate engagement is changing, with several avant-garde corporations pushing forward thinking about the role of the firm and opportunities to build peace. Yet, Tunisian firms do not face pressure to engage in peacebuilding, even if they have previously behaved poorly.

The evidence presented here suggests that reputation-building is part of the incentive behind firm-led peacebuilding, but that this depends on the state of norms that promote corporate responsibility. Negative reports make investing in peacebuilding in the interest of the firm when the public has expectations about how firms should behave.

What Are the Results of Firm-Led Peacebuilding?

I explore whether and how engaged corporations can prevent violence. The rational choice theory of civil war onset and termination and business research on the role private firms play in preventing civil wars suggests firms are uniquely situated in their ability to raise the cost of violence. I argue that proactive firms can significantly increase a country's peace years. Conversely, firms can make it significantly harder to reach an agreement in states with ongoing conflict since firms act as an additional veto player in the negotiating process.

Lesson 1: Engaged Firms Reduce the Occurrence of Violence

I argue that proactive firm engagement in peacebuilding helps foster a system where violence is a less attractive option for individuals. This suggests that, at a national level, we should see less violence in countries that have firms engaged in peacebuilding. I therefore hypothesize that states with an active private sector are less likely to experience violence.

The quantitative evidence suggests that countries with an active private sector are significantly less likely to experience violence. The data show that the mere presence of engaged firms, higher numbers of firms engaged in peacebuilding, and greater proportions of firms that are engaged, reduce the probability that a country experiences violent conflict. Also, I show that countries with more engaged firms are less likely to experience violent conflict than those with only one or two firms actively building peace.

Firms in Colombia were not engaged firms in the years leading up to the violent conflict between FARC and the government. Firms became markedly more involved over the course of the conflict, however. At the national level, Colombia's private firms clearly played an active role in encouraging the peace process and promoting its implementation, although it is challenging to isolate correlates of Colombia's peace accord with FARC from the many other factors that played into its creation. Since the signing of the 2016 peace accord, there is evidence that Colombia's firms have positively contributed in ways that encourage potential rebels to choose peace. Through rural development projects, economic opportunities, and social programs, businesses in Colombia are making the life of a rebel less appealing. Individuals have access to training and opportunities that were absent for many years. When we consider peace at the level of individual choice, the role of the private sector has been and will be key in encouraging nonviolence.

Northern Ireland also lacked positive firm engagement for many years. Throughout the Troubles, businesses and large corporations remained uninvolved, although they were frequently targeted with violence. Since the signing of the Good Friday Agreement, the norm of corporate engagement has spread. Still, many of Northern Ireland's domestically headquartered companies do little to actively engage existing local and national challenges. Laws have been written to prevent discrimination in hiring, but communities remain exceptionally segregated. Both the Catholic and Protestant communities face the challenges of poverty and intergenerational unemployment. Violence could become more widespread should a catalyst occur. While some domestically headquartered companies are offering training and community engagement programs, transnational firms have more aggressively worked to address these challenges.

Tunisia's Jasmine Revolution could easily have turned violent, as almost all of the other Arab Spring states had some level of violence associated with popular demands for change. Strong business organizations and unions were key in ensuring the peaceful transition during political unrest. While many domestic and foreign firms fled Tunisia during and after the revolution, civil society elites collaborated to avoid violence and demobilize public unrest. While these actors may normally have divergent policy views, they were able to work together during the democratic transition. It is likely that the power of the unions to reach and coordinate large portions of the population enabled these actors to have a greater impact on preventing violence than individual or groups of private firms possibly could have had.

The cases and data suggest that, broadly speaking, engaged firms encourage more peaceful societies. The quantitative results show countries with engaged firms have a low probability of experiencing violence. The cases suggest that when there is unrest, firm engagement can help to prevent violence, as experienced in Tunisia, and solidify peace, as experienced in Colombia and Northern Ireland. While firm activities, or lack thereof, are not likely to be the key explanation of how peaceful or violent a society is, the findings here suggest their efforts are making a difference.

Lesson 2: Engaged Firms Prolong Ongoing Violence

Countries with ongoing violence have more difficulty ending this violence when firms engage in peacebuilding-related activities after conflict has begun. While corporate peacebuilding efforts decrease the probability of armed conflict, these efforts have an inverse effect on the probability that armed conflict ends. Active firm engagement after violence has begun prolongs these conflicts, since corporations add their own preferences to negotiations. States with an active private sector are less likely to experience armed civil violence but unlikely to end it quickly. I hypothesize that states with ongoing violence and an active private sector have longer periods of armed conflict.

The data reveal a trend that ongoing conflicts are less likely to end when there are more firms engaged in peacebuilding and when the proportion of engaged firms increases. The probability of violence ending decreases for each additional firm that is engaged in peacebuilding and as the proportion of engaged firms moves from zero to one. The probability that violence ends decreases even with only one firm engaged in peacebuilding. The quantitative findings suggest that corporate engagement adds to the complexities of the conflict environment and prolongs violence.

In Colombia, the failure of firms to engage in peacebuilding allowed the conflict between FARC and government forces to become increasingly violent. Firms became actively engaged in the peace process as violence moved into urban areas and became more costly. Business leaders were included in the negotiating team, which helped to provide the legitimacy and resources required to support the fledgling peace process. However, business leaders had their own interests to consider. The process of modifying the agreement to have the support of the business community likely prolonged the peace process.

In Northern Ireland, the direct and indirect costs of violence compiled and eventually compelled companies to push for peace. Their action took the form of a neutral push for peace, argued on the basis of a peace dividend. Throughout their involvement, business organizations remained neutral, nonpolitical proponents of peace. Their main goals were to promote a single peace message through engaging the general population with grassroots movements and civil society campaigns. This involvement suggests that corporate peacebuilding during ongoing conflict does not always prolong violence and that neutral engagement can effectively move peace processes forward. While Northern Ireland still faces long-term challenges in building peace and reconciliation, proper private firm engagement can help to further these processes by addressing some of the underlying structural factors that lead to the onset of violence.

The findings suggest that firm engagement in peacebuilding can lead to positive and negative policy outcomes, depending on how and when the engagement occurs. It is important to consider the nature and circumstances of engagement. The data suggest that countries with ongoing violence are less likely to end the conflict when firms are engaged in peacebuilding. When corporations become involved in national peace processes, the addition of their opinions and concerns can prolong the violence, as was the case in Colombia. When firm-led peacebuilding is neutral, as was the case in Northern Ireland, their action can help push the peace process forward in important ways.

Reconnecting with Existing Research and Practitioners

The research findings presented here have important implications for scholars working on various puzzles involving conflict and its prevention, as well as those exploring business activities. In addition, there are important policy implications for practitioners and organizations looking to more effectively incorporate private firms in building more peaceful societies.

Conflict Management

Research on the topic of both binding and nonbinding third-party conflict management mechanisms has exploded in the last twenty years, as academics have increasingly endeavored to understand the many ways the international community can end violent conflict (see Beardsley et al. 2006; Greig 2005; Regan and Stam 2000; Bercovitch 1997). This scholarship has helped to generate much stronger knowledge about the role of third-party states, international organizations, and regional organizations play in resolving conflict and the circumstances that encourage their involvement. Evidence presented here suggests that a critical actor is missing from these studies: the private business sector. While related research has shown that trade can increase peaceful bilateral relationships (Gartzke et al. 2001; Gartzke and Li 2003), conflict management scholars do not consider how firms may change the dynamics of conflict. This omission suggests many of the conclusions may be biased, attributing outcomes to the actors under examination without considering all the actors influencing conflict dynamics.

The cases of Tunisia and Northern Ireland, as well as the quantitative analysis in chapter 5, suggest both the domestic and international private sectors help to prevent and resolve civil conflict. Firms can be partners in the peace process, and may help explain the success of other international actors (such as mediators). In the Colombian case and the empirical evidence presented in chapter 6, however, we see this involvement is not always a positive contribution. These results suggest a private sector that engages after the conflict has begun can hinder third-party conflict resolution efforts by complicating negotiations. And yet, the role of international businesses in the Northern Ireland peace process suggests that when businesses act in a strictly neutral capacity, they can help bring peace in conflict-torn states. These findings imply that business actors in some cases (like that of Colombia) are likely adding to the challenges facing those working toward negotiating peace deals, and in others (like in Northern Ireland) may be aiding their work. In either case, the findings presented here suggest a need for conflict management scholars to account for the role of business actors in their studies of conflict management processes.

Business and Peace

Much of the business and peace literature focuses on frameworks for business operations. For example, the CSR and CSV movements both approach community outreach and local issues related to conflict from the business perspective. The findings here suggest that not all corporate engagement makes positive contributions to society. Involvement in national peace negotiations when business interests contradict those of the disputants (as in Colombia) can further complicate already complex negotiations. And yet, when the private sector does not show interests in an outcome beyond peaceful conflict resolution (as transnational firms did in Northern Ireland), they can effectively move peace processes forward. This speaks directly to findings in the "peace through commerce" literature that discusses how business leaders reduce tensions in conflict zones (Getz and Oetzel 2009; Oetzel, Getz, and Ladek 2007).

An important caveat is that I have chosen a broad-based approach to corporate engagement, a phenomenon that has inherent heterogeneous characteristics (such as the nature of the firm in terms of size, industry, and relationship with their community). It is likely that the nature of corporate engagement has implications for its outcomes. Since existing business and peace research also avoids this challenge by either focusing on theoretical approaches to why and how private firms can contribute to peace (Fort 2007, 2015) or examining individual cases of corporate engagement (Miklian and Schouten 2019), we do not fully understand the implications of variations in the characteristics of the corporation and its involvement.

Moving Forward

To understand how firm engagement might best promote peace, we must account for the ongoing political circumstances of the country. Countries at peace offer corporations the opportunity to invest in peacebuilding activities, and these actions can help ensure the country has a peaceful future. They can also help a country successfully avoid violence during periods of instability, as was the case in Tunisia's revolution. Firms can also make important contributions for countries with ongoing violence. In Colombia, their engagement helped bring resources and legitimacy to the peace process but also brought additional preferences to already complicated negotiations. In Northern Ireland, corporate engagement helped bring a peace agenda forward, and the neutral approach avoided prolonging violence. Finally, firms can be an important partner in implementing peace agreements and building stability in post-conflict societies. While businesses alone cannot create peace, they can complement the peace process and are essential to ensuring postagreement economic growth and stability.

These findings add to an existing literature on the benefits of commerce more broadly. Much of this scholarship has its roots in liberal perspectives, suggesting economic development improves social conditions, creating an economic middle class that demands greater political and civil rights as a by-product of economic interdependence and free trade (Harrelson-Stephens and Callaway 2003; Milner 2002). Similarly, transnational mergers and acquisitions help strengthen workers' rights, empowerment, physical integrity, and women's economic rights (Kim and Trumbore 2010). Broader research on globalization and trade openness suggests an active private sector can help encourage peaceful societies domestically and in respect to other countries, improving domestic conditions and decreasing the probability of civil war as well as encouraging peaceful international relations.

The substantial evidence showing that states with strong trade ties are less likely to go to war with one another suggests the finding here may have broader implications. Trade can increase peaceful bilateral relationships through several avenues, including offering nonmilitary ways of communicating resolve (Gartzke, Li, and Boehmer 2001) and forcing leaders to choose between economic stability and political goals (Gartzke and Li 2003). As economic ties have important implications for peace, it is possible that peacebuilding efforts led by transnational firms play a different, although also salient, role in the levels of peace and violence a country experiences. Such efforts may have implications both for interstate and intrastate conflict and should be explored in future research.

In addition, this book has focused on how national characteristics may increase or decrease the probability of armed conflict and its end. Future research should work to adopt more aggregated measures of firm involvement and account for dyadic-level characteristics (Cunningham, Skrede Gleditsch, and Salehyan 2009). Creating more geographically specific measures of the locations of corporate engagement programs, for example, could take advantage of similar advances in event-based data on armed conflict (Sundberg and Melander 2013). The results I report here offer a starting point for such projects, suggesting there is a need for exploring these avenues of research.

The COPC data used to generate the results presented in chapters 4 and 5 offer initial quantitative evidence of corporate behavior and conflict processes. However, additional data collection is necessary and desirable, especially if we are to understand changes and trends in firm-led peacebuilding across time. This study suggests important peacebuilding actions are occurring, but it should be built on with more extensive data. Additionally, it is pertinent to explore the effects of these activities on the societies where they occur to ensure they are having the desired effect. Additionally, this study researches large, domestically headquartered corporations in unstable regions. How does this compare to peacebuilding conducted by multinational corporations, smaller businesses, and those operating in other parts of the world? This chapter offers an initial step in creating a broader understanding of how the private sector may help build more peaceful societies, but developing a complete understanding of the complexities of corporate peacebuilding is beyond the scope of a single book.

Finally, the research here leaves room for exploration of the effect an active private sector has on post-conflict stability and peace. An active private sector may help to rebuild institutions and infrastructure after the end of conflict, and such engagement may have implications for creating a more durable peace. Firm-led peacebuilding efforts may add to the contributions of third-party guarantees and security sector reforms that research shows can create long-lasting peace (Toft 2009; Fortna 2004). If this is indeed the case, corporate investment in peacebuilding may be especially important in post-conflict societies as a way to avoid the risk of renewed violence.

The very purpose of a private firm is to create profit, and companies have an obligation to shareholders to do so. Innovative approaches to engaging a society beyond economic transactions can both ensure long-term value and profits and benefit societies. In the private sector, numerous stakeholder- and industry-led initiatives, such as the World Diamond Council and the International Coffee Organization, exist to assist companies in implementing responsible business practices. The private sector has an opportunity to shape conflict-prone environments in important and positive ways. Increasing our knowledge and understanding of the firm's role in promoting peace generates important evidence useful for encouraging positive future firm involvement in peacebuilding.

Chapter 4 Appendix

Table A.4.1 Summary Statistics

	Observations	Mean	Standard Deviation	Minimum	Maximum
Variable					
Outcome					
Peacebuilding	20,328	.011	.104	0	1
Filling Governance "Gaps"					
Government Effectiveness	16,632	.44	.58	–1.89	1.97
Rule of Law	16,632	.27	.59	–2.25	1.62
Regulatory Quality	16,632	.41	.56	–2.27	1.54
Responding to Instability					
Ongoing Violence	20,404	.118	.323	0	1
Peace Years	20,328	9.920	6.91	0	22
Violence Years	20,328	1.58	4.14	0	18
Autocratic Shift	17,266	.005	.074	0	1
Protecting Reputation					
"Bad" Behavior	19,404	.007	.082	0	1
Controls					
Years Global Compact Member	20,328	.335	1.75	0	18
FDI	13,588	21.965	1.868	13.964	25.339

Each measure is lagged one year to ensure the direction of causality.

Table A.4.2 Variation in Peacebuilding-Related Activities across UCDP Armed Conflict Data Events and Outcomes, 1998–2018

	Peacebuilding	No Peacebuilding	Total
Ongoing Violence in Previous Year	8	2,287	2,295
Ongoing Civil War in Previous Year	3	178	181
Ongoing Armed Conflict in Previous Year	5	2,109	2,114
Event Ends in Previous Year	2	497	499

Table A.4.2 looks more deeply into the trends in corporate peacebuilding-related behavior across levels of UCDP violence (Pettersson and Öberg 2020). Corporations are clearly not motivated to invest in peace due to recent violent events or civil war. Since the UCDP armed conflict data measure violence at the national level, however, it is unclear that these events directly affect the companies being examined. Future research should explore subnational violence located near corporate sites to see whether the proximity of violence events encourages businesses to work toward peace.

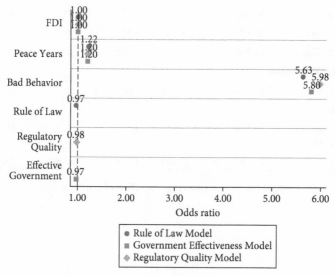

Figure A.4.1 Plot of Odds Ratios from Table 4.1

Figure A.4.1 plots the odds ratios across the model in Table A.4.1. Each measure of governance has an odds ratio value of less than one, meaning these decrease the odds of peacebuilding activities. The values for peace years and previous bad behavior both suggest increases in the odds of peacebuilding.

Table **A.4.3** Random Effects Models of Firm-Led Peacebuilding across Measures of Instability (1998–2018)

	Model 1: Years of Peace & Violence	Model 2: Recent Violence	Model 3: Polity Instability	Model 4: Country Fixed Effects
Variable				
Filling Governance "Gaps"				
Government *Effectiveness*	−0.0256** (0.0092)	−0.0272** (0.0091)	−0.0260** (0.0087)	0.0582 (0.0391)
Responding to Stability				
Years of Violence	0.0979 (0.0677)			0.6702 (0.4290)
Years of Peace	0.1803*** (0.0412)			0.3857*** (0.0691)
Recent Violence		−0.7035 (0.6217)		
Autocratic Shift			2.2436*** (0.5986)	
Protecting Reputation				
"Bad" Behavior	1.7579* (0.8348)	1.9115* (0.8153)	1.7811* (0.8340)	1.3741 (1.1113)
Controls				
Global Compact *Member*	0.0619 (0.0554)	0.0959 (0.0542)	0.0989 (0.0542)	−0.2107* (0.1026)
Foreign Investment	0.0000* (0.0000)	0.0000*** (0.0000)	0.0000*** (0.0000)	−0.0000* (0.0000)
Constant	−6.5120*** (0.8123)	−4.2885*** (0.5857)	−4.4842*** (0.5709)	
N	11,044	11,044	11,016	766
N (groups)	850	850	849	59
LR test	9.65***	7.68***	7.34***	

Robust standard error in parentheses; Two-tailed test $*p \leq .05$; $**p \leq .01$; $***p \leq .001$

Table A.4.3 shows that corporations are not responsive to different measures of recent, national instability but respond to long-term trends in peace. Recent, ongoing UCDP Armed Conflicts (Gleditsch et al. 2002) does not have a significant effect on the rate of corporate engagement. Firms do, however, respond to years of stability. The more years of peace or violence a country has experienced, the more likely a company is to engage in efforts to build on that peace.

Since violence and civil war are most likely to occur during times of political transition (Cederman, Hug, and Krebs 2010; Hegre 2004), firms may be especially sensitive to political change and its potential to threaten stability and investments. In addition, domestic institutional change can have consequences on economic performance (North 1990). It seems likely that corporations are sensitive to these changes, as they create the incentive structures of the economy. To measure political instability, I use the Polity IV database to create a dichotomous variable of whether there is an *autocratic shift* or *democratic shift* in governance from the previous year (Marshall and Jaggers 2004). (I also test the World Governance Indicator's measure of political stability and find that general instability does not explain corporate engagement [results available on request].) I find corporate behavior is not sensitive to recent political shifts unless they are autocratic. As shown in Model 3, corporations are more likely to engage when there has been a shift toward autocracy in the last year. This finding builds on work suggesting a complex relationship between peacebuilding and democratization (Jarstad and Sisk 2008).

In Model 4, I estimate the same model with country fixed effects, which controls for country-specific characteristics. This model controls for the effects of state characteristics such as level of democracy, size of the economy, and population. That the governance effectiveness measure is no longer significant suggests that much of the variation in governance being explained is across countries, rather than within countries. The same is true that "bad" behavior is no longer a significant predictor, meaning our strongest explanation is across rather than within companies. Both of the findings are likely due to the lack of variation in governing capacity and bad media reports over time. In other words, we can say that companies that have had negative media coverage are more likely to engage in peacebuilding compared to those that have not and companies are more likely to engage when they are headquartered in a country with low governance scores. I cannot, however, make conclusions about when a company changes its policies toward engagement.

Chapter 5 Appendix

Table A.5.1 Chi Square Tests of Value Creation and Violence Prevention: Number of Companies

Number of Companies Creating Value	No Violence	Violence	Total
0	1,954	77	2,031
1	56	10	66
2	16	2	18
3	13	0	13
4	7	0	7
5	3	0	3
6	3	0	3
7	3	0	3
8	1	0	1
9	2	0	2
12	1	0	1
28	1	0	1
Total	2060	89	2149

Pearson $chi^2(7) = 24.452$ Pr $= 0.011$

Table A.5.2 Chi Square Tests of Value Creation and Violence Prevention: Any Companies

Any Companies Creating Value	No Violence	Violence	Total
0	1,954	77	2,031
1	106	12	118
Total	2,060	89	2,149

Pearson $chi2(7) = 11.428$ Pr $= 0.001$

These chi square tests for independence suggest that knowing the number of corporations working to build peace helps us predict whether the country experiences violence in a given year. Similarly, knowing whether or not there are any companies creating value helps us predict whether there is violence in a country in a given year. While this test cannot help us establish a causal relationship, it does suggest there is a trend that merits further exploration. The chi square test does not consider other possible causes of violence, such as economic and government characteristics.

Table A.5.3 OLS Model of Violence Duration (in Days)

	Proportion of Engaged Firms	Number of Engaged Firms	Any Engaged Firms
Variable			
Value (Proportion)	0.0006*		
	(0.0002)		
Value (Number)		598.7216*	
		(176.9621)	
Value (0/1)			598.7216**
			(176.9621)
Controls			
Recent Deaths	−1.1837	−1.1837	−1.1837
	(1.0903)	(1.0903)	(1.0903)
Total Deaths	0.2991	0.2991	0.2991
	(0.1870)	(0.1870)	(0.1870)
Population	−0.04	-.046	−0.046
	(868.9238)	(868.9238)	(868.9238)
Democracy	.003	0.003	0.0035**
	(.001)	(.001)	(0.0011)
GDP per capita	.007**	.007**	0.007***
	(.001)	(.001)	(0.001)
Constant	-.0004	-.0004*	−0.0004**
	(.0001)	(.0001)	(0.0001)
N	42	42	42
R^2	0.92	.92	.92
PRE	91.92	91.92	91.92
Log Likelihood	−373.38	−373.38	−373.38

Robust standard error in parentheses; Clustered by country; Two-tailed test *$p \leq .05$; **$p \leq .01$; ***$p \leq .001$

Additionally, I test how private sector engagement effects the duration of conflict using "duration of violence," a count of the number of days a conflict is ongoing. I examine the length of violence using a basic linear OLS specification in Table A.5.3. Countries experiencing ongoing violence are also more likely to experience longer periods of violence when the private sector is actively engaged in the community (see Table A.5.3 and Figure 4.3). Higher numbers of engaged firms and higher proportions of engaged firms both prolong periods of violence. While this analysis only includes conflicts that have a recorded end date (thereby excluding the cases that have yet to end), having an active private sector leads to a 600 percent increase in the duration of conflict.

Predicted Length of Violence across Firm Engagement Levels

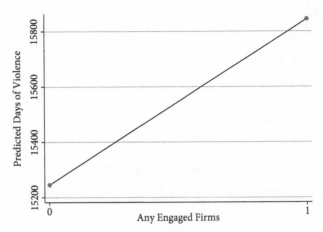

Figure A.5.1 Predicted Duration of Violence: Any Engaged Firms

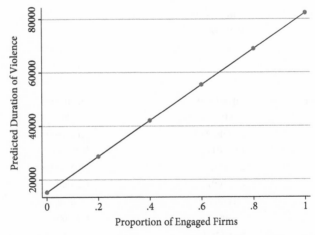

Figure A.5.2 Predicted Duration of Violence: Proportion of Engaged Firms

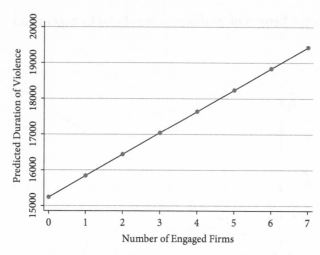

Figure A.5.3 Predicted Duration of Violence: Number of Engaged Firms

Table A.5.4 Hazard Model of Violence Duration

	Number of Engaged Firms	Any Engaged Firms
Variable		
Value (Number)	−40.1479***	
	(0.9659)	
Value (0/1)		−40.1479***
		(0.9659)
Controls		
Recent Deaths	−0.0011***	−0.0011***
	(0.0002)	(0.0002)
Total Deaths	−0.0006***	−0.0006***
	(0.0001)	(0.0001)
Democracy	−5.9571***	−5.9571***
	(0.7600)	(0.7600)
Population	−0.0000**	−0.0000**
	(0.0000)	(0.0000)
GDP per capita	0.0007***	0.0007***
	(0.0001)	(0.0001)
Large Companies	−0.1649***	−0.1649***
	(0.0230)	(0.0230)
N	48	48
N(failures)	12	12
Log Likelihood	−22.929***	−22.929***

Robust standard error in parentheses; Clustered by country; Two-tailed test *$p \leq .05$; **$p \leq .01$; ***$p \leq .001$

Above is an analysis of the duration of ongoing conflicts, modeled using Cox hazard analysis. Hazard analysis was developed in the health sciences as a way to test risk of death, and so the results are presented a increasing or decreasing the risk of an event. The method enables me to test how the risk of conflict varies across different levels of firm engagement, whereas the linear analysis shows variation in the number of conflict days. The below figure shows differences in the risk that a conflict ends according to the presence or absence of engaged firms. When controlling for recent and accumulated casualties, democracy, population, per capita GDP, and the number of large companies, a country is at greater risk of experiencing prolonged violence when private firms are engaged.

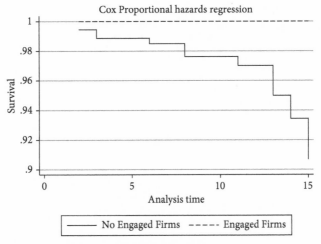

Figure A.5.4 Survival Curve of Ongoing Conflicts

Chapter 6 Appendix

Table A.6.1 Urban Deaths by Year in Colombia's Largest Cities

| Year | Total Deaths | | |
	Bogotá	Cali	Medellin
1989	0	0	0
1990	0	12	14
1991	9	2	2
1992	3	4	9
1993	3	0	1
1994	9	0	8
1995	4	0	0
1996	8	2	2
1997	14	0	5
1998	2	0	1
1999	16	7	14
2000	12	4	2
2001	4	1	1
2002	38	35	58
2003	4	0	4
2004	11	3	6
2005	0	0	5
2006	0	10	4
2007	2	6	0
2008	0	0	4
2009	3	1	0
2010	0	0	0
2011	0	7	0
2012	2	0	0
2013	0	0	0
2014	0	0	0
2015	0	0	0
2016	1	0	0
2017	2	0	0
2018	0	0	0

Source: UCDP Geo-referenced Event Data.

Table A.6.2 Kidnappings Targeting Corporate Leadership by Year

Year	Total Kidnappings	Firm-Related Kidnappings	Top-Management Kidnappings	Firms' Owners Kidnappings
1996	1091	220	3	1
1997	1671	249	2	0
1998	3023	453	25	32
1999	3349	575	52	77
2000	3697	NA	NA	NA
2001	3050	265	23	60
2002	2986	223	22	43

Source: Fon del Libertad Database, considers only FARC-perpetrated kidnappings.

Changes reflect a strategic shift from "simple kidnappings," where no ransom is demanded, toward "extortive kidnappings," which quadrupled from 2008 to 2013 (2014).

Chapter 8 Appendix

Table A.8.1 Pearson's χ^2 test of Significant Differences in Violence across Time in Armagh, Dungannon, and Omagh

	Casualties						
year	0	1	2	3	4	29	Total
1989	0	5	1	0	0	0	6
1990	1	7	2	0	1	0	11
1991	0	2	1	2	0	0	5
1992	0	2	0	0	1	0	3
1993	0	8	1	0	0	0	9
1994	0	2	0	0	0	0	2
1997	0	1	0	0	0	0	1
1998	0	0	0	0	0	1	1
2011	0	1	0	0	0	0	1
Total	1	28	5	2	2	1	39

Pearson chi^2(40) = 64.4369 Pr = 0.008

Table A.8.2 Armagh, Dungannon, and Omagh Annual Casualties 1969–1994

Year	Armagh Casualties	Dungannon Casualties	Omagh Casualties
1969	1	4	0
1970	0	0	0
1971	1	0	0
1972	6	3	0
1973	4	0	8
1974	3	4	0
1975	3	0	0
1976	3	6	0
1977	1	0	0
1978	0	0	0
1979	7	4	0
1980	1	0	0
1981	4	0	0
1982	10	0	0
1983	7	2	0
1984	3	2	0
1985	2	0	0
1986	2	0	0
1987	2	0	0
1988	1	0	0
1989	1	0	0
1990	7	0	0
1991	3	0	0
1992	2	0	0
1993	2	2	0
1994	4	0	0
1995	0	0	0
1996	0	0	0
1997	0	0	0
1998	0	0	29

From McKittrick et al. (2001) and Sutton (2001).

Notes

Chapter 1

1. The companies employ former fighters through the Colombian Agency for Reintegration (ACR), which helps former fighters prepare for civilian life (Aldenwinckle 2015).

Chapter 3

1. I use the term "peacebuilding-related" interchangeably with "peacebuilding" to refer to activities that are seeking to prevent conflict or occur in the post-conflict context.
2. While this study focuses on domestic firms, the theoretical logic applies more broadly.
3. Engaging may result in lost profits or damaged relationships if a firm is seen as part of an unpopular peace process.
4. This baseline is chosen for feasibility purposes, especially given that large firms have been shown to be better at communicating and reporting community engagement activities compared to small firms (see https://link.springer.com/article/10.1007/s10551-013-1827-7). One of the challenges with working with business data is that the majority of the corporate world is interested in current information and not information over time; so the list of firms is created off 2015 earnings.
5. Only a few corporations were covered for adopting peacebuilding programs before the year 2000, likely because the concept of corporate engagement was expanding and just starting to attract media attention.
6. These are the raw number of events rather than the percent of companies engaged in peacebuilding, because the percent of companies engaging is extremely small (there are 925 companies each year).
7. This includes Mexichem, Grupo Mexico, Desarrolladora Homex, Kimberly-Clark de Mexico, PEMEX, and Comision Federal de Electricidad.
8. Neither the foundation nor the DJSI index is coded over time, so they are not included in time series estimates. This is due to the limited availability of information over time.

Chapter 4

1. Not all of Colombia celebrated, as several agreement terms were revised after being voted down in a referendum.

2. Masglo, a Colombian cosmetics company, donates a portion of proceeds to women's projects in conflict regions.

3. Club Colombia imprints "soy capaz de creer" on their bottle caps as part of the SoyCapaz peace campaign of 100 national private sector firms and the Colombia National Industry Association. A similar campaign occurred in Sri Lanka with the "Sri Lanka First" initiative, which is an initiative for peace that "highlights the costs of war, and the socio-economic benefits of the peace dividend" (Tripathi and Gündüz 2008, 21).

4. Alpina dairy company also participates in SoyCapaz and ran ads encouraging national unity.

5. The need for quantitative research is discussed at length in Wolf, Deitelhoff, and Engert (2007). Oetzel and Getz's (2012) analysis of survey results is the only existing cross-national evidence to the author's knowledge.

6. Although examples like Pearson's partnership with Save the Children in the "Every Child Learning" program, which provides educational and psychosocial support to Syrian refugees, suggest some companies choose to engage in peacebuilding beyond where they operate.

7. Markets respond to peace processes, as investors responded negatively to Colombia's failed peace referendum (Repoza 2016). Broadly, global capital responds to crises, and the trade-offs between political goals and economic stability have pacifying effects (Gartzke and Li 2003).

8. Domestic firms are the focus of this study, a choice that is further discussed in the empirical section.

9. It is possible that a firm might lose money by being a part of an unpopular peace process or damage relations with the ruling politicians.

10. Colombia's business sector is not unique in its response, as is exemplified by the active private sectors in Sri Lanka after its decades-long civil war (for an analysis of firm-led peacebuilding in the Sri Lankan case, see Alert 2005).

11. While the level of analysis is focused on individual firm actions, reports involving their collective efforts in partnership with international organizations or governments are included.

12. As there is little variation in the outcome variable within companies, a fixed-effects specification would drop a vast majority of the cases.

13. I generate similar results using the number of years of ongoing UCDP Armed Conflicts (Gleditsch et al. 2002), if there was armed conflict ongoing in the previous year, and the number of years since a failed coup attempt (Powell and Thyne 2011) (see appendix).

14. Estimating the same model with country fixed effects, which controls for country-specific characteristics, suggests that much of the variation in governance being explained is across countries, rather than within countries, and across rather than within companies (see appendix).

15. I also tested the intensity level of the conflict in a given year as a proxy for the conflict phase (see Wolf, Deitelhoff, and Engert 2007, for a theoretical justification). The results were not significant.

Chapter 5

1. The UCDP data focuses on civil wars since the end of World War II.
2. The companies employ former fighters through the Colombian Agency for Reintegration (ACR), which helps former fighters prepare for civilian life (Kim and Trumbore 2010).
3. The global mean of per capita GDP was $17,300.

Chapter 6

1. For an overview of the conflict in Colombia, see Bouvier (2009).
2. The companies employ former fighters through the Colombian Agency for Reintegration (ACR), which helps former fighters prepare for civilian life, see Aldenwinckle (2015).
3. Colombia's business sector is not unique in its response, as is exemplified by the active private sectors in Sri Lanka after its decades long civil war. For an analysis of firm-led peacebuilding in the Sri Lankan case, see Alert (2005).
4. In Congo, the African mobile phone giant Celtel, benefited from doing business in conflict zones since there was no competition, but also made clear its position not to pay brides despite the opportunity to own a sizable investment in infrastructure (Oetzel and Miklian 2017).

Chapter 7

1. For a more thorough overview of the Arab Spring and Tunisia's transition, see Diamond and Plattner (2014).
2. Mohamud Bouazizi was a Tunisian street vendor who set himself on fire on December 17, 2010 in response to the confiscation of his wares and the harassment inflicted on him by a municipal official. The event is widely seen as a catalyst for the Tunisian Revolution.
3. According to the Worldwide Governance Indicators, the MENA countries have average government effectiveness, regulatory quality, and rule of law scores in the range of 45th to 50th percentile, whereas upper middle-income states score in 50th percentile for each measure of capacity.

Chapter 8

1. Indeed, The Apprentice Boys group in Derry/Londonderry, parades annually to mark the ending of the siege of the town in 1689. Protestants in the city closed the gates to

keep out the advancing Jacobite army of deposed Catholic King James II, who was attempting to regain the crown from Protestant King William III.

2. The nature of "home rule" in Northern Ireland and the actual body carrying it out has been contested and taken different forms over time. So-called transferred matters are areas of policymaking that are given over to Northern Ireland as a part of the Northern Ireland Act of 1998, but similar policymaking structures existed from 1921 to 1972 under the Government of Ireland Act of 1920. The administration of Northern Ireland directly by the United Kingdom was practiced between 1972 and 1998 as a result of the Troubles. However, the point here is precisely that we cannot rely on UK data to understand governance issues in Northern Ireland.

3. The G7 included the Hospitality Association for Northern Ireland, the Institute of Directors, the Northern Ireland Chamber of Commerce and Industry, the Northern Ireland Growth Challenge, the Northern Ireland Economic Council and the Northern Ireland Committee of the Irish Congress of Trade Unions.

References

2018. "Colombian Edgar Montenegro Wins International 2018 Oslo Business for Peace Award." *Business Call to Action*. https://www.businesscalltoaction.org/news/colombian-edgar-montenegro-wins-international-2018-oslo-business-for-peace-award.

Aas Rustad, Siri Camilla, Halvard Buhaug, Åshild Falch, and Scott Gates. 2011. "All Conflict Is Local: Modeling Sub-National Variation in Civil Conflict Risk." *Conflict Management and Peace Science* 28 (1):15–40.

Acemoglu, Daron, and James A. Robinson. 2013. *Why Nations Fail: The Origins of Power, Prosperity, and Poverty*. Danvers, MA: Crown Business.

Agency, Northern Ireland Statistics and Research. 2011. "Census 2011." https://www.nisra.gov.uk/statistics/census/2011-census.

Agency, Northern Ireland Statistics and Research. 2015. "VAT and PAYE Registered Businesses in Northern Ireland." Accessed February 5, 2020. https://www.nisra.gov.uk/sites/nisra.gov.uk/files/publications/IDBR%20Publication%202015_0.pdf.

Alamaro, Moshe. 2002. "The Economics of Peace." *Harvard Business Review* 80 (11):26–27.

Aldenwinckle, Jack. 2015. "A Civil Education: How Colombia Plans to Turn 32,000 Ex-Jungle-Dwelling Gorillas into Useful Members of Society." *Quartz*, May 31, 2015.

Aldwinckle, Jack. 2015. "How Colombia plans to turn 32,000 ex-jungle-dwelling guerrillas into useful members of society." *Quartz*. https://qz.com/413831/how-colombia-plans-to-turn-32000-ex-jungle-dwelling-guerrillas-into-useful-members-of-society/.

Aliyev, Vahid. 2017. *The Role of Business in Northern Ireland's Peace Process*. London: Democratic Progress Institute.

Allanson, Marie, Margareta Sollenberg, and Lotta Themnér. 2013. "Armed Conflict in the Wake of the Arab Spring." In *SIPRI Yearbook 2013*. Oxford, UK: Oxford University Press. https://www.sipriyearbook.org/view/9780199678433/sipri-9780199678433-div1-8.xml#.

Allison, Graham T. 1973. "Military Capabilities and American Foreign Policy." *Annals of the American Academy of Political and Social Science* 406:17–37.

Alluri, Rina M. 2009. "The Role of Tourism in Post-Conflict Peacebuilding in Rwanda." Working Paper 2. Bern, Switzerland.

Alsema, Adriaan. 2009. "Bogotá Authorities Arrest Two Suspects for Blockbuster Bomb." *Colombia Report*. Accessed January 18, 2017. http://colombiareports.com/bogota-authorities-arrest-two-suspects-for-blockbuster-bomb/.

Alsema, Adriaan. 2017. "Colombia Cement Cartel Receives $68 Million Fine after Price Fixing Scandal." *Colombia Reports*. Medellín, Colombia. https://colombiareports.com/colombia-cement-cartel-receives-68-million-fine-after-price-fixing-scandal/..

Amico, Alissa. 2014. "Corporate Governance Enforcement in the Middle East and North Africa: Evidence and Priorities (No. 15)." OECD Publishing.

Andersson, Jan Joel, Tobias Evers, and Gunnar Sjöstedt. 2011. *Private Sector Actors & Peacebuilding: A Framework for Analysis*. Stockholm: Swedish Institute of International Affairs.

Andrews, Tony, Bernarda Elizalde, Philippe Le Billon, Chang Hoon Oh, David Reyes, and Ian Thomson. 2017. "The Rise in Conflict Associated with Mining Operations: What Lies Beneath?" *Canadian International Resources and Development Institute (CIRDI)*, Vancouver, Canada.

Angrist, Michele Penner. 2013. "Understanding the Success of Mass Civic Protest in Tunisia." *Middle East Journal* 67 (4):547–564.

Aoudi, Houssem. 2019. *Cogite*. Edited by Molly M. Melin. Tunis, Tunisia, January 28, 2019.

Arias, María Alejandra, Adriana Camacho, Ana María Ibáñez, Daniel Mejía, and Catherine Rodriguez. 2014. *Costos económicos y sociales del conflicto en Colombia¿ Cómo construir un posconflicto sostenible?*. Bogotá: Universidad de los Andes-Cede.

Assaad, Ragui, and Ghada Barsoum. 2019. "Public Employment in the Middle East and North Africa." *IZA World of Labor* 463. doi: 10.15185/izawol.463.

Atehortúa, Clara, Jorge Salcedo, and Roberto Vidal. 2013. "Internally Displaced outside of Camps and the Role of Local Authorities in Colombia: A Comparative Study of Bogotá DC and Cali." Brookings Institution.

Austin, Jonathan Luke, and Achim Wennmann. 2017. "Business Engagement in Violence Prevention and Peace-Building: The Case of Kenya." *Conflict, Security, and Development* 17 (6):451–472.

Avant, Deborah, and Virginia Haufler. 2018. "Public–Private Interactions and Practices of Security." In *The Oxford Handbook of International Security*, edited by Alexandra Gheciu and William Wohlforth, 350. Oxford: Oxford University Press.

Avina, Jeffrey. 2013. "The Evolution of Corporate Social Responsibility (CSR) in the Arab Spring." *Middle East Journal* 67 (1):77–92.

Ayeb, Habib, and Ray Bush. 2014. "Small Farmer Uprisings and Rural Neglect in Egypt and Tunisia." *Middle East Report* 272 (44). http://www.hlrn.org/img/documents/Ayeb-Bush_Small_Farmer_Uprisings.pdf.

Ayeb, Habib, and Ray Bush. 2019. *Food Insecurity and Revolution in the Middle East and North Africa: Agrarian Questions in Egypt and Tunisia*. New York: Anthem Press.

Aw, Bee Yan, Mark J. Roberts, and Tor Winston. 2007. "Export Market Participation, Investments in R&D and Worker Training, and the Evolution of Firm Productivity." *World Economy* 30 (1):83–104.

Azam, Jean-Paul. 1995. "How to Pay for the Peace? A Theoretical Framework with References to African Countries." *Public Choice* 83 (1):173–184.

Baghdadi, Salma. 2019. *BIAT Foundation*. Edited by Molly M. Melin. Tunis, Tunisia, February 1, 2019.

Bais, Karolien, and Mijnd Huijser. 2005. *The Profit of Peace: Corporate Responsibility in Conflict Regions*. Sheffield, UK: Greenleaf Publishing.

Ballentine, Karen, and Virginia Haufler. 2005. *Enabling Economies of Peace: Public Policy for Conflict-Sensitive Business*. New York: Global Compact.

Ballentine, Karen, and Heiko Nitzschke. 2004. "Business and Armed Conflict: An Assessment of Issues and Options." *Die Friedens-Warte* 79 (1/2): 35–56.

BanColombia, Grupo. 2015. "Annual Management and Corporate Responsibility Report 2015."

Banfield, Jessica, Canan Gündüz, and Nick Killick, eds. 2006. *Local Business Local Peace: The Peacebuilding Potential of the Domestic Private Sector*. London: International Alert.

Banfield, Jessica, Virginia Haufler, and Damien Lilly. 2005a. "Transnational Corporations in Conflict-Prone Zones: Public Policy Responses and a Framework for Action." *Oxford Development Studies* 33 (1):133–147.

Barkemeyer, Ralf, Philippe Givry, and Frank Figge. 2018. "Trends and Patterns in Sustainability-Related Media Coverage: A Classification of Issue-Level Attention." *Environment and Planning C: Politics and Space* 36 (5):937–962.

Baron, David P. 2001. "Private Politics, Corporate Social Responsibility, and Integrated Strategy." *Journal of Economics and Management Strategy* 10 (1):7–45.

Baron, David P. 2007. "Corporate Social Responsibility and Social Entrepreneurship." *Journal of Economics and Management Strategy* 16 (3):683–717.

Barro, Robert J. 1991. "A Cross-Country Study of Growth, Saving, and Government." In *National Saving and Economic Performance*, edited by B. Douglas Bernheim and John B. Shoven, 271–304. Chicago: University of Chicago Press.

Bausch, Andrew W. 2015. "Democracy, War Effort, and the Systemic Democratic Peace." *Journal of Peace Research* 52 (4):435–447.

Bauza, Vanessa. 2017. "In Colombia, High Hopes That Roads Will Boost Jobs, Incomes." *International Finance Group*. https://www.ifc.org/wps/wcm/connect/news_ext_content/ifc_external_corporate_site/news+and+events/news/colombia-roads-boosts-jobs-incomes.

Beardsley, K., and N. Lo. 2013. "Democratic Communities and Third-Party Conflict Management." *Conflict Management and Peace Science* 30 (1):76–93. doi: 10.1177/0738894212456954.

Beardsley, Kyle. 2006a. "Not All Mediators Are Created Equal: Choosing Who Mediates." Annual Meeting of the American Political Science Association, Washington, DC.

Beardsley, Kyle. 2006b. "Politics by Means Other Than War: Understanding International Mediation." Political Science, University of California, San Diego.

Beardsley, Kyle. 2010. "Pain, Pressure, and Political Cover: Explaining Mediation Incidence." *Journal of Peace Research* 47 (4):1–12.

Beardsley, Kyle. 2011. *The Mediation Dilemma*. Ithaca, NY: Cornell University Press.

Beardsley, Kyle, David E. Cunningham, and Peter B. White. 2018. "Mediation, Peacekeeping, and the Severity of Civil War." *Journal of Conflict Resolution* 63 (7):1682–1709. doi: 0022002718817092.

Beardsley, Kyle, David M. Quinn, Bidisha Biswas, and Jonathan Wilkenfeld. 2006. "Mediation Style and Crisis Outcomes." *Journal of Conflict Resolution* 50 (1):58–86.

Bebbington, Anthony, and Jeffrey Bury. 2013. *Subterranean Struggles: New Dynamics of Mining, Oil, and Gas in Latin America*. Vol. 8. Austin: University of Texas Press.

Beittel, June S. 2015. *Peace Talks in Colombia*. Washington, DC: Library of Congress, Congressional Research Service.

Bell, Amy, and Andres Schipani. 2015. "Colombia Prioritises Infrastructure Plans: Roads, Bridges and Tunnels Are Top Priorities." *Financial Times*. https://www.ft.com/content/39e07b96-4b3d-11e5-b558-8a9722977189.

Bennett, Juliette. 2002. "Public Private Partnerships: The Role of the Private Sector in Preventing Funding Conflict." *Vanderbilt Journal of Transnational Law* 35:711.

Benoit, David. 2019. "Move over, Shareholders: Top CEOs Say Companies Have Obligations to Society." *Wallstreet Journal*, Markets. https://www.wsj.com/articles/business-roundtable-steps-back-from-milton-friedman-theory-11566205200.

Bercovitch, Jacob. 1997. "Mediation in International Conflict: An Overview of Theory, a Review of Practice." In *Peacemaking in International Conflict: Methods and Techniques*, edited by William Zartman and J. Lewis Rasmussen, 163–194. Washington, DC: United States Institute of Peace Press.

Bercovitch, Jacob. 1998. "The Study of International Mediation: Empirical Research and the State of the Art." The Conference on Civilian Conflict Resolution, Castle Hunnigen.

Bercovitch, Jacob. 1999. The International Conflict Management Dataset: Official Codebook for the International Conflict Management Dataset.

Bercovitch, Jacob, and Allison Houston. 1996. "The Study of International Mediation." In *Resolving International Conflicts*, edited by Jacob Bercovitch, 11–35. Boulder, CO: Lynne Rienner Publishers.

Berliner, Daniel, and Aseem Prakash. 2012. "From Norms to Programs: The United Nations Global Compact and Global Governance." *Regulation and Governance* 6 (2):149–166.

Blainey, Geoffrey. 1973. *The Causes of War*. London: Macmillan.

Blasco, José Luis, and Adrian King. 2017. "KPMG Survey of Corporate Responsibility Reporting 2017." KPMG International Cooperative.

Board, Editorial. 2016. "Colombia's Revised Peace Accord." *New York Times*. https://www.nytimes.com/2016/11/15/opinion/colombias-revised-peace-accord.html.

Bond, Carol. 2018. *Business and Peace-Building: The Role of Natural Resources Companies*. London: Routledge.

Bonini, Sheila, Timothy M. Koller, and Philip H. Mirvis. 2009. "Valuing Social Responsibility Programs." *McKinsey on Finance* 32 (Summer):11–18.

Boudon, Lawrence. 1996. "Guerrillas and the State: The Role of the State in the Colombian Peace Process." *Journal of Latin American Studies* 28 (2):279–297.

Boudreaux, Karol C. 2008. "Economic Liberalization in Rwanda's Coffee Sector: A Better Brew for Success." In *Yes Africa Can*, edited by Pum Chuhan-Pole and Manka Angwafo, 185–199. Washington, DC: World Bank.

Boukhars, Anouar. 2015. *The Reckoning: Tunisia's Perilous Path to Democratic Stability*. Vol. 2. Washington, DC: Carnegie Endowment for International Peace.

Bouslah, Kais. 2015. "Responsible Investment in Tunisia." In *The Routledge Handbook of Responsible Investment*, edited by James P. Hawley Tessa Hebb, Andreas G. F. Hoepner, Agnes L. Neher, and David Wood, 125–137. Sheffeld: Routledge.

Boutros-Ghali, Boutros. 1992. "An Agenda for Peace: Preventive Diplomacy, Peacemaking, and Peacekeeping." *International Relations* 11 (3):201–218.

Bouvier, Virginia Marie. 2009. *Colombia: Building Peace in a Time of War*. Washington, DC: US Institute of Peace Press.

Bowen, Jeremy. 2013. *The Arab Uprisings: The People Want the Fall of the Regime*. New York: Simon and Schuster.

Brahimi, Lakhdar. 2000.*Report of the Panel on United Nations Peace Operations*. New York: United Nations.

Braithwaite, John, and Toni Makkai. 1991. "Testing an Expected Utility Model of Corporate Deterrence." *Law and Society Review* 25 (1):7–40.

Brown, Abby. 1987. "Is Ethics Good Business?" *Personnel Administrator* 32 (2):67–74.

Brück, Tilman. 1997. "Macroeconomic Effects of the War in Mozambique." Queen Elizabeth House Working Paper 11.

Bryan, Dominic. 2019. Professor, School of History, Anthropology, Philosophy and Politics. Edited by Molly M. Melin. Belfast: Queens University, June 21, 2019.

Buhaug, Halvard, Kristian Skrede Gleditsch, Helge Holtermann, Gudrun Østby, and Andreas Forø Tollefsen. 2011. "It's the Local Economy, Stupid! Geographic Wealth Dispersion and Conflict Outbreak Location." *Journal of Conflict Resolution* 55 (5):814–840.

Butterworth, Robert. 1978. "Do Conflict Managers Matter? An Empirical Assessment of Interstate Security Disputes and Resolution Efforts, 1945–1974." *International Studies Quarterly* 22 (2):195–214.

Camacho, Adriana, and Catherine Rodriguez. 2013. "Firm Exit and Armed Conflict in Colombia." *Journal of Conflict Resolution* 57 (1):89–116.

Carothers, Thomas. 2018. "Tunisia in Transition: A Comparative View." In *Project on Middle East Democracy*, edited by Amy Hawthorne. Carnegie Endowment for International Peace. https://carnegieendowment.org/2018/05/30/tunisia-in-transition-comparative-view-pub-76501.

CBI, The. 2003. NI 2003. Confederation of Business Industry.

Cederman, Lars-Erik, Kristian Skrede Gleditsch, and Halvard Buhaug. 2013. *Inequality, Grievances, and Civil War*. Cambridge: Cambridge University Press.

Cederman, Lars-Erik, Simon Hug, and Lutz F. Krebs. 2010. "Democratization and Civil War: Empirical Evidence." *Journal of Peace Research* 47 (4):377–394.

Ch, Rafael, Jacob Shapiro, Abbey Steele, and Juan F. Vargas. 2018. "Endogenous Taxation in Ongoing Internal Conflict: The Case of Colombia." *American Political Science Review* 112 (4):996–1015.

Chakravarthy, Jivas, Ed DeHaan, and Shivaram Rajgopal. 2014. "Reputation Repair after a Serious Restatement." *The Accounting Review* 89 (4):1329–1363.

Chebbi, Nejib. 2019. Tunisian Opposition Party Leader; Democratic Progressive Party Founder. Edited by Molly M. Melin. Tunis, Tunisia, January 29, 2019.

Chen, Al Y. S., Roby B. Sawyers, and Paul F. Williams. 1997. "Reinforcing Ethical Decision Making through Corporate Culture." *Journal of Business Ethics* 16 (8):855–865. doi: 10.1023/a:1017953517947.

Clark, Gordon L., Andreas Feiner, and Michael Viehs. 2015. "From the Stockholder to the Stakeholder: How Sustainability Can Drive Financial Outperformance." Available at SSRN 2508281.

Clayton, Govinda, and Han Dorussen. 2021. "The Effectiveness of Mediation and Peacekeeping for Ending Conflict." *Journal of Peace Research*. doi: 0022343321990076. https://www.research-collection.ethz.ch/bitstream/handle/20.500.11850/487973/1/0022343321990076.pdf.

Cochrane, Feargal. 2007. "Irish-America, the End of the IRA's Armed Struggle and the Utility of Soft Power." *Journal of Peace Research* 44 (2):215–231.

Collier, Paul. 1999. "On the Economic Consequences of Civil War." *Oxford Economic Papers* 51 (1):168–183.

Collier, Paul. 2007. "Bottom Billion." *The Blackwell Encyclopedia of Sociology* (23): 1–3.

Collier, Paul, Lani Elliott, Håvard Hegre, Anke Hoeffler, Marta Reynal-Querol, and Nicholas Sambanis. 2003. *Breaking the Conflict Trap: Civil War and Development Policy*. Oxford, UK: World Bank and Oxford University Press.

Collier, Paul, and Anke Hoeffler. 1998. "On Economic Causes of Civil War." *Oxford Economic Papers* 50 (4):563–573.

Collier, Paul, and Anke Hoeffler. 2000. "Greed and Grievance in Civil War." World Bank Policy Research Working Paper 2355. *World Bank*. http://www.worldbank.org/research/PDF.

Collier, Paul, and Anke Hoeffler. 2002. "The Political Economy of Secession." *Development Research Group, World Bank* 23. Washington, DC.

Collier, Paul, and Anke Hoeffler. 2004. "Greed and Grievance in Civil War." *Oxford Economic Papers* 56 (4):563–595.

Collier, Paul, Anke Hoeffler, and Måns Söderbom. 2004. "On the Duration of Civil War." *Journal of Peace Research* 41 (3):253–273.

Collier, Paul, and Nicholas Sambanis. 2002. "Understanding Civil War: A New Agenda." *Journal of Conflict Resolution* 46 (1):3–12.

Coogan, Tim Pat. 1993. *The IRA: A History*. London: Palgrave Macmillan.

Cox, Michael, Adrian Guelke, and Fiona Stephen. 2006. *A Farewell to Arms? Beyond the Good Friday Agreement*. Manchester, UK: Manchester University Press.

Crèmer, Jacques. 1993. "Corporate Culture and Shared Knowledge." *Industrial and Corporate Change* 2 (3):351–386. doi: 10.1093/icc/2.3.351.

Cuéllar, Alfonso. 2016. "Oil and Peace in Colombia: Industry Challenges in the Post-War Period." https://www.wilsoncenter.org/publication/oil-and-peace-colombia-industry-challenges-the-post-war-period.

Cunningham, David. 2006. "Veto Players and Civil War Duration." *American Journal of Political Science* 50 (4):875–892.

Cunningham, David E. 2010. "Blocking Resolution: How External States Can Prolong Civil Wars." *Journal of Peace Research* 47 (2):115–127.

Cunningham, David E., Kristian Skrede Gleditsch, and Idean Salehyan. 2009. "It Takes Two: A Dyadic Analysis of Civil War Duration and Outcome." *Journal of Conflict Resolution* 53 (4):570–597.

Dashwood, Hevina S. 2012. *The Rise of Global Corporate Social Responsibility: Mining and the Spread of Global Norms*. Cambridge: Cambridge University Press.

Davies, Norman. 1996. *Europe: A History*. New York: Oxford University Press.

Davis, Keith. 1973. "The Case for and against Business Assumption of Social Responsibilities." *Academy of Management Journal* 16 (2):312–322.

Davis, Peter. 2012. *Corporations, Global Governance and Post-Conflict Reconstruction*. London: Routledge.

De Mesquita, Bruce Bueno. 1988. "The Contribution of Expected Utility Theory to the Study of International Conflict." *Journal of Interdisciplinary History* 18 (4):629–652.

De Soysa, Indra. 2002. "Paradise Is a Bazaar? Greed, Creed, and Governance in Civil War, 1989–99." *Journal of Peace Research* 39 (4):395–416.

De Soysa, Indra, and Eric Neumayer. 2007. "Resource Wealth and the Risk of Civil War Onset: Results from a New Dataset of Natural Resource Rents, 1970–1999." *Conflict Management and Peace Science* 24 (3):201–218. doi: 10.1080/07388940701468468.

Dealbook. 2020. "Greed Is Good. Except When It's Bad." *New York Times*, September 13, 2020, Business & Policy.

Decker, Wayne H. 2012. "A Firm's Image Following Alleged Wrongdoing: Effects of the Firm's Prior Reputation and Response to the Allegation." *Corporate Reputation Review* 15 (1):20–34.

Dedeke, Nick. 2019. "Is Corporate Vigilantism a Threat to Democracy?" In *Commentary*: Real Clear Politics. May 4, 2019. https://www.realclearpolitics.com/articles/2019/05/04/is_corporate_vigilantism_a_threat_to_democracy_140218.html.

Deitelhoff, Nicole. 2009. "The Business of Security and the Transformation of the State." *TranState Working Papers* 87. Universität Bremen.

Deitelhoff, Nicole, Moira Feil, Susanne Fischer, Andreas Haidvogl, Klaus Dieter Wolf, and Melanie Zimmer. 2010. "Business in Zones of Conflict and Global Security Governance: What Has Been Learnt and Where to from Here?" In *Corporate Security Responsibility?*, 202–226. New York: Springer.

Deitelhoff, Nicole, and Klaus Dieter Wolf. 2010. *Corporate Security Responsibility? Corporate Governance Contributions to Peace and Security in Zones of Conflict, Global Issues.* New York, NY: Palgrave Macmillan.

Democratic Progress Institute, The. 2017. *Peace and the Economy: The Role of Business and the Private Sector in Peace Processes.* Dublin, Belfast, Dundalk: Democratic Progress Institute.

DeRouen, Karl, Jr., Mark J. Ferguson, Samuel Norton, Young Hwan Park, Jenna Lea, and Ashley Streat-Bartlett. 2010. "Civil War Peace Agreement Implementation and State Capacity." *Journal of Peace Research* 47 (3):333–346.

DeRouen, Karl R., Jr., and David Sobek. 2004. "The Dynamics of Civil War Duration and Outcome." *Journal of Peace Research* 41 (3):303–320.

Deshpande, Rohit, and John U. Farley. 1999. "Corporate Culture and Market Orientation: Comparing Indian and Japanese Firms." *Journal of International Marketing* 7 (4): 111–127.

Deutsch, M. 1973. *The Resolution of Conflict.* New Haven, CT: Yale University Press.

Diamond, Larry, and Marc F Plattner. 2014. *Democratization and Authoritarianism in the Arab World.* Baltimore: Johns Hopkins University Press.

Dillinger, Jessica. 2017. "Most Expensive Terrorist Attacks in the World." *WorldAtlas*, April 25, 2017.

Dixon, William J. 1996. "Third-Party Techniques for Preventing Conflict Escalation and Promoting Peaceful Settlement." *International Organization* 50 (4):653–681.

Doyle, Michael W., and Nicholas Sambanis. 2000. "International Peacebuilding: A Theoretical and Quantitative Analysis." *American Political Science Review* 94 (4):779–801.

Drake, Charles J. M. 1991. "The Provisional IRA: A Case Study." *Terrorism and Political Violence* 3 (2):43–60.

Dunning, Thad. 2005. "Resource Dependence, Economic Performance, and Political Stability." *Journal of Conflict Resolution* 49 (4):451–482.

Dunning, Thad, and Leslie Wirpsa. 2004. "Oil and the Political Economy of Conflict in Colombia and Beyond: A Linkages Approach." *Geopolitics* 9 (1):81–108.

Econometrics, Cambridge. 2000. "The Northern Ireland Economic Research Centre (1990)." *Regional Economic Prospects: Analysis and Forecasts to the Year.*

Ecopetrol. 2009. "Sustainability Report." https://www.unglobalcompact.org/system/attachments/8851/original/Ecopetrol_-_Sustainability_Report_2009.pdf?1292961088.

Eisenstadt, Todd A., A. Carl LeVan, and Tofigh Maboudi. 2015. "When Talk Trumps Text: The Democratizing Effects of Deliberation during Constitution-Making, 1974–2011." *American Political Science Review* 109 (3):592–612.

Eisenstadt, Todd A., A. Carl LeVan, and Tofigh Maboudi. 2017. *Constituents before Assembly: Participation, Deliberation, and Representation in the Crafting of New Constitutions.* Cambridge: Cambridge University Press.

Elliott, John H. 2006. *Empires of the Atlantic World: Britain and Spain in America 1492–1830.* New Haven, CT: Yale University Press.

Eskandarpour, Azar, and Achim Wennmann. 2011. "Strengthening Preventative Diplomacy: The Role of Private Actors." Strengthening International Support for Conflict Prevention, Geneva.

Fassihian, Dokhi. 2018. *Democratic Backsliding in Tunisia: The Case for Renewed International Attention*. Washington, DC: Freedom House.

Favretto, Katja. 2005. "Bargaining in the Shadow of War: Bias and Coercion in U.S. mediation, 1945–1990." Annual Meeting of the American Political Science Association, Washington DC.

Favretto, Katja. 2009. "Should Peacemakers Take Sides? Major Power Mediation, Coercion and Bias." *American Political Science Review* 103 (2):248–263. doi: 10.1017/S0003055409090236.

Fearon, James D., and David D. Laitin. 2003. "Ethnicity, Insurgency, and Civil War." *American Journal of Political Science* 97 (1):75–90.

Fearon, James D. 1995. "Rationalist Explanations for War." *International Organization* 49 (3):379–414.

Feng, Yi. 2001. "Political Freedom, Political Instability, and Policy Uncertainty: A Study of Political Institutions and Private Investment in Developing Countries." *International Studies Quarterly* 45 (2):271–294.

Fielding, David. 2003. "Investment, Employment, and Political Conflict in Northern Ireland." *Oxford Economic Papers* 55 (3):512–535.

Fink, Larry. 2019. "Larry Fink's 2019 Letter to CEOs: Purpose & Profit." Blackrock. Accessed July 24, 2018. https://www.blackrock.com/corporate/investor-relations/larry-fink-ceo-letter.

Fjelde, Hanne, and Indra De Soysa. 2009. "Coercion, Co-Optation, or Cooperation? State Capacity and the Risk of Civil War, 1961–2004." *Conflict Management and Peace Science* 26 (1):5–25.

Flannery, Nathaniel Parish. 2017. "Will Peace Talks Really Help Colombia's Economy?" *Forbes*. https://www.forbes.com/sites/nathanielparishflannery/2017/09/25/will-peace-talks-really-help-colombias-economy/?sh=3d5a239b6904.

Ford, Jolyon. 2015. *Regulating Business for Peace: The United Nations, the Private Sector, and Post-Conflict Recovery*. Cambridge: Cambridge University Press.

Forrer, John, Timothy Fort, and Raymond Gilpin. 2012. *How Business Can Foster Peace*. Washington, DC: United States Institute of Peace.

Forrer, John, and Conor Seyle. 2016. *The Role of Business in the Responsibility to Protect*. Cambridge, MA: Cambridge University Press.

Fort, Timothy. 2007. *Business, Integrity, and Peace: Beyond Geopolitical and Disciplinary Boundaries (Business, Value Creation, and Society)*. Cambridge, MA: Cambridge University Press.

Fort, Timothy L. 2008. *Prophets, Profits, and Peace: The Positive Role of Business in Promoting Religious Tolerance*. New Haven, CT: Yale University Press.

Fort, Timothy L. 2009. "Peace through Commerce: A Multisectoral Approach." *Journal of Business Ethics* 89:347–350.

Fort, Timothy. 2015. *Diplomat in the Corner Office: How Business Contributes to Peace*. Palo Alto, CA: Stanford University Press.

Fort, Timothy L., and Cindy A. Schipani. 2004. *The Role of Business in Fostering Peaceful Societies*. Cambridge: Cambridge University Press.

Fortna, Virginia Page. 2004. *Peace Time: Ceasefire Agreements and the Durability of Peace*. Princeton, NJ: Princeton University Press.

Frazier, Derrick, and William J. Dixon. 2006. "Third-Party Intermediaries and Negotiated Settlements, 1946–2000." *International Interactions* 32 (4):385–408.

Freeman, R. Edward. 2010. *Strategic Management: A Stakeholder Approach*. Cambridge: Cambridge University Press.

Freeman, R. Edward, and John McVea. 2001. "A Stakeholder Approach to Strategic Management." In *The Blackwell Handbook of Strategic Management*, edited by Henry W. Lane, Martha L. Maznevski, Mark E. Mendenhall, and Jeanne McNett, 189–207. New York: John Wiley & Sons.

Friedman, Milton. 1970. "A Friedman Doctrine: The Social Responsibility of Business Is to Increase Its Profits." *New York Times Magazine* 13 (1970):32–33.

Gaibulloev, Khusrav, Justin George, Todd Sandler, and Hirofumi Shimizu. 2015. "Personnel Contributions to UN and non-UN Peacekeeping Missions." *Journal of Peace Research* 52 (6):727–742. doi: 10.1177/0022343315579245.

Gall, Carlotta. 2016. "Tunisia Seeks Foreign Investment to Cement Democratic Gains." *New York Times*, November 30, 2016, Africa. https://www.nytimes.com/2016/11/30/world/africa/tunisia-investment-arab-spring.html.

Galvis, Miguel. 2016. "Colombia: Refinery Fraud Tops $4 Billion." *Latin Correspondent*. http://latincorrespondent.com/2016/02/colombia-refinery-fraud-tops-4-billion.

Ganson, Brian. 2011. "Business and Conflict Prevention: Towards a Framework for Action." Strengthening International Support for Conflict Prevention, Geneva.

Gartner, Scott Sigmund. 2011. "Signs of Trouble: Regional Organization Mediation and Civil War Agreement Durability." *Journal of Politics* 73 (2):380–390. doi: 10.1017/S0022381611000090.

Gartner, Scott Sigmund, and Jacob Bercovitch. 2006. "Overcoming Obstacles to Peace: The Contribution of Mediation to Short-Lived Conflict Settlements." *International Studies Quarterly* 50 (4):819–840.

Gartner, Scott Sigmund, and Randolph M. Siverson. 1996. "War Expansion and War Outcome." *Journal of Conflict Resolution* 40 (1):4–15.

Gartzke, Erik, and Quan Li. 2003. "War, Peace, and the Invisible Hand: Positive Political Externalities of Economic Globalization." *International Studies Quarterly* 47 (4):561–586.

Gartzke, Erik, Quan Li, and Charles Boehmer. 2001. "Investing in the Peace: Economic Interdependence and International Conflict." *International Organization* 55 (2):391–438.

Gaviria, Alejandro. 2002. "Assessing the Effects of Corruption and Crime on Firm Performance: Evidence from Latin America." *Emerging Markets Review* 3 (3):245–268.

Gehlbach, Scott, and Edmund J. Malesky. 2010. "The Contribution of Veto Players to Economic Reform." *Journal of Politics* 72 (4):957–975.

Gent, Stephen. 2003. "Instability, Intervention, and Inter-Power Politics." Empirical Implication of Theoretical Models Summer Institute, Ann Arbor, Michigan.

Gerring, John, and Rose McDermott. 2007. "An Experimental Template for Case Study Research." *American Journal of Political Science* 51 (3):688–701.

Getz, Kathleen A. 1990. "International Codes of Conduct: An Analysis of Ethical Reasoning." *Journal of Business Ethics* 9 (7):567–577.

Getz, Kathleen A., and Jennifer Oetzel. 2009. "MNE Strategic Intervention in Violent Conflict: Variations Based on Conflict Characteristics." *Journal of Business Ethics* 89 (4):375–386. doi: 10.1007/s10551-010-0412-6.

Gherib, Jouhaina. 2014. "Influences on Commitment of Companies in Sustainable Development: Empirical Evidence from Tunisia." *East-West Journal of Economics and Business* 17 (1):85–106.

Gilardi, Fabrizio. 2012. "Transnational Diffusion: Norms, Ideas, and Policies." *Handbook of International Relations* 2:453–477.

Gleditsch, Kristian Skrede. 2002. "Expanded Trade and GDP Data." *Journal of Conflict Resolution* 46 (5):712–724.

Gleditsch, Nils Petter, Peter Wallensteen, Mikael Eriksson, Margareta Sollenberg, and Håvard Strand. 2002. "Armed Conflict 1946–2001: A New Dataset." *Journal of Peace Research* 39 (5):615–637.

Golan, Guy J. 2008. "Where in the World Is Africa? Predicting Coverage of Africa by US Television Networks." *International Communication Gazette* 70 (1):41–57.

Greig, J. Michael. 2005. "Stepping into the Fray: When Do Mediators Mediate?" *American Journal of Political Science* 49 (2):249–266.

Greig, J. Michael, Andrew P. Owsiak, and Paul F. Diehl. 2019. *International Conflict Management*. New York: Polity Press.

Greig, J. Michael, and Patrick Regan. 2008. "When Do They Say Yes? An Analysis of the Willingness to Offer and Accept Mediation in Civil Wars." *International Studies Quarterly* 52 (4):759–781.

Grossman, Herschel I. 1992. "Foreign Aid and Insurrection." *Defence and Peace Economics* 3 (4):275–288.

Guáqueta, Alexandra. 2006. "Case Study Colombia." In *Local Business, Local Peace: The Peacebuilding Potential of the Domestic Private Sector*. London: International Alert.

Guáqueta, Alexandra. 2013. "Harnessing Corporations: Lessons from the Voluntary Principles on Security and Human Rights in Colombia and Indonesia." *Journal of Asian Public Policy* 6 (2):129–146.

Guáqueta, Alexandra, and Yadaira Orsini. 2007. *Business and Reintegration: Cases, Experiences and Lesson*. Bogotá: Fundación Ideas para la Paz.

Gudgin, Graham. 2019. "Discrimination in Housing and Employment under the Stormont Administration." In *The Northern Ireland Question*, edited by Patrick John Roche and Brian Barton, 97–121. London: Routledge.

Gudgin, Graham, and Stephen Roper. 1990. *The Northern Ireland Economy: Review and forecasts to 1995*: NIERC (Northern Ireland Economic Research Centre).

Guelke, Adrian. 1996. "The United States, Irish Americans and the Northern Ireland Peace Process." *International Affairs* 72 (3):521–536.

Gurr, Ted Robert. 2015. *Why Men Rebel*. London: Routledge.

Halliday, Colin. 2019. "Resurgam Trust." Belfast, June 21, 2019.

Handley, Antoinette. 2019. *Business and Social Crisis in Africa*: Cambridge University Press.

Hanieh, Adam. 2015. "Shifting Priorities or Business as Usual? Continuity and Change in the post-2011 IMF and World Bank Engagement with Tunisia, Morocco and Egypt." *British Journal of Middle Eastern Studies* 42 (1):119–134.

Hansen, Holley, Sara McLaughlin Mitchell, and Stephen Nemeth. 2008. "IO Mediation of Interstate Conflicts: Moving Beyond the Global vs. Regional Dichotomy." *Journal of Conflict Resolution* 51 (4):721–737.

Hanson, Stephanie. 2009. "FARC, ELN: Colombia's Left-Wing Guerrillas." www.cfr.org.

Harding, Kieran. 2020. "Business in the Community Director." In *Business in the Community*, edited by Molly M. Melin. Belfast, January 8, 2020.

Harrelson-Stephens, Julie, and Rhonda Callaway. 2003. "Does Trade Openness Promote Security Rights in Developing Countries? Examining the Liberal Perspective." *International Interactions* 29 (2):143–158.

Haufler, Virginia. 1997. *Dangerous Commerce: State and Market in the International Risks Insurance Regime.* Ithaca: Cornell University Press.

Haufler, Virginia. 2001a. "Is There a Role for Business in Conflict Management?" In *Turbulent Peace: The Challenges of Managing International Conflict,* edited by Chester A. Crocker, Fen O. Hampson, Pamela R. Aall, and Pamela Aall, 659–675. Washington, DC: United States Institute of Peace Press.

Haufler, Virginia. 2001b. *A Public Role for the Private Sector: Industry Self-Regulation in a Global Economy.* Washington, DC: The Brookings Institution Press.

Haufler, Virginia. 2004. "International Diplomacy and the Privatization of Conflict Prevention." *International Studies Perspectives* 5 (2):158–163. doi: 10.1111/j.1528-3577.2004.00166.x.

Haufler, Virginia. 2005. "Foreign Investors in Conflict Zones: New Expectations." In *Guns and Butter: The Political Economy of International Security.* Boulder, CO: Lynne Rienner. https://www.researchgate.net/profile/Virginia-Haufler-2/publication/266495882_ FOREIGN_INVESTORS_IN_CONFLICT_ZONES_NEW_EXPECTATIONS/links/ 5554b8ae08aeaaff3bf45223/FOREIGN-INVESTORS-IN-CONFLICT-ZONES-NEW-EXPECTATIONS.pdf.

Haufler, Virginia. 2010a. "Disclosure as Governance: The Extractive Industries Transparency Initiative and Resource Management in the Developing World." *Global Environmental Politics* 10 (3):53–73. doi: 10.1162/GLEP_a_00014.

Haufler, Virginia. 2010b. "Governing Corporations in Zones of Conflict: Issues, Actors and Institutions." In *Who Governs the Globe?,* edited by Deborah D. Avant, Martha Finnemore, and Susan K. Sell, 102–130. Cambridge: Cambridge University Press.

Hauge, Wenche. 2010. "When Peace Prevails: The Management of Political Crisis in Ecuador, Madagascar, Tunisia, and Venezuela." *Alternatives* 35 (4):469–493.

Hearnden, Keith, and Alec Moore. 1999. *The Handbook of Business Security: A Practical Guide to Managing Security Risks.* London: Kogan Page Publishers.

Hegre, Håvard. 2004. "The Duration and Termination of Civil War." *Journal of Peace Research* 41 (3):243–252.

Hegre, Håvard, and Håvard Mokleiv Nygård. 2015. "Governance and Conflict Relapse." *Journal of Conflict Resolution* 59 (6):984–1016.

Hegre, Håvard, Tanja Ellingsen, Scott Gates, and Nils Petter Gleditsch. 2001. "Towards a Democratic Civil Peace? Democracy, Political Change, and Civil war, 1816–1992." *American Political Science Review* 95 (1):33–48.

Heldt, Birger, and Mats Hammarström. 2002. "The Diffusion of Military Intervention: Testing a Network Position Approach." *International Interactions* 28 (4):355–377.

Henke, Marina E. 2016. "Great Powers and UN Force Generation: A Case Study of UNAMID." *International Peacekeeping* 23 (3):468–492.

Hinds, Róisín. 2014. "Conflict Analysis of Tunisia." GSDRC.

Hirshleifer, Jack. 1995. "Theorizing about Conflict." *Handbook of Defense Economics* 1:165–189.

Hirshleifer, Jack. 2001. *The Dark Side of the Force: Economic Foundations of Conflict Theory.* Cambridge: Cambridge University Press.

Hönke, Jana. 2013. *Transnational Companies and Security Governance: Hybrid Practices in a Postcolonial World*. London: Routledge.

Hoskisson, Robert E., Lorraine Eden, Chung Ming Lau, and Mike Wright. 2000. "Strategy in Emerging Economies." *Academy of Management Journal* 43 (3):249–267.

Houry, Yehia. 2019. *Flat 6 Labs*. Edited by Molly M. Melin. Tunis, Tunisia, January 31, 2019.

Hufbauer, G. C., and Jeffrey J. Schott. 1983. *Economic Sanctions in Support of Foreign Policy Goals*. Washington, DC: Institute for International Economics.

Huisken, Ron. 1982. *Armaments and Development, Militarization and Arms Production*. New York: St. Martin's.

Hultman, Lisa, Jacob Kathman, and Megan Shannon. 2013. "United Nations Peacekeeping and Civilian Protection in Civil War." *American Journal of Political Science* 57 (4):875–891.

Hutchison, Marc L., and Kristin Johnson. 2011. "Capacity to Trust? Institutional Capacity, Conflict, and Political Trust in Africa, 2000–2005." *Journal of Peace Research* 48 (6):737–752.

Ibáñez, Ana M., and Christian Jaramillo. 2006. "Oportunidades de desarrollo económico en el posconflicto: propuesta de política." *Coyuntura Económica* 36 (2):93–127.

Iff, Andrea, and Rina M. Alluri. 2016. "Business Actors in Peace Mediation Processes." *Business and Society Review* 121 (2):187–215.

Iff, Andrea, Damiano Sguaitamatti, Rina M. Alluri, and Daniela Kohler. 2010. "Money Makers as Peace Makers? Business Actors in Mediation Processes."

Institute for Economics and Peace, The. 2017. Global Peace Index.

International Alert. 2005. *Peace through Profit: Sri Lankan Perspectives on Corporate Social Responsibility*. London: International Alert. https://www.international-alert.org/sites/default/files/SriLanka_PerspectivesOnCSR_EN_2005.pdf.

International Finance Corporation, The. 2017. "Banking on Women in Tunisia." World Bank Group.

Jackson, Brian A. 2005. "Provisional Irish Republican Army." In *Aptitude for Destruction, Volume 2: Case Studies of Organizational Learning in Five Terrorist Groups*, edited by Brian A. Jackson, John C. Baker, Kim Cragin, John Parachini, Horacio R. Trujillo, and Peter Chalk, 93–140. Los Angeles: RAND Corporation.

Jackson, Ira A., and Jane Nelson. 2004. *Profits with Principles: Seven Strategies for Delivering Value with Values*. New York: Broadway Business.

Jakobsen, Tor Georg, Indra De Soysa, and Jo Jakobsen. 2013. "Why Do Poor Countries Suffer Costly Conflict? Unpacking Per Capita Income and the Onset of Civil War." *Conflict Management and Peace Science* 30 (2):140–160. doi: 10.1177/0738894212473923.

Jarstad, Anna K., and Timothy D. Sisk. 2008. *From War to Democracy: Dilemmas of Peacebuilding*. Cambridge: Cambridge University Press.

Jimenez, Nicolas. 2017. "The Colombian Peace Process: Challenges to Implementation and the Role of Business in the Post-Conflict." *The MacMillan Center News*. https://macmillan.yale.edu/news/colombian-peace-process-challenges-implementation-and-role-business-post-conflict.

Johnson, Adrian. 2019. The International Fund for Ireland. Edited by Molly M. Melin. Derry, June 23, 2019.

Johnston, Kevin. 2008. *In the Shadows of Giants*. Dublin: Gill & Macmillan.

Joras, Ulrike. 2007. "The Role of the Private Business Sector in Peace Negotiations: Lessons from Guatemala." *Sicherheit und Frieden (S+ F)/Security and Peace* 25 (4):177–183.

Jrad, Abdesslem. 2019. UGTT. Edited by Molly M. Melin. Tunis, Tunisia, February 1, 2019.

Kaplan, Oliver, and Enzo Nussio. 2018. "Explaining Recidivism of Ex-Combatants in Colombia." *Journal of Conflict Resolution* 62 (1):64–93.

Karray, Bassem. 2019. "Proposals, Intermediation, and Pressure: The Three Roles of the UGTT in Tunisia's Post-Revolutionary Constitutional Process." In *Socioeconomic Protests in MENA and Latin America*, edited by Irene Weipert-Fenner and Jonas Wolff, 123–144. London: Palgrave.

Kathman, Jacob, and Megan Shannon. 2011. "Oil Extraction and the Potential for Domestic Instability in Uganda." *African Studies Quarterly* 12 (3):23–45.

Kechiche, Amina, and Richard Soparnot. 2012. "CSR within SMEs: Literature Review." *International Business Research* 5 (7):97.

Keethaponcalan, S. I. 2001. "Mediation Dilemmas: Resolving the Ethnic Conflict in Sri Lanka." *Pakistan Horizon* 54 (2):79–98.

Kell, Georg. 2018. "The Future of Corporate Responsibility." *Forbes.* Accessed July 24, 2019. https://www.forbes.com/sites/georgkell/2018/06/18/the-future-of-corporate-responsibility/?sh=56a1f8fb6105.

Kim, Dong-Hun, and Peter F. Trumbore. 2010. "Transnational Mergers and Acquisitions: THE impact of FDI on Human Rights, 1981–2006." *Journal of Peace Research* 47 (6):723–734.

Kindleberger, Charles P. 1969. "American Business Abroad." *The International Executive* 11 (2):11–12. doi: 10.1002/tie.5060110207.

King, Charles. 2001. "The Benefit of Ethnic War: Understanding Eurasia's Unrecognized States." *World Politics* 53 (4):524–552.

Klapper, Leora, Christine Richmond, and Trang Tran. 2013. *Civil Conflict and Firm Performance: Evidence from Cote d'Ivoire.* Washington, DC: The World Bank.

Klare, Michael. 2001. *Resource Wars: The New Landscape of Global Conflict.* Stugart: Macmillan.

Kleiboer, Marieke. 1996. "Understanding Success and Failure of International Mediation." *Journal of Conflict Resolution* 40 (2):360–389.

Knox, Colin, and Padraic Quirk. 2000. *Peacebuilding in Northern Ireland, Israel and South Africa.* New York: Springer.

Koenig-Archibugi, Mathias. 2004. "Transnational Corporations and Public Accountability." *Government and Opposition* 39 (2):234–259. doi: 10.1111/j.1477-7053.2004.00122.x.

Kolk, Ans, and François Lenfant. 2010. "MNC Reporting on CSR and Conflict in Central Africa." *Journal of Business Ethics* 93 (2):241–255.

Kolk, Ans, and François Lenfant. 2012. "Business–NGO Collaboration in a Conflict Setting: Partnership Activities in the Democratic Republic of Congo." *Business and Society* 51 (3):478–511. doi: 10.1177/0007650312446474.

Kolk, Ans, and François Lenfant. 2015. "Partnerships for Peace and Development in Fragile States: Identifying Missing Links." *Academy of Management Perspectives* 29 (4):422–437.

König, Thomas, George Tsebelis, and Marc Debus. 2010. *Reform Processes and Policy Change: Veto Players and Decision-Making in Modern Democracies.* Vol. 16. New York: Springer Science & Business Media.

Koubi, Vally. 2005. "War and Economic Performance." *Journal of Peace Research* 42 (1):67–82.

Kreutz, Joakim. 2010. "How and When Armed Conflicts End: Introducing the UCDP Conflict Termination Dataset." *Journal of Peace Research* 47 (2):243–250.

Kroc Institute for International Peace Studies. 2019. *Peace Accords Matrix*. South Bend: University of Notre Dame.

Kugler, Jacek, and Marina Arbetman, eds. 2018. *Political Capacity and Economic Behavior*. London: Routledge.

Kydd, Andrew H. 2006. "When Can Mediators Build Trust?" *American Political Science Review* 100 (3):449–462.

Le Billon, Philippe. 2001. "The Political Ecology of War: Natural Resources and Armed Conflicts." *Political Geography* 20 (5):561–584.

Leary, Jennifer C. 2007. "Talisman's Sudanese Oil Investment: The Historical Context Surrounding Its Entry, Departure, and Controversial Tenure." Duke University, Trinity College.

Lederach, John Paul. 1997. *Building Peace: Sustainable Reconciliation in Divided Societies*. Vol. 4. Washington, DC: United States Institute of Peace Press.

Lee-Jones, Krista. 2019. "Tunisia: An Overview of Corruption and Anti-Corruption." In *Anti-Corruption Help Desk Brief*. Berlin, Germany: Transparency International. https://knowledgehub.transparency.org/helpdesk/tunisia-overview-of-corruption-and-anti-corruption.

Li, Chien-pin. 1993. "The Effectiveness of Sanctions Linkages: Issues and Actors." *International Studies Quarterly* 37 (3):349–370.

Lieberfeld, Daniel. 1995. "Small Is Credible: Norway's Niche in International Dispute Settlement." *Negotiation Journal* 11 (3):201–207.

Lieberfeld, Daniel. 2002. "Evaluating the Contributions of Track-Two Diplomacy to Conflict Termination in South Africa, 1984–90." *Journal of Peace Research* 39 (3):355–372.

Lindgreen, Adam, José-Rodrigo Córdoba, François Maon, and José María Mendoza. 2010. "Corporate Social Responsibility in Colombia: Making Sense of Social Strategies." *Journal of Business Ethics* 91 (2):229–242.

Lindgren, Göran. 1984. "Review Essay: Armaments and Economic Performance in Industrialized Market Economies." *Journal of Peace Research* 21 (4):375–387.

Lujala, Paivi. 2009. "Deadly Combat over Natural Resources: Gems, Petroleum, Drugs, and the Severity of Armed Civil Conflict." *Journal of Conflict Resolution* 53 (1):50–71.

Lynn Dobbs, Kirstie, and Peter J. Schraeder. 2019. "Evolving Role of North African Civil Society Actors in the Foreign Policymaking Process: Youth, Women's, Labour and Human Rights Organisations." *Journal of North African Studies* 24 (4):661–681.

MacGinty, Roger. 1997. "American Influences on the Northern Ireland Peace Process." *Journal of Conflict Studies* 17 (2). https://journals.lib.unb.ca/index.php/JCS/article/download/11750/12522.

Mack, Raymond, and Richard Snyder. 1957. "An Analysis of Social Conflict: Toward an Overview and Synthesis." *Journal of Conflict Resolution* 1:212–248.

Maher, David, and Andrew Thomson. 2018. "A Precarious Peace? The Threat of Paramilitary Violence to the Peace Process in Colombia." *Third World Quarterly* 39 (11):1–32. doi: 10.1080/01436597.2018.1508992.

Malek, Chiheb. 2019. UTIC. Edited by Molly M. Melin. Tunis, Tunisia, January 28, 2019.

Management, Rotterdam School of. 2015. "Establishing a Fund for Connecting Rural People to a Natural Gas Network." Accessed January 11. https://www.rsm.nl/fileadmin/Images_NEW/Faculty_Research/Partnership_Resource_Centre/Cases/case_naturalgas_final.pdf.

Mandri-Perrott, Cledan. 2010. "Connecting Colombia's Poor to Natural Gas Services: Lessons Learned from a Completed Output-Based Aid Project." *OBApproaches*, World Bank 31.

Mansfield, Edward D., and Jack Snyder. 2009. "Pathways to War in Democratic Transitions." *International Organization* 63 (2):381–390.

Maoz, Zeev. 2004. "Conflict Management and Conflict Resolution—A Conceptual and Methodological Introduction." In *Multiple Paths to Knowledge in International Politics: Methodology in the Study of Conflict Management and Conflict Resolution*, edited by Zeev Maoz, Alex Mintz, Clifton T. Morgan, and Glenn Palmer. Lexington, MA: Lexington Books.

Marshall, Monty G., and Keith Jaggers. 2004. "Polity IV Project: Political Regime Characteristics and Transitions, 1800–2003." http://www.systemicpeace.org/polity/polity4.htm.

Marshall, Shelley, and Kate Macdonald. 2013. *Fair Trade, Corporate Accountability and Beyond: Experiments in Globalizing Justice*. Hampshire, UK: Ashgate Publishing.

Martin, Lisa L. 1993. "Credibility, Costs, and Institutions: Cooperation and Economic Sanctions." *World Politics* 45 (3):406–432.

Mason, David T., and Patrick J. Fett. 1996a. "How Civil Wars End: A Rational Choice Approach." *Journal of Conflict Resolution* 40 (4):546–568.

Mason, T. David, and Patrick J. Fett. 1996b. "How Civil Wars End a Rational Choice Approach." *Journal of Conflict Resolution* 40 (4):546–568.

Mattes, Michaela, and Burcu Savun. 2009. "Fostering Peace after Civil War: Commitment Problems and Agreement Design." *International Studies Quarterly* 53 (3): 737–759.

McAdam, Doug, Sidney Tarrow, and Charles Tilly. 2003. "Dynamics of Contention." *Social Movement Studies* 2 (1):99–102.

McKittrick, David, Seamus Kelters, Brian Feeney, and Chris Thornton. 2001. *Lost Lives: The Stories of the Men, Women and Children Who Died as a Result of the Northern Ireland Troubles*. New York: Random House.

McNamara, Kevin. 2009. *The MacBride Principles: Irish America Strikes Back*. Liverpool, UK: Liverpool University Press.

Melin, Molly M. 2005. "A Time for War and a Time for Peace: The Issue of Timing and the Expansion of Militarized Interstate Disputes." Masters, Political Science, University of California, Davis.

Melin, Molly M. 2011. "The Impact of State Relationships on If, When and How Conflict Management Occurs." *International Studies Quarterly* 55:1–25.

Melin, Molly M. 2013. "When States Mediate." *Penn State Journal of Law and International Affairs* 2 (1):78–90.

Melin, Molly M., Scott Sigmund Gartner, and Jacob Bercovitch. 2013. "Fear of Rejection: The Puzzle of Unaccepted Mediation Offers in International Conflict." *Conflict Management and Peace Science* 30 (4):354–368.

Melin, Molly M., and Isak Svensson. 2009. "Incentives for Talking: Accepting Mediation in International and Civil Wars." *International Interactions* 35 (3):249–271.

Miklian, Jason. 2017. "Mapping Business-Peace Interactions: Opportunities and Recommendations." *Business, Peace and Sustainable Development* 10 (10):3–27.

Miklian, Jason, Rina M. Alluri, and John Elias Katsos. 2019. *Business, Peacebuilding and Sustainable Development*. London: Routledge.

Miklian, Jason, and Juan Pablo Medina Bickel. 2020. "Theorizing Business and Local Peacebuilding through the 'Footprints of Peace' Coffee Project in Rural Colombia." *Business and Society* 59 (4):676–715.

Miklian, Jason, and Angelika Rettberg. 2019. "From War-Torn to Peace-Torn? Mapping Business Strategies in Transition from Conflict to Peace in Colombia." In *Business, Peacebuilding and Sustainable Development*, edited by Jason Miklian, Rina M. Alluri, and John Elias Katsos, 110–128. Abingdon: Routledge.

Miklian, Jason, and Peer Schouten. 2019. "Broadening 'Business,' Widening 'Peace': A New Research Agenda on Business and Peace-Building." *Conflict, Security, and Development* 19 (1):1–13.

Milner, Wesley T. 2002. "Economic Globalization and Rights." In *Globalization and Human Rights*, edited by Alison Brysk, 77. Oakland: University of California.

Mintz, Alex, and Chi Huang. 1990. "Defense Expenditures, Economic Growth, and the 'Peace Dividend.'" *American Political Science Review* 84 (4):1283–1293.

Miroff, Nick. 2016. "The Staggering Toll of Colombia's War with FARC Rebels, Explained in Numbers." *Washington Post*, August 24, 2016, Worldviews. https://www.washingtonpost.com/news/worldviews/wp/2016/08/24/the-staggering-toll-of-colombias-war-with-farc-rebels-explained-in-numbers/?utm_term=.f49b9870710b.

Morgan, T. Clifton, and Glenn Palmer. 2000. "A Model of Foreign Policy Substitutability: Selecting the Right Tools for the Right Job(s)." *Journal of Conflict Resolution* 44 (1):11–32.

Mosley, Hugh G. 1985. *The Arms Race: Economic and Social Consequences*. Glencoe: Free Press.

Most, Benjamin A., and Harvey Starr. 1980. "Diffusion, Reinforcement, Geopolitics and the Spread of War." *American Political Science Review* 74 (4):932–946.

Most, Benjamin A., and Harvey Starr. 1984. "International Relations Theory, Foreign Policy Substitutability, and 'Nice' Laws." *World Politics* 36 (3):383–406.

Most, Benjamin A., and Harvey Starr. 1989. *Inquiry, Logic, and International Politics*. Columbia: University of South Carolina Press.

Murdoch, James C., and Todd Sandler. 2004. "Civil Wars and ECONOMIC GROWTH: SPATIAL dispersion." *American Journal of Political Science* 48 (1): 138–151.

Murphy, Helen. 2012. "Colombia Names Team for Peace Talks with FARC Rebels." *Reuters*, September 5, 2012. http://www.reuters.com/article/us-colombia-farc-idUSBRE8841KO20120905.

Murphy, Peter. 2015. "Ecopetrol Pipeline Bombing Spills More Oil into Colombian River." *Reuters*. Accessed January 18, 2017. http://www.reuters.com/article/us-ecopetrol-pipeline-idUSKBN0P22CH20150622.

Nelson, Jane. 2000. *The Business of Peace*. London: Prince of Wales Business Forum, International Alert and Council on Economic Priorities.

Norris, Pippa. 2000. *A Virtuous Circle: Political Communications in Postindustrial Societies*. Cambridge: Cambridge University Press.

North, Douglass C. 1990. *Institutions, Institutional Change and Economic Performance*. Cambridge: Cambridge University Press.

North, Douglass C., and Barry R. Weingast. 1989. "Constitutions and Commitment: The Evolution of Institutions Governing Public Choice in Seventeenth-Century England." *Journal of Economic History* 49 (4):803–832.

OECD. 2018. *OECD Economic Surveys: Tunisia*. Paris: OECD Publishing.

OECD. 2014. "SME Policy Index: The Mediterranean Middle East and North Africa 2014 Implementation of the Small Business Act for Europe: Implementation of the Small Business Act for Europe." OECD, The European Commission, European Training Foundation.

OECD. 2020. "Official Development Assistance Flows." OECD. Accessed March 5, 2020. http://www.oecd.org/dac/financing-sustainable-development/development-finance-data/aid-at-a-glance.htm.

Oetzel, Jennifer. 2005. "Smaller May Be Beautiful but Is It More Risky? Assessing and Managing Political and Economic Risk in Costa Rica." International Business Review 14 (6):765–790.

Oetzel, Jennifer, and Kathleen Getz. 2012. "Why and How Might Firms Respond Strategically to Violent Conflict?" Journal of International Business Studies 43 (2):166–186.

Oetzel, Jennifer, Kathleen A. Getz, and Stephen Ladek. 2007. "The Role of Multinational Enterprises in Responding to Violent Conflict: A Conceptual Model and Framework for Research." American Business Law Journal 44 (2):331–358. doi: 10.1111/j.1744-1714.2007.00039.x.

Oetzel, Jennifer, and Jason Miklian. 2017. "Multinational Enterprises, Risk Management, and the Business and Economics of Peace." Multinational Business Review 25 (4):270–286.

Oetzel, Jennifer, Michelle Westermann-Behaylo, Charles Koerber, Timothy L. Fort, and Jorge Rivera. 2009. "Business and Peace: Sketching the Terrain." Journal of Business Ethics 89 (4):351–373.

Omari, Torkin. 2018. "Profiles: Luis Carlos Villegas." Colombia Reports. http://colombiareports.com/luis-carlos-villegas/.

Omri, M. 2015. "No Ordinary Union: UGTT and the Tunisian Path to Revolution and Transition." Workers of the World: International Journal on Strikes and Social Conflict 1 (7):14–29.

Osborne, R. D. 2003. "Progressing the Equality Agenda in Northern Ireland." Journal of Social Policy 32 (3):339–360.

Osborne, Robert D. 1980. "Religious Discrimination and Disadvantage in the Northern Ireland Labour Market." International Journal of Social Economics 7 (4):206–223.

Osborne, Robert D., and R. J. Cormack. 1986. "Unemployment and Religion in Northern Ireland." Economic and Social Review 17 (3):215–225.

Otis, John. 2017. "Faced with Peace, Former Rebels in Colombia Find New Ways to Survive." In Latin America. National Public Radio.

Ott, M. 1972. "Mediation as a Method of Conflict Resolution." International Organization 26:595–618.

Owsiak, Andrew P. 2014. "Conflict Management Trajectories in Militarized Interstate Disputes: A Conceptual Framework and Theoretical Foundations." International Studies Review 16 (1):50–78.

Owsiak, Andrew P. 2020. "Conflict Management Trajectories: Theory and Evidence." International Interactions 47 (1):23–55. doi: 10.1080/03050629.2020.1814767.

Palmer, Glenn, and Archana Bhandari. 2000. "The Investigation of Substitutability in Foreign Policy." Journal of Conflict Resolution 44 (1):3–10.

Pastrana, Nathaly Aya, and Krishnamurthy Sriramesh. 2014. "Corporate Social Responsibility: Perceptions and Practices among SMEs in Colombia." Public Relations Review 40 (1):14–24.

Patterson, Glenn. 2016. Gull. London: Head of Zeus.

Pauly, Louis W., and Simon Reich. 1997. "National Structures and Multinational Corporate Behavior: Enduring Differences in the Age of Globalization." *International Organization* 51 (1):1–30.

Pearson, Frederic S. 1974. "Geographic Proximity and Foreign Military Intervention." *Journal of Conflict Resolution* 18 (3):432–460.

Pettersson, Therese, Stina Hogbladh, and Magnus Oberg. 2019. "Organized Violence, 1989–2018 and Peace Agreements." *Journal of Peace Research* 56 (4):589–603.

Pettersson, Therése, and Magnus Öberg. 2020. "Organized Violence, 1989–2019." *Journal of Peace Research* 57 (4):597–613.

Pettersson, Therése, and Peter Wallensteen. 2015. "Armed Conflicts, 1946–2014." *Journal of Peace Research* 52 (4):536–550.

Peyronel, Valérie. 2017. "US Investment in Northern Ireland: Strategies, Incentives and Perspectives." In *Revisiting the UK and Ireland's Transatlantic Economic Relationship with the United States in the 21st Century*, edited by Anne Groutel, Marie-Christine Pauwels, and Valérie Peyronel, 75–91. London: Palgrave Macmillan.

Phayal, Anup, Prabin B. Khadka, and Clayton L. Thyne. 2015. "What Makes an Ex-Combatant Happy? A Micro-Analysis of Disarmament, Demobilization, and Reintegration in South Sudan." *International Studies Quarterly* 59 (4):654–668.

Pigman, Geoffry Allen. 2013. "The Diplomacy of Global and Transnational Firms." In *The Oxford Handbook of Modern Diplomacy*, edited by Andrew F. Cooper, Jorge Heine, and Ramesh Thakur, 193–208. Oxford, UK: Oxford University Press.

Porter, Michael E., and Mark R. Kramer. 2006. "The Link between Competitive Advantage and Corporate Social Responsibility." *Harvard Business Review* 84 (12):78–92.

Porter, Michael E., and Mark R. Kramer. 2019. "Creating Shared Value." In *Managing Sustainable Business*, edited by Gilbert G. Lenssen and N. Craig Smith, 323–346. New York: Springer.

Portland Trust, The. 2013. *The Role of Business in Peacemaking: Lessons from Cyprus, Northern Ireland, South Africa and the South Caucasus*. London: The Portland Trust.

Poverty, Business Fights. 2010. "World Business and Development Award Winners Show That Fighting Poverty Can Also Benefit Business." http://community. businessfightspoverty.org/profiles/blogs/world-business-and-development.

Powell, Jonathan M., and Clayton L. Thyne. 2011. "Global Instances of Coups from 1950 to 2010 a New Dataset." *Journal of Peace Research* 48 (2):249–259.

Prakash, Aseem, and Matthew Potoski. 2006. "Racing to the Bottom? Trade, Environmental Governance, and ISO 14001." *American Journal of Political Science* 50 (2):350–364.

Preston, Lee E. 1981. "Research on Corporate Social Reporting: Directions for Development." *Accounting, Organizations and Society* 6 (3):255–262.

Preston, Lee E., and James E. Post. 1981. "Private Management and Public Policy." *California Management Review* 23 (3):56–62.

Pruitt, Dean G. 1981. *Negotiator Behavior*. New York, NY: Academic Press.

Pshisva, Rony, and Gustavo A. Suarez. 2006. "Captive Markets: The Impact of Kidnappings on Corporate Investment in Colombia." *Federal Reserve*. https://www.federalreserve. gov/econres/feds/39captive-markets39-the-impact-of-kidnappings-on-corporate-investment-in-colombia.htm.

Regan, Patrick. 1996. "Conditions of Successful Third-Party Intervention in Intrastate Conflicts." *Journal of Conflict Resolution* 40 (2):336–359.

Regan, Patrick. 2000. "Substituting Policies during U.S. Interventions in Internal Conflicts: A Little of This, a Little of That." *Journal of Conflict Resolution* 44 (1):90–106.

Regan, Patrick, and Allan C. Stam. 2000. "In the Nick of Time: Conflict Management, Mediation Timing, and the Duration of Interstate Disputes." *International Studies Quarterly* 44 (2):239–260.

Reidenbach, R. Eric, and Donald P. Robin. 1991. "A Conceptual Model of Corporate Moral Development." *Journal of Business Ethics* 10 (4):273–284.

Reilly, Charles. 2008. *Peace-Building and Development in Guatemala and Northern Ireland.* New York: Springer.

Rekik, Haifa Chtourou. 2016. "The Determinants of the Commitment to Corporate Social Responsibility: Case of Tunisia." *Journal of Accounting, Business and Management* 23 (1):15–30.

Remili, Boujemaa. 2019. *IDEA Consult.* Edited by Molly M. Melin. Tunis, Tunisia, February 1, 2019.

Reno, William. 2004. "Order and Commerce in Turbulent Areas: 19th Century Lessons, 21st Century Practice." *Third World Quarterly* 25 (4):607–625. doi: 10.2307/3993736.

Repoza, Kenneth. 2016. "What Investors Still Like about Colombia." *Forbes*, October 7, 2016. https://www.forbes.com/sites/kenrapoza/2016/10/07/what-investors-still-like-about-colombia/#533b09d5e71d.

Rettberg, Angelika. 2003. "The Business of Peace in Colombia: Assessing the Role of the Business Community in the Colombian Peace Process." Annual Meeting of the Latin American Studies Association (LASA). Dallas, Texas, USA.

Rettberg, Angelika. 2007. "The Private Sector and Peace in El Salvador, Guatemala, and Colombia." *Journal of Latin American Studies* 39 (3):463–494.

Rettberg, Angelika. 2008. "Exploring the Peace Dividend: Perceptions of Armed Conflict Impacts on the Colombian Private Sectors." International Alert.

Rettberg, Angelika. 2009. "Business and Peace in Colombia: Responses, Challenges, and Achievements." In *Colombia: Building Peace in a Time of War*, edited by Virginia Marie Bouvier, 191–204. Washington, DC: US Institute of Peace Press.

Rettberg, Angelika. 2013. "Peace Is Better Business, and Business Makes Better Peace: The Role of the Private Sector in Colombian Peace Processes." GIGA Working Papers 240. https://www.jstor.org/stable/resrep07632?seq=1#metadata_info_tab_contents.

Rettberg, Angelika. 2004. "Business-Led Peacebuilding in Colombia: Fad or Future of a Country in Crisis?" Working Paper 56. London: Crisis States Programme, Development Research Centre, DESTIN, LSE.

Rettberg, Angelika. 2019. "The Colombian Private Sector in Colombia's Transition to Peace." In *Civil Action and the Dynamics of Violence*, edited by Deborah Avant, Marie E. Berry, Erica Chenoweth, Rachel Epstein, Cullen Hendrix, Oliver Kaplan, and Timothy Sisk, 255–278. Oxford, UK: Oxford University Press.

Rettberg, Angelika, Ralf J. Leiteritz, and Carlo Nasi. 2011. "Entrepreneurial Activity in the Context of Violent Conflict: Business and Organized Violence in Colombia." *Journal of Small Business and Entrepreneurship* 24 (2):179–196.

Reuters. 2014. "Colombia's Argos to Donate Land, Money to Peace Charity." Thomas Reuters Foundation News. Accessed January 7. http://news.trust.org//item/20141023174947-9n5x4.

Reuters. 2017. "Bombings Halted Pumping at Colombia's Cano-Limon Oil Pipeline." https://www.reuters.com/article/us-colombia-oil/bombings-halted-pumping-at-colombias-cano-limon-oil-pipeline-idUSKBN15611Y.

Reuters. 2018. "ELN Rebels Bomb Colombia's Cano Limon Oil Pipeline: Sources." September 5, 2018. https://www.reuters.com/article/us-colombia-oil/eln-rebels-bomb-colombias-cano-limon-oil-pipeline-sources-idUSKCN1LL209.

Rivoal, Catherine. 2012. "Social Responsibility in Agriculture." In *MediTERRA 2012 (English)*, edited by Ciheam Bari, 197–210. Paris: Presses de Sciences Po.

Robbins, Nick. 2006. *The Corporation that Changed the World: How the East India Company Shaped the Modern Multinational*. London: Pluto Press.

Roddy, Jim. 2019. City Center Initiative Derry Manager. Edited by Molly M. Melin. Derry, Northern Ireland, June 23, 2019.

Romdhane, Mahmoud Ben. 2019. Former Tunisian Minister of Transport; Former Tunisian Minister of Social Programs. Edited by Molly M. Melin. Tunis, Tunisia, January 28, 2019.

Roosevelt, Theodore. 1985. *Theodore Roosevelt, An Autobiography*. New York: Da Capo Press.

Roper, Stephen. 1996. "Grant Deadweight and Profitability: The Case of Northern Ireland." *Applied Economics* 28 (4):499–508.

Ross, Michael L. 2003a. "The Natural Resource Curse: How Wealth Can Make You Poor." In *Natural Resources and Violent Conflict: Options and Actions*, edited by Ian Bannon and Paul Collier, 17–42. Washington, DC: World Bank Publications.

Ross, Michael L. 2003b. "Oil, Drugs, and Diamonds: The Varying Roles of Natural Resources in Civil War." In *The Political Economy of Armed Conflict: Beyond Greed and Grievance*, edited by Karen Ballentine and Jake Sherman, 47–70. Boulder, CO: Lynne Rienner.

Ross, Michael L. 2004. "What Do We Know about Natural Resources and Civil War?" *Journal of Peace Research* 41 (3):337–356. doi: 10.1177/0022343304043773.

Rowthorn, B., and N. Wayne. 1988. *Northern Ireland: The Political Economy of Conflict*: Boulder, CO: Westview Press.

Russo, Angeloantonio, and Francesco Perrini. 2010. "Investigating Stakeholder Theory and Social Capital: CSR in Large Firms and SMEs." *Journal of Business Ethics* 91 (2):207–221.

Sachs, Jeffrey D., and Andrew M. Warner. 2001. "The Curse of Natural Resources." *European Economic Review* 45 (4):827–838.

Sambanis, Nicholas. 2002. "A Review of Recent Advances and Future Directions in the Quantitative Literature on Civil War." *Defence and Peace Economics* 13 (3):215–243.

Savun, Burcu. 2005. "Information, Bias and Mediation Success." Annual Meeting of the International Studies Association, San Diego, CA.

Schepers, Donald H. 2006. "The Impact of NGO Network Conflict on the Corporate Social Responsibility Strategies of Multinational Corporations." *Business and Society* 45 (3):282–299.

Schloss, M. J. 2008. "Governance and Policy Framework for Extractive Industries' Performance." *Oil, Gas and Energy Law Journal (OGEL)* 6 (3). https://www.ogel.org/article.asp?key=2807.

Schmidt, Holger. 2004. "Regime Type and Conflict Management by International Organizations: The Case of the UN, 1945–2001." Annual Meeting of the International Studies Association, Montreal, Canada.

Schouten, Peer, and Jason Miklian. 2017. "The Business–Peace Nexus: 'Business for Peace' and the Reconfiguration of the Public/Private Divide in Global Governance." *Journal of International Relations and Development* 23 (2):414–435.

Schraeder, Peter J., and Hamadi Redissi. 2011. "The Upheavals in Egypt and Tunisia: Ben Ali's Fall." *Journal of Democracy* 22 (3):5–19.

Schraeder, Peter J., and Hamadi Redissi. 2014. "Ben Ali's Fall." In *Democratization and Authoritarianism in the Arab World*, edited by Larry Diamond and Marc F. Plattner. Baltimore, MD: Johns Hopkins University Press.

Scott, Martin. 2009. "Marginalized, Negative or Trivial? Coverage of Africa in the UK Press." *Media, Culture, and Society* 31 (4):533–557.

Shannon, Megan. 2009. "Preventing War and Providing the Peace? International Organizations and the Management of Territorial Disputes." *Conflict Management and Peace Science* 26 (2):144–163.

Siverson, Randolph M., and Harvey Starr. 1991. *The Diffusion of War: A Study of Opportunity and Willingness*. Ann Arbor: University of Michigan Press.

Smith, N. Craig. 2015. "Size Matters? How the Business Case for CSR can Apply to Any Company, No Matter the Size." *Huffpost*. https://www.huffpost.com/entry/size-matters-how-the-busi_b_8073490.

Sperr, Anneken Kari. 2013. "Mediation in Norway: 'Faster, Cheaper and More Friendly.'" In *Mediation: Principles and Regulation in Comparative Perspective*, edited by Klaus J. Hopt and Felix Steffek, 1137–1164. New York: Oxford University Press.

Spreitzer, Gretchen. 2007. "Giving Peace a Chance: Organizational Leadership, Empowerment, and Peace." *Journal of Organizational Behavior* 28 (8):1077–1095.

Staines, Nicholas. 2004. *Economic Performance over the Conflict Cycle*. Washington, DC: International Monetary Fund.

Starik, Mark, and Archie B. Carroll. 1990. "In Search of Beneficence: Reflections on the Connections between Firm Social and Financial Performance." Proceedings of the International Association for Business and Society. San Diego, CA, March 16–18.

Starr, Harvey. 2000. "Substitutability in Foreign Policy: Theoretically Central, Empirically Elusive." *Journal of Conflict Resolution* 44 (1):128–138.

Statistics, Northern Ireland, and Research Agency Staff. 2002. *Northern Ireland Annual Abstract of Statistics*. Belfast: Stationery Office.

Steelman, Toddi A., and Jorge Rivera. 2006. "Voluntary Environmental Programs In the United States: Whose Interests Are Served?" *Organization and Environment* 19 (4):505–526.

Stel, Nora. 2014. "Business in Genocide: Understanding the How and Why of Corporate Complicity in Genocides." Working Paper 28. https://ideas.repec.org/p/msm/wpaper/2014-28.html.

Stepan, Alfred. 2012. "Tunisia's Transition and the Twin Tolerations." *Journal of Democracy* 23 (2):89–103.

Sternberg, Elaine. 2009. "Corporate Social Responsibility and Corporate Governance." *Economic Affairs* 29 (4):5–10.

Stevenson, Richard W. 1994. "Peace in a Northern Ireland Factory." *New York Times*, September 8, 1994, 1, D. https://www.nytimes.com/1994/09/08/business/peace-in-a-northern-ireland-factory.html.

Stiftung, Bertelsmann. 2014. *BTI 2014-Tunisia Country Report*. Gütersloh: Bertelsmann Stiftung.

Suarez, Carolina, and Juan David Ferreira. 2016. "Forum Futuro Colombia, an Opportunity to Reinforce the Peace Building Process and the SDGs." SDG Funders: SDG Philanthropy Forum. Accessed January 11, 2017. http://sdgfunders.org/blog/forum-futuro-colombia-an-opportunity-to-reinforce-the-peace-building-process-and-the-sdgs/.

Sundberg, Ralph, and Erik Melander. 2013. "Introducing the UCDP Georeferenced Event Dataset." *Journal of Peace Research* 50 (4):523–532.

Sutton, Malcolm. 2001. *Bear in Mind These Dead . . . An Index of Deaths from the Conflict in Ireland 1969–2001*. Belfast: Beyond the Pale Publications.

Svendsen, Ann. 1998. *The Stakeholder Strategy: Profiting from Collaborative Business Relationships*. Oakland, CA: Berrett-Koehler Publishers.

Svensson, Isak. 2006. "Elusive Peacemakers: A Bargaining Perspective on Mediation in Internal Armed Conflicts." Department of Peace and Conflict Research, Uppsala University.

Switzer, Jason. 2002. "Conflicting Interests." *International Institute for Sustainable Development*. Accessed February 5, 2017. http://www.iisd.org/pdf/2002/envsec_conflicting_interests.pdf.

Sweetman, Derek. 2009. *Business, Conflict Resolution and Peacebuilding: Contributions from the Private Sector to Address Violent Conflict*. London: Routledge.

Teegan, Hildy, and Jonathan P. Doh. 2003. *Globalization and NGOs: Transforming Business, Government and Society*. Westport, CT: Praeger Publishers.

teleSUR. 2017. "Colombian Companies Charged for Crimes against Humanity." February 4, 2017. http://www.telesurtv.net/english/news/Colombian-Companies-Charged-for-Crimes-Against-Humanity--20170204-0010.html.

Terris, Leslie G., and Zeev Maoz. 2005. "Rational Mediation: A Theory and a Test." *Journal of Peace Research* 42 (5):563–583.

Tevault, Ashley. 2013. "How Institutional and Business Power Theory Shapes Business Strategy in Fragile States: The Case of Sierra Leone." *Business, Peace and Sustainable Development* 2013 (1):43–62. doi: 10.9774/GLEAF.8757.2013.se.00005.

Thies, Cameron G. 2010. "Of Rulers, Rebels, and Revenue: State Capacity, Civil War Onset, and Primary Commodities." *Journal of Peace Research* 47 (3):321–332.

Thomas, Melissa A. 2010. "What Do the Worldwide Governance Indicators Measure?" *European Journal of Development Research* 22 (1):31–54.

Thornton, Christopher. 2014. "The Rocky Path from Elections to a New Constitution in Tunisia: Mechanisms for Consensus-Building and Inclusive Decision-Making." Oslo Forum. https://www.africaportal.org/publications/the-rocky-path-from-elections-to-a-new-constitution-in-tunisia-mechanisms-for-consensus-building-and-inclusive-decision-making/.

Thorp, Rosemary, and Francisco Durand. 1997. "A Historical View of Business-State Relations: Colombia, Peru, and Venezuela Compared." In *Business and the state in developing countries*, edited by Sylvia Maxfield and Ben Ross Schneider, 216–236. Ithaca, New York: Cornell University Press.

Thyne, Clayton L. 2006. "ABC's, 123's, and the Golden Rule: The Pacifying Effect of Education on Civil War, 1980–1999." *International Studies Quarterly* 50 (4):733–754.

Tierney, Michael J., Daniel L. Nielson, Darren G. Hawkins, J. Timmons Roberts, Michael G. Findley, Ryan M. Powers, Bradley Parks, Sven E. Wilson, and Robert L. Hicks. 2011. "More Dollars than Sense: Refining Our Knowledge of Development Finance Using AidData." *World Development* 39 (11):1891–1906.

Toft, Monica Duffy. 2009. *Securing the Peace: The Durable Settlement of Civil Wars*. Princeton, NJ: Princeton University Press.

Townroe, Peter, and Ron Martin. 1992. *Regional Development in the 1990s: The British Isles in Transition*. Vol. 4. London: Psychology Press.

Tripathi, Salil, and Canan Gündüz. 2008. *A Role for the Private Sector in Peace Processes? Examples, and Implications for Third-Party Mediation*. Geneva: HD Centre for Humanitarian Dialogue.

Tsebelis, George. 2002. *Veto Players: How Political Institutions Work*. Princeton, NJ: Princeton University Press.

Tures, John A., and Paul R. Hensel. 2000. "Measuring Opportunity and Willingness for Conflict: A Preliminary Application to Central America and the Caribbean." Annual Meeting of the American Political Science Association, Washington, DC.

Ullmann, Arieh A. 1985. "Data in Search of a Theory: A Critical Examination of the Relationships among Social Performance, Social Disclosure, and Economic Performance of US Firms." *Academy of Management Review* 10 (3):540–557.

UNICEF. 2019. *Child labor*. New York: UNICEF.

United Nations. "United Nations Peacebuilding Fund." Accessed August 29, 2019. http://www.unpbf.org/application-guidelines/what-is-peacebuilding/#fnref-1937-2.

Van Tulder, Rob, and Ans Kolk. 2001. "Multinationality and Corporate Ethics: Codes of Conduct in the Sporting Goods Industry." *Journal of International Business Studies* 32 (2):267–283.

Vivarta, Veet, and Guilherme Canela. 2006. "Corporate Social Responsibility in Brazil." *Journal of Corporate Citizenship* 21 (1):95–106.

Vives, Antonio. 2006. "Social and Environmental Responsibility in Small and Medium Enterprises in Latin America." *Journal of Corporate Citizenship* (21):39–50.

Vogel, David. 1997. "Trading Up and Governing Across: Transnational Governance and Environmental Protection." *Journal of European Public Policy* 4 (4):556–571.

Walker, Edward T. 2013. "Signaling Responsibility, Deflecting Controversy: Strategic and Institutional Influences on the Charitable Giving of Corporate Foundations in the Health Sector." *Research in Political Sociology* 21:181–214.

Walsh, Dermott. 2000. *Bloody Sunday and the Rule of Law in Northern Ireland*. New York: Springer.

Walter, Barbara F. 2004. "Does Conflict Beget Conflict? Explaining Recurring Civil War." *Journal of Peace Research* 41 (3):371–388.

Walter, Barbara F. 2009. "Bargaining Failures and Civil War." *Annual Review of Political Science* 12:243–261.

Ward, Michael D., and David R. Davis. 1992. "Sizing Up the Peace Dividend: Economic Growth and Military Spending in the United States, 1948–1996." *American Political Science Review* 86 (3):748–755.

WBCSD. 2002. *Corporate Social Responsibility: The WBCSD's Journey*. Geneva: World Business Council for Sustainable Development.

Weede, Erich, and Edward N. Muller. 1998. "Rebellion, Violence and Revolution: A Rational Choice Perspective." *Journal of Peace Research* 35 (1):43–59.

Weiss, Thomas G. 1999. "Sanctions as a Foreign Policy Tool: Weighing Humanitarian Impulses." *Journal of Peace Research* 36 (5):499–509.

Wenger, Andreas, and Daniel Möckli. 2003. *Conflict Prevention: The Untapped Potential of the Business Sector*. Boulder, CO: Lynne Rienner.

Wennmann, Achim. 2016. "Business and the UN Peace and Security Agenda." Geneva Peacebuilding Platform, Brief.

Werner, Suzanne. 2000. "Deterring Intervention: The Stakes of War and Third Party Involvement." *American Journal of Political Science* 44 (4):720–732.

Westermann-Behaylo, Michelle K. Kathleen Rehbein, and Timothy Fort. 2015. "Enhancing the Concept of Corporate Diplomacy: Encompassing Political Corporate Social Responsibility, International Relations, and Peace through Commerce." *Academy of Management Perspectives* 29 (4):387–404.

Westhues, Martina, and Sabine Einwiller. 2006. "Corporate Foundations: Their Role for Corporate Social Responsibility." *Corporate Reputation Review* 9 (2):144–153.

Wheeler, David, and Maria Sillanpää. 1997. *The Stakeholder Corporation: A Blueprint for Maximizing Stakeholder Value*. London: Pittman.

Williams, Margaret. 2016. "Youth, peace, and security: A new agenda for the Middle East and North Africa." *Journal of International Affairs* 69 (2):103–114.

Williams, Oliver F., ed. 2008. *Peace through Commerce: Responsible Corporate Citizenship and the Ideals of the United Nations Global Compact*. 1st ed. John W. Houck Notre Dame Series in Business Ethics. South Bend, IN: University of Notre Dame Press.

Wolf, Klaus Dieter, Nicole Deitelhoff, and Stefan Engert. 2007. "Corporate Security Responsibility: Towards a Conceptual Framework for a Comparative Research Agenda." *Cooperation and Conflict* 42 (3):294–320.

World Bank. 2014. *Towards Sustainable Peace, Poverty Eradication, and Shared Prosperity*. Washington, DC: World Bank Group.

World Bank. 2015. "Policy Research Note No.3: Ending Extreme Poverty and Sharing Prosperity: Progress and Policies." http://pubdocs.worldbank.org/en/109701443800596288/PRN03Oct2015TwinGoals.pdf.

World Bank. 2018a. *Case Study: Dairy Sector Supply Chain Development in a Conflict-Affected Region of Colombia*. Washington, DC: World Bank Group.

World Bank. 2018b. "Foreign Direct Investment, Net Inflows." https://data.worldbank.org/indicator/BX.KLT.DINV.CD.WD.

World Bank. 2019. *Doing Business Report*. Washington, DC: World Bank Group.

World Bank. 2020. "The World Bank in Tunisia: Country Overview." The World Bank, accessed March 2, 2020. https://www.worldbank.org/en/country/tunisia/overview.

Wright, Norman S., and Hadyn Bennett. 2011. "Business Ethics, CSR, Sustainability and the MBA." *Journal of Management and Organization* 17 (5):641–655.

Yoon, Mi Yung. 1997. "Explaining U.S. Intervention in Third World Internal Wars, 1945–1989." *Journal of Conflict Resolution* 41 (4):580–602.

Yoon, Yeosun, Zeynep Gürhan-Canli, and Norbert Schwarz. 2006. "The Effect of Corporate Social Responsibility (CSR) Activities on Companies with Bad Reputations." *Journal of Consumer Psychology* 16 (4):377–390.

Zielinski, Rosella Cappella. 2016. *How States Pay for Wars*. Ithaca, NY: Cornell University Press.

Index